CRISTINA, THE BEST TO YOU. Carl Baehr

From the Emerald Isle to the Cream City

A HISTORY OF THE IRISH IN MILWAUKEE

Carl Baehr

Everything Goes Media
Milwaukee, Wisconsin
www.everythinggoesmedia.com

From the Emerald Isle to the Cream City:
A History of the Irish in Milwaukee
Carl Baehr

Everything Goes Media
www.everythinggoesmedia.com
Published October 2018

Publisher's Cataloging-In-Publication Data

Names: Baehr, Carl, author.
Title: From the Emerald Isle to the Cream City : a history of the Irish in Milwaukee / Carl Baehr.
Description: Includes bibliographical references and index. | Milwaukee, WI: Everything Goes Media, 2018.
Identifiers: ISBN 978-1-893121-39-3 | LCCN 2018953506
Subjects: LCSH Irish Americans--Wisconsin--Milwaukee--History. | Milwaukee (Wis.)--History. | Milwaukee (Wis.)--Ethnic relations. | BISAC HISTORY / United States / State & Local / Midwest (IA, IL, IN, KS, MI, MN, MO, ND, NE, OH, SD, WI)
Classification: LCC F589.M69 B34 2018 | DDC 977.5/950049162--dc23

22 21 20 19 18   10 9 8 7 6 5 4 3 2 1

Cover Image: Courthouse Square, later known as Cathedral Square.
(History of Milwaukee, Wisconsin, John Gregory, 1931)

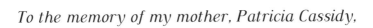

To the memory of my mother, Patricia Cassidy,

and

to my grandchildren, Sean, Shannon, Devin, and Aidan.

Table of Contents

Table of Contents

Table of Contents

Acknowledgments

Special thanks to Ellen Baehr, my wife, for her assistance in helping with this history by going on research trips, reading the text multiple times, and offering suggestions to improve it. Thanks to my good friend George Wagner for listening to me talk about the topics included in this book for many years, and for reading the text and recommending changes. Thank you to Sharon Woodhouse for the many improvements she has made to the book. The text has benefited from the comments made by my friend Terry Duffey and my brother-in-law Pete Fromm, as well those made by Dennis McBride. Thank you also to my late friend Jerry Kearney for his interest.

Thanks to the archivists and librarians of the Milwaukee Archdiocesan Archives, the Milwaukee County Historical Society, City of Milwaukee Legislative Reference Bureau, and the Humanities Department of the Milwaukee Public Library for preserving historical materials and for providing access to them.

Without the online newspapers, censuses, and other documents, the job of researching the material for this book would have been almost impossible in my lifetime. Thank you to those responsible for these resources.

Note on Street Names

The current names of streets are used in this book. The list below indicates the former names.

- N. Broadway was Main Street until 1870.

- E. Clybourn Street was Huron Street until 1926.

- E. Juneau Avenue was Division Street until 1885.

- E. Kilbourn Avenue was Biddle Street until 1929.

- W. Kilbourn Avenue was Cedar Street until 1929.

- W. Michigan Street was Sycamore Street until 1926.

- E. St. Paul Avenue was Detroit Street until 1965.

- E. State Street was Martin Street until 1926.

- W. State Street was Tamarack Street until 1866.

- N. Water Street was E. Water Street until 1926.

- E. Wells Street was Oneida Street until 1926.

- E. Wisconsin Avenue was Wisconsin Street until 1926.

- W. Wisconsin Avenue was Spring Street until 1876, then Grand Avenue until 1926.

Maps

Milwaukee in 1856. (American Geographical
Society Library, University of Wisconsin-
Milwaukee Libraries)

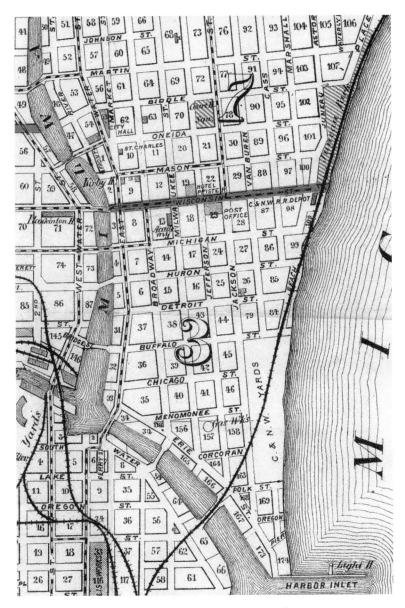

Milwaukee in 1888 – Third Ward and Juneautown. (American Geographical Society Library, University of Wisconsin-Milwaukee Libraries)

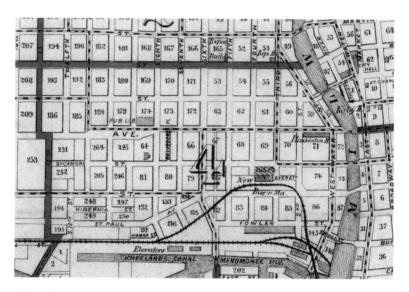

Milwaukee in 1888 – Hibernia Street, St. Paul Avenue, and Hinman Street were all in Tory Hill. (American Geographical Society Library, University of Wisconsin-Milwaukee Libraries)

Chapter 1
1835–1839

In Milwaukee today, on the third weekend of each August, more than 100,000 people gather on the Summerfest grounds in the Historic Third Ward to steep themselves in Irish culture at the largest festival of its kind in the world. Irish music, dancing, theater, sports, history, genealogy, and culture are all celebrated.

Irish music, dancing, and storytelling first came to the Third Ward more than 180 years ago. The Ward, south of Downtown and east of the Milwaukee River, would become the largest Irish neighborhood in the city. Immigrants from Ireland arrived in Milwaukee seeking the American Dream, with its ideals of democracy, liberty, equality, and the opportunity to prosper. The city's Irish would work hard to achieve better lives. But they had their setbacks.

The Third Ward saw the highest fatality rates in the city during the cholera epidemics of 1849 and 1850. And only a decade later, it was a place of unimaginable grief when the sinking of the *Lady Elgin* claimed the lives of many of its residents, as well as the lives of Irish from other neighborhoods. The Third Ward was the location of the calamitous 1883 Newhall House hotel fire, in which more of the city's Irish perished. But the final disaster occurred when the Third Ward itself burned in 1892, putting an end to the neighborhood with the city's largest concentration of Irish, and scattering its residents to other parts of the city.

The Beginning

There were two classes of Irish Catholics who came to Milwaukee in the mid-1830s. Most of them were poor, illiterate peasants from the rural areas of Ireland. They had come to Milwaukee after working their way west, many working on constructing canals in New York, Pennsylvania, Ohio, Indiana, and Michigan, or laboring in factories in East Coast cities. A much smaller group consisted of middle-class merchants and professionals from the cities and towns of Ireland, as well as those few who owned large farms there. Many of them arrived in Milwaukee by way of Canada and the eastern United States.

There were also different groups of Irish Protestants who became Milwaukeeans. Some were Anglo-Irish, who were born in Ireland and were descendants of Englishmen who had settled there. They generally belonged to the Church of Ireland, an arm of the Church of England, and they attended Episcopalian churches here. Among them were Dublin-born Hans Crocker, who would become an early mayor of Milwaukee, and Alderman Wilson Graham from County Armagh.

Some well-to-do Catholics in Ireland had faced giving up their property under the English penal laws unless they gave up Catholicism, so they converted to Protestantism. For example, the Fitzgerald family had become Episcopalians in Ireland. A descendant of the family, seafaring John Fitzgerald, came to Milwaukee and was the grandfather of Edmund Fitzgerald, whose name will perpetually be linked to the sinking of his namesake ship, the *SS Edmund Fitzgerald*.

Most of the Irish Protestants, though, were Scotch-Irish, a term they used to differentiate themselves from Irish Catholics. They or their ancestors were Scots who had settled in Ireland, and they were generally Presbyterians or Methodists. In Milwaukee, the Protestants and Catholics usually did not mix. Irish Protestants did not generally live in Irish neighborhoods and did not get involved in Irish issues as the Catholics did.

In Ireland, a series of laws beginning in the late 1600s, known as the penal laws, helped to create the two classes of Catholics. The English, who had invaded Ireland centuries earlier, enacted the penal laws against the native population. The laws forbade Catholics to teach or run schools in Ireland, or to leave the country for an education. They also prohibited Catholics from practicing law or holding any government office. Other laws restricted the right of Catholics to vote, own weapons, or practice their religion.

But the main function of the penal laws was to take land ownership away from Catholics and put it in the hands of the followers of the Church of Ireland. Catholics were not allowed to buy land. When a Catholic landowner died, his land was required to be distributed equally among all male heirs. The result was that each heir had a smaller portion of land than that held by his father. When those inheritors died, their male descendants were left with still smaller plots of land. The effect over time was to produce tiny farms that could not support the owner and his family. The rural farmers slipped into poverty and ignorance during the enforcement of the penal laws. By 1750, Protestants owned 95% of the land in Ireland.[1]

Since the merchant and manufacturing classes of Catholics lived in cities and towns and did not own agricultural land, they were not the focus of the penal laws. Many of these rules were not enforced with them or did not affect them. Consequently, they had wealth and education that their rural brethren did not.

Compounding the poverty problem was the large increase in the population of Ireland from the last decade of the 1700s through the early decades of the 1800s, resulting in the number of inhabitants on the island jumping from about 5 million to 8 million, about 1.5 million more than today's population. The end of the Napoleonic wars in 1815 brought about a drop in agricultural prices, causing English owners of Irish land to convert farmland to pastures for grazing animals. Peasants who tended the fields and raised the crops were no longer needed and large numbers of them were evicted. For many, there was no other option but to emigrate. The large farms of some Catholics who had managed to retain them became unprofitable when the prices dropped. The poor economic climate throughout the country also led to the emigration of many in the middle classes.

Beginning in 1815 and up to the beginning of the famine in 1845, about a million Irish came to the United States.[2] Many single women without money or education worked as servants for middle-class and wealthy families. Men worked in factories, built canals, or filled other laborer positions. Those with sufficient money bought farmland or started businesses in cities and towns. As tribal lands were opened up

3

Evictions of Irish peasants occurred throughout the nineteenth century. A battering ram was used to destroy the house after the eviction. (Wikipedia – Evictions)

by treaties in the 1820s and 1830s, new farmland, new towns, and new canals offered opportunities for Yankees from the East Coast and for European immigrants. Most of the Europeans coming to the United States at that time were from the British Isles—Irish as well as English, Scottish, and Welsh.

Early Milwaukee

The settling of Milwaukee began when French-Canadian fur trader Solomon Juneau and Yankee lawyer Morgan L. Martin platted their village, Juneautown, on the east side of the Milwaukee River in 1835.

Juneau had a fur trading post and old log house near N. Water Street and E. Wisconsin Avenue, while a new frame home for his large family was built a block south at E. Michigan Street. Juneau's wife was Josette Vieau, the daughter of French-Canadian fur trader Jacques Vieau and Angelique Roy, of French-Canadian and Menomonee ancestry. Nearby were Menomonee Indians as well as other French Canadians, relatives of Juneau and Vieau. Potawatomi were also scattered throughout the area. But by 1840, most of the Native Americans, many themselves refugees from lands to the east, were forced to go west as they were cleared from a place that their people had inhabited for thousands of years to make way for the white men coming in from the East.

Simultaneous to Juneau and Martin's development, Byron Kilbourn and his associates planned another village, Kilbourntown, on the west side of the river. George Walker eventually developed a third settlement south of the Menomonee River known as Walker's Point. The three villages would later unite to become the city of Milwaukee.

Milwaukee in 1837. The cluster of buildings in center-left are in Juneautown, with the undeveloped Third Ward to its left. (*Medical History of Milwaukee*, Louis Frank, 1915)

The new villages drew hundreds of people from the East and by 1837 they held nearly 1,000 inhabitants. The terrain was not city-ready. The confluence and margins of the rivers were marshy, and the bluffs along the river valleys were generally high and steep. There were eight-to eighty-foot bluffs stretching along today's E. Michigan Street from Lake Michigan to a footpath next to the Milwaukee River. There the bluffs turned north and paralleled the current N. Water Street. Most of the Third Ward south of the cliffs was swampland. On the west side of the river, the bluffs began near W. Clybourn and N. Fifth streets and extended northerly along the Milwaukee River and westerly along the Menomonee River. On the south side of the Menomonee River Valley, the bluffs ran to the west along W. Oregon Street and southward roughly along S. Second Street. The land below the bluffs was mostly marshy.

Early visitors described the area as pleasant, charming, and beautiful. They were impressed with the views of the rivers and the lake from the bluffs. They looked out at the bay and judged it the best on the western shore of Lake Michigan. But neither bluffs nor swamps were conducive to travel within the community. Bluffs needed to be cut down to create sloping hills that could be navigated by man and beast, and swamps had to be filled in. Bridges were needed over the rivers to connect the villages. Cutting and grading of streets was necessary.

Providing an easy way to enter the city from Lake Michigan was a major requirement. The land route from Chicago or Green Bay was a very difficult journey, so the vast majority of people coming into the city came by ship. Reaching the bay was the easy part; getting from the shore to the new villages developing along the Milwaukee River was difficult. The Milwaukee, Menomonee, and Kinnickinnic rivers flowed together and entered the lake east of the current E. Greenfield Avenue. The trip from the outlet up to the downtown area was difficult for larger boats. Consequently, passengers and freight were offloaded from lake vessels to smaller craft that could navigate the river to the new villages, or bring them to shore near E. Clybourn Street.

New arrivals were greeted by a shoreline covered with white cedar and oaks a foot and a half to two feet in diameter. The whole area was covered with a wide variety of trees, bushes, and wildflowers. High ground was covered in places with scrub and brambles that were impenetrable to humans but not to rabbits, bobcats, and other animals. Wild rice grew in marshes teeming with wildlife.

The first step in Milwaukee's citymaking was taken when the Indian trail along today's N. Water Street between E. Michigan Street and E. Wisconsin Avenue was graded and became the city's first street. E. Clybourn Street was filled in from N. Water Street to Lake Michigan, where small watercraft would bring passengers to the shore. Work was slowly underway to create other streets, although they still left much to be desired. Parts of the bluffs in Juneautown were cut down and the excess material was used to begin filling in the marshes, work made to order for Irish laborers.

Early Irish Arrivals

New Irish residents came from all four of Ireland's provinces, with northernmost Ulster leading the way, followed by immigrants from Leinster in the east. The southwestern province of Munster contributed the George Furlong family of County Cork. The Furlongs had agricultural land in Ireland that became unprofitable after the Napoleonic wars. They left their native country in 1821 for Quebec, Canada, where they established a farm. After a decade in Quebec, they migrated west to Detroit, and in 1835 they arrived in Milwaukee. They purchased land for a farm in the Town of Greenfield, where George Furlong died in 1837 at the age of 57.

His sons, John and William, both in their early 20s when they arrived, became prosperous and influential in Milwaukee. Their sister, 20-year-old Ellen, had married David Curtin of County Limerick while the family lived in Detroit. There, the Curtins' son, Jeremiah, who would become a famed linguist and folklorist, was born. Shortly after his birth, the Curtins moved to Milwaukee and started a farm in Greenfield near the Furlongs.[3]

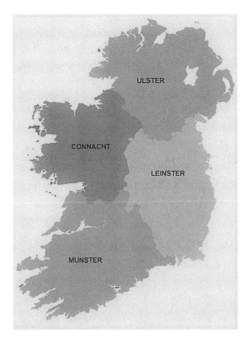

Map of Ireland's four provinces. (Wikipedia – Provinces of Ireland)

More typical of the Irishmen who came to Milwaukee was James Keenan. He arrived in the United States from County Mayo (in Ireland's fourth province, Connaught, in the west) in 1816 without any skills. He worked as a laborer in the East, where his son, Matthew, was born. The family continued west until they reached Milwaukee in 1837. James was then in his 50s and Matthew was 12. Because there were no bridges over the Milwaukee River, the Keenans operated a ferry that crossed the river at Wisconsin Avenue. James died penniless in 1843, but Matthew attained wealth and prominence before his death in 1898.[4]

Michael Finnegan, 28, came to Milwaukee in 1836 after four years in the United States. The immigrant from County Louth worked his way west as an employee of a surveying party. Here he married Annie Davlin in Solomon Juneau's home, and he planted the first trees in Cathedral Square. He worked as a laborer, then a policeman, and finally as a letter carrier while raising a family of four children.

It was a time of prosperity and inflation in the United States until the Panic of 1837 burst the bubble. Prices for land, which had been on the rise, collapsed. Businesses went bankrupt and thousands of workers lost their jobs, and those that kept their employment saw their wages decline. The villages that made up Milwaukee suffered along with the rest of the country. The crisis left little money for promoters of the villages to hire the labor to upgrade their communities. The flow of newcomers became a trickle and about half of the city's 1,000 inhabitants moved on.

Among the trickle still arriving was 29-year-old John Boyd who arrived in 1838, six years after coming to America from Ireland. Boyd worked in cotton mills in the East and as a laborer in Milwaukee until he accumulated enough money to reach the American dream—starting his own farm. He farmed in Granville until his retirement, when he returned to the city and lived in the Tory Hill neighborhood.

Another Irishman who became a Milwaukeean, if only briefly, during the 1830s was John O'Rourke. Solomon Juneau hired O'Rourke to be the first editor of the *Milwaukee Sentinel*. Juneau paid for the 24-year-old O'Rourke's trip from New York, along with the printing equipment he would need. The Irishman began his duties and, on June 27, 1837, the first issue of the *Sentinel* hit the streets. After three months as editor, O'Rourke was unable to continue his duties due to tuberculosis. He died

Map of Ireland's 32 counties. (Wikipedia – Counties of Ireland)

in December.

An Irishman who left his mark on the city during this time was Patrick O'Kelly, Milwaukee's first resident priest. Priest missionaries had served Milwaukee Catholics, including Solomon Juneau, since 1834, usually holding services in Juneau's home. The visiting priests came infrequently, requiring some Catholics like the Juneaus and the Furlongs to travel to Chicago for their children's baptisms. In 1839, O'Kelly was sent from the Detroit Archdiocese to live in Milwaukee and minister to the city's Catholics. O'Kelly was born in County Kilkenny in 1795 and was in his mid-40s when he arrived. One of his first tasks was to build a church here. It was located on the corner of N. Jackson and E. State streets and was called St. Luke's for the first three years of its existence.

O'Kelly's assistant, Thomas Morrissey, born in County Waterford, visited mission churches in Kenosha, Racine, and Waukesha counties, some in rural areas that were very difficult to reach on poor to nonexistent roads. Morrissey was an Irish-speaker who was able to communicate with those Irishmen who did not speak English.

O'Kelly ministered to churches in Milwaukee County, which served predominately English-speaking Irish. But one problem for O'Kelly was that some of his St. Luke's parishioners spoke German or French and he only spoke English. Another problem for O'Kelly was his view on drinking alcohol; he was against it and was not afraid to say so. A compatriot in this temperance crusade was Theobald Mathew, a priest in Cork, Ireland. Mathew was wildly successful in spearheading a movement there to get an estimated five million Irish men and women to take a pledge to never take a drink. In Milwaukee, O'Kelly's nagging on the matter just irritated his congregation. Solomon Juneau complained about O'Kelly to his superior in Detroit, Bishop Peter Lefevre. All of this was a strain on O'Kelly and he became ill.[5]

Patrick O'Kelly was transferred to a parish in Michigan in 1842 and was replaced by Martin Kundig, a priest who could speak English, German, and French, and consequently could conduct services in the native tongue of virtually all his congregation. He changed the name of the church from St. Luke's to St. Peter's to honor his bishop's patron saint and he kept his views on temperance more low-key than O'Kelly had.

Chapter 2
1840–1849

The 1840 census showed that the population of the city was rebounding from the pre-recession number of 1,000. The city now had over 1,300 residents, about 200 of them Irish, making that group about 15 percent of the total. Germans, who would eventually be the largest immigrant group in the city, made up a smaller part of the population, with Yankees in the vast majority.

More Irish Arrivals

The Panic of 1837 had closed mills in New England, leaving Irish workers there without jobs. Many Irish worked their way west and some settled in Milwaukee in the late 1830s and early 1840s, many of them from Fall River, Massachusetts.[1] Discrimination against the Irish in Eastern cities also drove many of them westward. The recession had loosened its grip as the 1840s arrived. More work was being done to change the Milwaukee area from its wild state to an urban center. Laborers, many of them Irish, were doing much of the work.

In 1841, industrious Irishman Jeremiah Coffee extended N. Water Street northward from E. Mason Street to E. Juneau Avenue, his plow pulled by a pair of black and white oxen. Coffee's shanty was located on the steep slope of W. Wells Street near N. Ninth Street. The upper floor exited onto N. Ninth Street, so his oxen were stabled on that floor, while he lived on the floor below. The N. Water Street job was just one of many carried out by Coffee. While working on bluff removal, Coffee's horse was the envy of his competitors because it allowed the Irishman to be more productive than they were. The horse was old and slow but intelligent. It pulled the cart filled with soil from the bluff to where it needed to be dumped without the benefit of a driver. It would then return for another load on its own. Coffee was killed in an accident while working on another fill project in 1848.

In 1843, handbills circulated in Eastern cities claiming that there was a need for 3,000 workers for harbor improvements in Milwaukee. Hundreds of Irish spent the last of their funds to get to Milwaukee, only to find that there was very little work for them here. It was believed that canal boat companies had produced the phony handbills to increase their business. Since there was little manufacturing here, people without skills could only find seasonal work, which would not provide for them throughout the year.

Canals, Piers, and Other Improvements

Many Irishmen worked their way westward by working on canal building. The Erie Canal across New York from the Hudson River to Lake Erie, completed in 1825, had shortened the trip from Atlantic seaports to the western shores of Lake Michigan. Thousands of miles of new canals were constructed after the Erie Canal was completed. The miserable work of digging in cold water and muck provided many Irish immigrants with a way to support their families as they worked through Pennsylvania, Ohio, Michigan, and Illinois. However, the canal building era was rapidly drawing to a close, thanks to the advent of the railroad.

Byron Kilbourn and his group, despite the growth of railroads, went ahead with their plans to dig a canal from E. North Avenue to the Rock River, which in turn would provide a water route to the Mississippi River. In the fall of 1840, the Milwaukee and Rock River Canal Company advertised for 40 to 50 laborers to begin work on preparing for the canal. They constructed a retaining wall along the bottom of the Milwaukee River bluffs and built earthworks in preparation. The first mile of the canal, and the North Avenue dam to control the water flow, were projected to be completed within a year. That goal was not met.

In 1841, a group of Irishmen who worked on the Illinois and Michigan Canal came to Milwaukee, but not to work on the canal. They realized that there was little future in canal building so they used their

The Rock River Canal paralleled the Milwaukee River. It was later filled in and named N. Commerce Street. (Photo courtesy of Jeff Beutner)

savings to buy farmland in Oak Creek. They formed a settlement there that included St. Matthew Church, near S. Chicago and W. Ryan roads. Besides Ryan Road, the names of other roads in that part of Oak Creek, like Fitzsimmons and O'Brien, reflect their former presence.

In addition to Oak Creek, there were two other Irish farming communities outside the city. One was in the Town of Granville, with St. Michael's Church, originally at W. Brown Deer and N. Green Bay roads, serving that area's Irish. The other was in the towns of Greenfield and Franklin, with the Irish attending St. Mary's Church in Hales Corners at S. 95th Street and W. Forest Home Avenue. Each of these churches, besides providing a meeting place for its members, included a burial ground for their final resting place.

In the fall of 1842, other Irish workers were drawn to the city to work on the earlier aborted canal project. After ten weeks the canal was a mile long, the dam was in place, and it was reported that work would resume the following spring. It never did. The canal was used to power mills along its route, but that was its only function. Years later it was filled in and named N. Commerce Street.

Yankees, Germans, Irish, and other European immigrants continued to pour into the city; some to stay and others on their way westward to create towns and farms inland. Access to the city was streamlined in 1843 with the opening of the first pier at the foot of E. Clybourn Street. At 1,200 feet long and 44 feet wide, it extended far enough into the lake to allow ships to dispense their passengers and goods on the dock.

Piers extended nearly a quarter of a mile into Lake Michigan in 1856. The Third Ward was developing south of E. Clybourn Street (in line with the right-hand pier). (Author's collection)

Competition for moving freight and passengers to town could sometimes become fierce. When one German passenger had a choice of five carts to take him from the pier to Downtown, he chose the German teamster rather than one of the four Irish drivers. Enraged, the Irish followed, yelling insults and throwing stones at the "Dutchman's" vehicle.[2]

Sculpting of the city continued, but not without controversy. Yankees complained that too much work was being done on improvements to E. Michigan Street in the Third Ward while the Yankee Hill neighborhood was being ignored. They claimed that Juneau favored the Third Ward Irish because they shared politics and religion—Democratic and Catholic.

Many of the Irish were squatters, living in small, crudely built one-room structures that were home to an entire family and maybe a few animals. They built these shanties, also called paddies-huts, on land no one else was interested in, like sandy areas along the lake and the filled-in marshes. However, some did live on potential prime real estate north of E. Wisconsin Avenue along the lake bluff with its scenic views. Because there was no water readily available in that area, the affluent were not interested in building on the bluffs until the 1870s, when the new municipal water system would allow the construction of grand homes there. City officials complained that the shanties were an eyesore and should be removed, and that the construction of a promenade to provide views of Lake Michigan would make better use of the bluffs.

The cores of Milwaukee's two early Irish neighborhoods were taking shape as the marshes were slowly being filled in. The bigger of the two was the Third Ward, the land south of Wisconsin Avenue and bordered by Lake Michigan and the Milwaukee River. In the other neighborhood, Tory Hill, the residents built homes on the side of the hill, between N. Sixth and N. Eighth streets south of W. Clybourn Street, that gave the neighborhood part of its name.

Immigrants Working Together

Excessive consumption of alcohol was very common in frontier areas during this time and abstinence was not the norm, but in February of 1843 the Wisconsin Catholic Total Abstinence Society was founded in Milwaukee. It included French, Irish, and German Catholics who took a pledge to abstain from intoxicating drinks. If any member was seen drinking they would be reported to the president of the society, whose duty it would be to publicly expel that person at the next meeting. Many Yankees in the city had taken the pledge as members of the Pioneer Temperance Society two years earlier, but a contemporary, James Buck, in looking over the list of those people years later, commented that many on the list had died from excessive drink. There is no reason to expect that Catholic temperance fared any better.

On St. Patrick's Day in 1843, members of the Wisconsin Catholic Total Abstinence Society put on the most spectacular parade that the young city had seen. Three thousand Catholics marched through Juneautown and Kilbourntown, amazing spectators. In addition to city residents, marchers came from the outlying areas of the county as well as from Kenosha, Waukesha, and Racine counties. It remained the biggest St. Patrick's Day celebration for the rest of the century.

A few days after the parade, the city's Germans, again joined by the Irish and French, staged another parade to celebrate the decision by the United States Congress to dredge and improve the harbor. The three ethnic groups wanted to display their commitment to the city's development. The improvements would solidify Milwaukee's position as the best harbor on the western shore of Lake Michigan. The Germans and Irish again impressed the Yankee population with their celebrations on the Fourth of July.

The city's Yankees, and Protestants from the British Isles, held the political power in Milwaukee at the time and dominated both political parties, the Whigs and the Democrats. They filled nearly every elected position in the villages from 1837 to 1843, with the primary exception being the French Canadian, Solomon Juneau. The Irish and many Germans supported the Democrats, who were friendly to immigrants, to gain some influence in the local political scene. Two Germans and two Irishmen, Andrew McCormick and Thomas J. Gilbert, were elected East Side trustees, with Gilbert selected as president of the combined Juneautown and Kilbourntown villages in 1844. Germans and Irish also banded together to fight the restrictions on immigrant voting on issues such as Wisconsin statehood, representatives to the constitutional convention, and the adoption of the constitution itself.

Bloody Third Ward

As the marshes of the Third Ward continued to be filled in, and the Irish population continued to increase, the Ward took on an Irish flavor. The Whigs never tired of insulting the Third Warders. In 1846 Edward McGarry, a Third Ward alderman, complained that the Whigs were referring to the Ward as the "Bloody Third Ward," presumably because of the fist fights and drunken brawls that took place there, but "knives, guns and clubs were unheard of."[3]

The Whigs also dubbed the Third Ward "Sodom and Gomorrah," implying that vice was prevalent. The *Daily Courier*, the Irish newspaper,

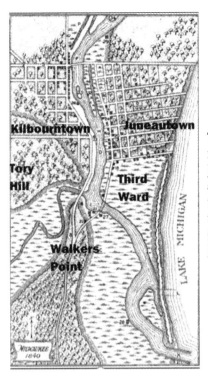

This early Milwaukee map of 1840 shows the three villages—Juneautown, Kilbourntown, and Walker's Point—as well as the two Irish neighborhoods, the Third Ward and Tory Hill. (*History of Milwaukee, Wisconsin*, John G. Gregory, 1931)

shot back that they hoped no Whigs would be turned to pillars of salt.

Businesses lined the Ward's northern section between E. Clybourn Street and E. Wisconsin Avenue and its western edge along N. Water Street and N. Broadway. The Irish were concentrated in homes south of E. Clybourn Street to E. Menomonee Street and from N. Milwaukee Street east to the lake.

Yankees owned most of the land in the Third Ward, which was within walking distance of jobs Downtown and on the waterways. Since walking was the primary means of locomotion, Ward land was increasing in value and higher rents could be charged compared with buildings farther from the city center. The first structures in the city were built quickly and cheaply. Most had ceilings that were barely six feet high. As they were replaced with more livable buildings with higher ceilings, landlords began moving the older, primitive buildings from other parts of the city to the Third Ward.[4] Most of the residents were renters and they paid a premium for living in these houses. Over the decades, many of these renters would become homeowners and by the end of the century, as Italians moved into the Ward, they would complain that Irish landlords were charging them

17

excessive rents for dilapidated housing.[5]

Tory Hill

The other, smaller Irish neighborhood, Tory Hill, had a higher concentration of Irish and their offspring than did the Third Ward. Tory Hill was located at the point where the bluffs along the west side of the Milwaukee River Valley met the bluffs on the north side of the Menomonee River Valley, near W. Clybourn and N. Fifth streets. The area between N. Sixth and N. Eighth streets, where a hill ran down from W. Clybourn Street to W. St. Paul Avenue, became known as Tory Hill. The Tory Hill neighborhood grew to include the area from N. 5th to N. 14th streets between W. Clybourn Street and the Menomonee River below. There were many Irish living on streets farther north, and the northern boundary of the Tory Hill neighborhood has at times been considered by historians to be either W. Michigan Street or W. Wisconsin Avenue rather than W. Clybourn Street.

For the first part of its name, we turn to Humphrey Desmond, a Milwaukee Irishman and local historian, as well as a lawyer and the owner and editor of the *Catholic Citizen*, a forerunner to today's *Catholic Herald Citizen*. He said the name "Tory" in Tory Hill was "not complimentary" and that it was "a name fastened on the Irish in the sixteenth and seventeenth centuries by the English invaders."[6] *The Oxford Companion to Irish History* tells us that the word "tory" came from the Irish word *toraidhe*, which means robber. The English initially used the term to refer to Irish outlaws or bandits but eventually they applied it to all Irish Catholics.

By the 1860s, the name of the neighborhood was firmly entrenched. In an article in a Milwaukee newspaper, *The Weekly Wisconsin*, in January 1863, a Milwaukee reporter touring New York's Central Park writes of the large number of swans in the park. He comments that "the good Irish people of Tory Hill furnish twice the number of swans and geese."[7]

Tory Hill was settled by squatters who erected one-room shanties clustered helter-skelter on the hillside. Inside most of the shacks were a stove, a table, and a bed or beds. Many shanty owners had pens for chickens, geese, swans, pigs, and cows, and the whole area reeked of farm odors. Some animals wandered freely. A few owners laid sod and transplanted trees, but the neighborhood would never become bucolic, with slaughterhouses, tanneries, and railroad yards in its future.[8]

Many neighborhood residents would not acquire the skills necessary to rise above the grinding poverty in which they were mired. Some turned to drink, which led to domestic violence, fights, and disorderly conduct. Some Tory Hillers were well known to the justice system, and as little as they could afford it, they would help pay for that system through fines that were levied for their crimes. For the rest of the nineteenth century the neighborhood was considered a ghetto with a less than ideal reputation. The unpleasant odors that emanated from it caused it to be referred to as a "fragrant" or "delectable locality."[9]

Idleness among youths led some of them to terrorize outsiders who came into the area, as well as people in nearby neighborhoods. Attacks on people on the fringes of Tory Hill scared users of Merrill's Grove, a mile away at N. 29th Street and W. Wisconsin Avenue, who reportedly feared "unpleasantness from the Tory Hill ruffians and other Irish ragamuffins."[10] James Kneeland, a wealthy Yankee investor and one-time owner of some Tory Hill land, wore as a badge of courage later in his life the fact that when he was young, he would walk through Tory Hill—alone.[11] The *Sentinel* editorialized that it was necessary to "skim the vile scum from that neighborhood."[12] Humphrey Desmond, editor of the *Catholic Citizen*, reported that drinking in Tory Hill "set back many promising careers and made wretched many homes."[13]

The policemen who were assigned to the neighborhood were Irish, but that seemed to have little impact. When policeman Jerry O'Connor tried to arrest Michael Conlan's wife, Conlan attacked O'Connor with an axe. Fellow Officer Costney Egan, like O'Connor a County Tipperary native, came to O'Connor's rescue and subdued Conlan. The *Sentinel* pointed out that it had been a while since a policeman, also known as a "peeler" by residents, could singlehandedly make an arrest in Tory Hill.

Decades later the situation had not changed. Policeman William Kelly was assigned to Tory Hill in the late 1880s. According to Kelly, "it was a custom for four or five of them to jump a cop when he was calling for a patrol wagon and take his prisoner away from him." In one such fight, Kelly hit a man with his club, and afterward said "it was the only time I raised my club and struck a man."[14]

Sometimes even two police officers were not enough. Policemen John O'Brien and Thomas Clark were arresting John O'Neill when they were

Milwaukee's founder, French-Canadian fur trader Solomon Juneau. (*History of Milwaukee, Wisconsin*, John G. Gregory, 1931)

attacked by Tory Hill rowdies. O'Brien suffered injuries to his face and neck, but it could have been worse. One of his attackers had called for an axe to make "mincemeat of the peelers."[15]

Milwaukee Becomes a City

In 1846, the villages of Juneautown, Kilbourntown, and Walker's Point were consolidated to form the city of Milwaukee. Solomon Juneau was elected the city's first mayor and three aldermen were elected from each of the five wards. Two of the Third Ward alderman were from Ireland: Wilson Graham, a Protestant lawyer, and Richard Murphy, an Irish Catholic grocer and hide dealer.

Irish Voting Illegally?

That same year, the "White Irishman," John White, did not fare as well in his run for County Sheriff. The Milwaukee *Sentinel*, a Whig newspaper, repeatedly charged that White had voted illegally in 1843. The city's Protestant clergy joined in the anti-White campaign because he was a foreigner and a Catholic. The city's Germans joined the Yankees in the belief that White and many of the Irish immigrants had not been in the United States long enough to vote legally. Generally, the rules required that an immigrant be in the country for two years before he could file his intention to become a citizen. After they filed, they could legally vote. Since many of the Germans came directly to Milwaukee from Germany, they assumed that the Irish came directly from Ireland and had not waited the required two years. But, as mentioned earlier, most Irish did not have the means to travel to Milwaukee directly but instead worked their way west over a period of years. An analysis of Irish naturalization records in Milwaukee from 1839 to 1843 shows that they were in the United States an average of six years before filing their intent to become a citizen. In John White's case, he filed his intent to become a citizen in Detroit in 1837. So, both the *Sentinel* and the Germans were incorrect in accusing the Irish generally, and John White in particular, of voting illegally.

The second step in the naturalization process was to wait several more years before the final papers for citizenship could be applied for and issued. Many immigrants, regardless of ethnicity, did not take this step because they were satisfied with their ability to vote and citizenship did not really give them many further tangible benefits, except to be eligible to hold public office. But some Irish, including John White, did complete the citizenship process, after an average stay of over nine years. Not content in claiming that White voted illegally, the *Sentinel* editorialized that he had not been a citizen long enough to run for sheriff, even though he was eligible immediately after he gained citizenship in 1844.

In 1849, John White would finally be elected to a political position when he won the county treasurer election. He was the first Irishman to hold that title, but he would not be the last. During the next 40 years, the Irish would have a virtual lock on the county treasurer position, filling it with 11 Irishmen while only 3 non-Irishmen were elected to the position in that time.

More Immigrants

The estimated population of Milwaukee in 1844 was 6,000 people. There is no recorded estimate of the ethnic breakdown, but the Irish were probably about 15 to 20 percent of the total. Because of the extended time that it took for Irish immigrants to work their way to Milwaukee, many had larger families at that point than they did when they reached North America. An example is Richard Reynolds and his wife, Christina Connors, who came from County Meath and who would eventually have nine children. They arrived in Milwaukee in 1837 with three children who were born in Ireland, one in New York, and two in Michigan. James Johnson from County Clare, Milwaukee's first Irish physician, came here with his wife, Catherine, in 1844. The first three of their eight children were born in New York and Ohio.

These American-born children would not officially be counted as part of the Irish population by the United States Census Bureau because they were not born in Ireland, but their non-Irish neighbors would certainly have considered them Irish. Many more Irish children would be born in Milwaukee and these too would not officially be classified as Irish. Similarly, American-born children of other immigrants to Milwaukee, like the Scots, Welsh, English, Swiss, Swedish, and Norwegians, would not be counted in a specific ethnic group. They would be counted as Yankees, giving a skewed picture of the ethnic makeup of city. The Irish numbers were affected more than other groups because of their larger families.

Attempt to Repeal the Acts of Union

In 1800, the Acts of Union were passed, which eliminated the Irish Parliament, giving the English Parliament full control over Irish affairs and creating the United Kingdom of Great Britain and Ireland. In the late 1830s and early 1840s, a movement to repeal that Union took place in Ireland, led by Irish leader Daniel O'Connell. The movement sought to repeal the Acts and restore the Irish Parliament, and to provide Ireland with some measure of independence.

In 1843, Irish in cities throughout America, including Milwaukee, formed Repeal Associations. Local groups were instrumental in calling attention to the movement and raising money to be sent to Ireland to support the issue. Milwaukee Irish arranged activities for the Fourth of July and St. Patrick's Day and held frequent meetings, often in association with the Catholic Temperance Society. The cause of freedom and independence in Ireland was supported by Milwaukee citizens of all ethnic groups, including the freedom-loving Yankees, some of whom thought that freedom in Ireland would keep Irishmen there and out of the United States.

To bring in more members, and more funds, the city's Irish founded the Wisconsin Repeal Association. Elected officers included Yankees and Germans. The fee for joining the organization was 25 cents, with

Ireland's emancipator, Daniel O'Connell.
(Portrait by Bernard Mulrenin)

twelve and a half cents due monthly after that. A rule prohibited religious or political discussions at meetings. A semi-monthly newspaper, *The Immigrant and Irish Repealer*, was published by John A. Brown, James Magone, and Daniel Fitzsimmons, the latter two being officers of the local association.

Daniel O'Connell gave a speech in Ireland during the summer of 1843 condemning slavery in the United States, causing him to lose the support of the Repeal Associations that had formed in the southern states. That autumn, O'Connell and other leaders of the repeal movement were arrested and charged with conspiracy by the British government. O'Connell was sentenced to a year of imprisonment for his "conspiracy," but was released after three months by the British House of Lords, who condemned his trial as unfair. But the Repeal Movement was dead after that, and so still, was Irish independence.

The Irish in Ireland felt an allegiance to their home county. A man from County Kerry was a Kerryman—and he would say so and be proud of it. People from Ulster or Dublin or Wexford felt similarly and would voice it. When they arrived in the United States, particularly if they were in a group from the same place in Ireland, they would continue to identify themselves that way.

But in Milwaukee, as the Irish mixed with those from other parts of Ireland and with people of other nationalities, they were more likely to refer to themselves as Irishmen rather than Sligomen or Corkmen. Issues that affected all of Ireland, like the repeal of the Acts of Union and the upcoming potato famine, drove away much of the provincialism of the past.

St. Patrick's Day

Milwaukee's celebration of St. Patrick's Day in 1844 was held at the Cottage Inn on N. Water Street south of E. Michigan Street and featured speakers, toasts, and food. Yankees, like the founder of Walker's Point, George Walker, spoke in favor of Irish independence. Other supporters for Irish freedom included Germans, Swedes, and French. Solomon Juneau sparked enthusiastic applause when he called for "the overthrow of British tyranny."[16]

But the highlight among the speakers was Edward Keogh, who was not yet nine years old, the son of Thomas Keogh, the school teacher at St. Peter's. The boy spoke of Ireland, a country that he left at age five, and "the masterly style and language in which it was expressed went directly to the hearts of his audience" and the "tear that sprang involuntary to the eyes of the hardy sons of the Emerald Isle, evinced that their feelings were touched by this youthful orator."[17] As an adult, Edward Keogh would be elected to represent the Third Ward in the state legislature and would serve there for a total of 20 years.

Irish Get Churches of Their Own

Milwaukee became the center of the Diocese of Wisconsin in 1843, with John Henni as its bishop and St. Peter's as its cathedral. The Irish and Catholic Germans shared St. Peter's Cathedral but the Germans were not content with the arrangement. They felt that their religion could be best served only in the German language, so they made plans to form their own parish. In April 1846, the cornerstone for St. Mary's Church on N. Broadway and E. Kilbourn Avenue was laid. In 1847, the church, now known as Old St. Mary's Church, was consecrated by the German-speaking Henni and his address to those present was in German.

This left St. Peter's to the English-speakers, who were overwhelmingly Irish. Churches in the diocese were referred to by the language in which they conducted their services, aside from the Mass, which was always in Latin. Therefore, if services were in German it was called a German church and if services were in English it was referred to as an English church. There were relatively few English-speaking Catholics who were not Irish, so ironically, Irish churches were referred to as English churches.

St. Peter's Cathedral, on E. State and N. Jackson streets, even without the Germans, was too small for the growing Irish population, and was not considered grand enough for a cathedral. The cornerstone for a new structure, the one still on that site today, was laid in 1847. Henni chose a new name, calling it the Cathedral of St. John the Evangelist for his patron saint. The site for the church was on N. Jackson Street across from Courthouse Square (now known as Cathedral Square). The funds to build the structure came from donations from Germany, France, Cuba, and Mexico. The Cathedral's parishioners were primarily from the Third

German Catholics built Old St. Mary's Church, leaving the Cathedral of St. John to the Irish. (Photograph by the author)

Ward and Tory Hill.

The same year the Cathedral's cornerstone was laid, plans were in the works for a second Irish church to better serve the needs of Tory Hill residents, as well as Irish living in Walker's Point. A new wood frame church, also built with European donations, was completed two years later on filled land at N. Second and W. Michigan streets. It was named for St. Gall, a sixth-century Irish missionary who worked to Christianize Switzerland and in whose honor the Abbey of St. Gall there was named. Milwaukee's Swiss-born archbishop, John Henni, had attended the abbey and he named St. Gall's Church. This was one of the few acts by the German-speaking Henni that received the whole-hearted approval of the city's Irish.

Potato Blight, the Great Hunger, and More Immigrants

In 1845, a year after the repeal movement failed, the potato crop in Ireland also began to fail. An organism attacked the potato plant through its leaves, leaving the tuber a black, gooey, inedible mess. About a third of Ireland's population relied on the potato as their main source of nourishment, and the blight caused the deaths by starvation and related diseases of a million to a million and a half people during the years 1845 to 1849.[18] More than two million Irish were forced to leave the country during that time and the years following.[19] The potato blight was also known as the Great Famine or, in the Irish language, as *An Gorta Mór*, The Great Hunger.

In 1846, Milwaukee's Irish organized to raise money to help feed starving Irish. Influential Irish citizens like John White and James Johnson were joined by Yankees Byron Kilbourn, Increase Lapham, Rufus King, and Alexander Mitchell in their effort. Milwaukeeans of all nationalities donated to the fund that raised over $1,700. The money was used to buy 425 barrels of flour to be sent to Ireland. The grain was shipped to Buffalo free of charge, but the cost of transporting it through the Erie Canal to New York and then to Irish ports used about 15 percent of the money collected. Ironically, English landowners shipped massive amounts of agricultural goods and livestock from Ireland to England and Scotland while Irishmen were dying of hunger and Americans were sending food to help. The Irish resentment toward English policies, always strong, increased tremendously and lasted for generations.

Milwaukee's Hibernian Benevolent Society was formed in 1847 to aid the sufferers of the Great Famine. It apparently was initially called the St. Patrick Benevolent Society and was also known as the Hibernian Mutual Benefit Society. Patrick McDonough, who was later lost in the 1860 sinking of the *Lady Elgin*, was its first recorded president and Thomas Shields, superintendent of Kilbourn's canal, its first vice-president.

The association also aided its members by visiting the sick and offering financial support while they were unable to work. It contributed to the expense of burying its members and provided funds to the deceased's family. Support was also given to charitable causes like evicted tenants and others in need in Ireland and elsewhere. Members met at St. Gall's hall.

The Great Hunger in Ireland brought many hundreds of Irish to Milwaukee during the famine years. In 1848, the lack of food resulted in a failed rebellion in Ireland, which brought still more Irish here. These extremely poor Irish immigrants came to Milwaukee much more quickly after arriving in North America than the previous Irish immigrants had. Travel costs to the Midwest had dropped significantly after the railroads built routes that followed the Erie Canal across the state of New York and charged lower rates, forcing canal transportation charges to drop

The potato crop failure led to the Great Famine, which meant starvation and death for many Irish. (*Illustrated London News*, Bridget O'Donnell and Her Two Children, 1849)

to meet the competition. Great Lakes ships from Buffalo then brought immigrants to Milwaukee and other port cities.

By 1848, the number of Irish in the city had increased from about 200 in 1840 to nearly 2,500, according to a city census taken that year, and they made up fifteen percent of the population. The number of Germans was more than double that of the Irish. The city's population was over 16,000 then, with the majority of Milwaukee inhabitants being immigrants.

William Gray, born in the city of Limerick about 1825, was typical of the famine immigrants, who came primarily from the south and west of Ireland. He brought his family to the United States in 1847 and made it to Milwaukee that same year. He had no skills and found it difficult to earn a living the first few years with the low wages paid to laborers. Then he began working on the construction of the gas works in the Third Ward, which brought lighting to some city buildings and streets. His wages increased when he became an employee of the gas works and his life became easier. He and his wife, Mary Slattery, had 13 children. The couple lived the rest of their lives on N. Jefferson Street in the Ward.

Another poor famine family, Patrick Cudahy Sr., his wife, Elizabeth Shaw, and the first four of their children, came to the city during the summer of 1849 from County Kilkenny. The Cudahys turned out to be anything but typical. They settled initially in Tory Hill and then moved further west along the Menomonee River Valley, where their other two children were born. The five sons worked in meatpacking plants as young men and then made their careers in the business. Four of them became millionaires and one of them, Patrick Jr., founded the Milwaukee suburb of Cudahy.

An Irish-American Militia—The City Guard

Many Irish militias in the United States could trace their existence to the failed Young Irelander Rebellion of 1848. Most of the Young Irelanders, a nationalist group that included both Catholics and Protestants, were graduates of Trinity College in Dublin. In February 1848, the overthrow of the French king sparked rebellions across Europe in Germany, Austria, Italy, Hungary, and Ireland. The Irish action took place in Ballingarry, County Tipperary, in July. After a gun battle of several hours between police and rebels, the rebellion was over, and the rebels were forced to flee and hide. A Milwaukee man, Thomas Shea, who became one of the city's wealthiest Irishmen, liked to tell the story of when he was a teenager in Boula, County Tipperary. After the skirmish he supplied food for members of the rebel group, including his heroes William Smith O'Brien and Thomas Francis Meagher, while they were on the run at Slievenamon. Shea emigrated to Milwaukee the following year in 1849.

Two of the revolutionaries, James Stephens and John O'Mahony, avoided arrest by escaping to Paris, while others were arrested and sent to a penal colony in Tasmania, Australia. Stephens would later found the Irish Republican Brotherhood in Ireland, the forerunner of the Irish Republican Army, while O'Mahony organized the Fenian Brotherhood in the United States. The defeat of the Young Irelanders kindled a nationalism that lasted for generations among the Irish and Irish Americans. In America, it led to the organization of militias throughout the country that, it was hoped, would someday free Ireland from dreaded England.

In reaction to the failed revolt, Milwaukee's Irish formed the City Guard that year. The founder and 35-year-old captain of the City Guard was John McManman, who was born in County Mayo and had previously served as an officer in an Irish militia company in Detroit. In 1844, McManman came to Milwaukee, where he married 20-year-old Anna Gannon before returning to Detroit. Two years later, the McManmans came back to Milwaukee and opened a wholesale and retail grocery business in a building owned by fellow Irishman, physician James Johnson, on N. Water Street between E. St. Paul Avenue and E. Clybourn Street.

John McManman was very confident of his military abilities. One of his critics claimed that he thought that the three greatest military leaders of the world were, in no particular order, Hannibal, Napoleon, and … well, McManman was too modest to mention the third. But that same critic conceded that McManman was a "generous, good fellow as ever lived."[20] The longer he resided in Milwaukee, the more he was respected and admired. One newspaperman said, "you would have to travel far and long to find as genial, painstaking and hospitable a host."[21] McManman moved among the influential men of Juneautown, putting him in the company of only a handful of the city's Irish. He was a supporter of the theater and was elected to the school board representing the Third Ward. He favored limiting the number of bridges over the river to the hated Kilbourntown, even though it was now part of Milwaukee. He, along with many others, lobbied the federal government to cut a channel from the Milwaukee River to Lake Michigan, which would give ships easy access to city warehouses and Downtown while eliminating the need for long piers into the lake.

Within months of McManman's arrival, the governor called for the formation of a state regiment to volunteer for service in the Mexican-American War, and he appointed McManman to the regimental staff. McManman was a strong supporter of the city's other three militia companies, all German: the Washington Guard, the Milwaukee Riflemen, and the Milwaukee Dragoons.

So, when McManman's Irish City Guard was formed in the autumn of 1848, the city had its fourth military company, all of them manned by foreign-born residents. The Guard's headquarters was on the third floor of Doctor Johnson's building on N. Water Street. The militia had 75 members and included a band and a full set of musical instruments. The Guard's uniforms consisted of a dark blue coat with tails, high collar and cuffs edged in white, and light blue trousers, spreading well over the foot. They wore white cross belts on their chests with glittering breastplates,

The genial John McManman, founder of the Irish City Guard, held the highest military post in the state, that of Adjutant General. (UCLA Libraries)

**The uniform of the City Guard included tall hats
and cross belts on the chest.** (Wikipedia)

and tall military hats with white braids and tassels, each with a large white
plume and a brass-colored chinstrap.[22]

The Guard drew members who could afford the expense of their
uniforms, which was usually covered by the dues they paid. Another
expense to many members was the pay lost while participating in Guard
activities. Consequently, members of the Guard were better off financially
than the majority of Irish, laborers who lived from hand to mouth.
Aside from the goal of eventually freeing Ireland, there were other, more
immediate reasons to join the Guard. For its leaders, the recognition
could, and often did, lead to political positions, business connections, and
elevated status in the community. Every high-ranking officer of the City
Guard had been, or would be, elected to some political office, a trend that
held true for most Irish military officers in the city for the rest of the
century, when nearly all Irish politicians served in Irish militias. For the
rank and file, the uniform and the parading drew the admiration of the

Irish community, and for the single men, the attention of young women in particular. In an era when Irish Catholics were generally detested and loathed, it was an opportunity to impress detractors.

The Guard's first two months of existence were spent in drilling. Their discipline paid off when Wisconsin Adjutant General Smith inspected them and, commenting that they were as good as any in the state, agreed to supply them with state-owned arms and accouterments. The Guard celebrated by holding a ball at their headquarters that included dancing, a midnight supper, then more dancing. The affair, put on with the help of McManman's lieutenants, Andrew McCormick and the white-clad John White, was described as being "the most brilliant military ball seen in the city."[23]

Most of the City Guard's activities consisted of monthly drills, occasional marches into the countryside for target practice, hosting their annual ball, and parading. They drew appreciative crowds as they marched on special occasions like St. Patrick's Day, Washington's Birthday, the commemoration of the Battle of New Orleans, and the Fourth of July parade, often with the German companies. By the end of the first year, McManman stepped up from captain of the City Guard to major and commander of the Milwaukee Battalion, which incorporated the city's four militia companies. John White was elected to replace him as captain of the City Guard.

The American Party and the German 48ers

The American Party, later known as the Know Nothing movement, began to build momentum in the late 1840s. Yankees resented the growing number of German and Irish immigrants and focused on Catholics in a predominately Protestant country, where anti-Catholicism could be traced to the Puritan days. The influx of immigrants caused a significant decline in factory wages, which created further hostility toward the newcomers. Because Milwaukee was a new city with no long-standing Protestant core and because it had a majority immigrant population, the Yankees could not promote the same anti-immigrant sentiment that was growing in eastern cities. While some Yankees did hold hostile views of the new immigrants, they could not take on the majority of their neighbors. They could, and did, repeat anti-Catholic rhetoric such as the pope's desire to be governor of Wisconsin or president of the United States.[24]

The most ardent foes of the Irish Catholic segment of the city during this time period though were the German Forty-Eighters. In 1848, the Forty-Eighters participated in rebellions in some European countries for more democratic governments and more human rights. They left Europe after they failed in their mission and many came to Milwaukee. The Forty-Eighters, also called Freethinkers, did not want the government to tamper with their drinking of alcohol and were anti-temperance, so the Irish would seem to have been natural supporters of the Freethinkers. But the Forty-Eighters were also anti-Catholic because the Catholic Church supported the governments the Freethinkers fought against in Europe. The Irish, who had clung to their religion through centuries of assault by the English, did not abandon it now. So, in addition to being anti-Catholic, the Forty-Eighters became anti-Irish. A leader of the Freethinkers in Milwaukee, Bernard Domschke, wrote, "The Irish are our natural enemies, not because they are Irishmen, but because they are the truest guards of Popery."[25] Although they detested the Irish, Freethinkers saved most of their wrath for the prominent Catholics in the city, the German Catholic clergy and German religious orders, whom they criticized in newspapers and harassed on city streets.

The Freethinkers founded a German language newspaper called the *Volksfreund*, with Frederick Fratney as editor. Fratney especially disliked Irish Catholics, but there is no record of any specific conflict between him and the Irish. Strangely, he married an Irish Catholic woman named Bridget Moran, and two of their children were baptized at the Cathedral of St. John's. Fratney died at the age of 37, perhaps due to some kind of internal conflict.

Plank Roads and Railroads

Irish laborers were kept busy working on the major projects of bluff removal, marsh filling, and street creation. In 1846, Tory Hill resident Owen Powderly, a native of County Meath, was working on the bluff near N. Fifth Street and W. Wisconsin Avenue when a section of the bluff collapsed, killing him and his team of horses and injuring several other workers.

Irish workers were also employed on the construction of the plank roads that radiated from the city to communities to the south, west, and north. In 1849, a new project was started—preparing a road bed for the city's first railroad, which would run from the foot of Tory Hill to the west. Its initial run was in November 1850 when it ran the five miles to Wauwatosa. In February 1851, the line was extended to Waukesha. The railroad, which would eventually be known as the Milwaukee Road, would employ hundreds of Irish workers during the rest of the century and ultimately reach the West Coast.

Time Difference

The two communities on opposite sides of the Milwaukee River did not agree on much. In 1849, three years after the villages joined to become the City of Milwaukee, they could not even agree on the time. There were no time zones in that era. The official local time was measured by its distance from Greenwich, England. Consequently, the time in Madison, 79 miles west of Milwaukee, would be earlier than the time in Milwaukee at any given instant. But the distance from Juneautown to Kilbourntown could not account for the difference of 12 minutes between the two communities, especially since the west village was 12 minutes later than the east village. West Siders were used to looking at watchmaker Cornelius Peters' great clock on N. Third Street to set their timepieces, while East Siders turned to N. Water Street watchmaker, Abner Kirby, for the correct time. But neither community's time was correct according to civil engineer Michael McDermott. The County Galway native calculated the city's distance from Greenwich and determined that Peters' time was six minutes fast while Kirby's was six minutes slow.

Cholera, 1849

In fleeing the famine in Ireland, tens of thousands of Irish people died on the "coffin" ships that transported them to North America. The ships generally lacked food, water, and sanitation. Many passengers starved and even the well-provisioned ships carried many more people than they should have, and the crowded conditions were perfect for spreading diseases like typhus, cholera, and smallpox. Overcrowding of people was dangerous even on Great Lakes ships, especially during an epidemic.

During the summer of 1849, the cholera epidemic was closing in on Milwaukee from the east, through the Great Lakes, and from the south along the Mississippi River. The epidemic hit Europe before coming to the United States and caused many deaths in Ireland, where malnourished famine sufferers were too weak to fight it off. Victims of the disease suffered severe diarrhea that could lead to dehydration, kidney failure, and death within a few hours or a few days.

It was not then known how the disease spread, but there were many ideas about how to avoid getting it. Stagnant water was thought to be a possible source, so newspapers called for filling in depressions in the Third Ward where puddles formed, and then covering them with lime. Another recommendation was to wake up at six in the morning, wash the whole body by rubbing hard, eat a lot of meat, drink a lot of water, and go to bed by ten o'clock at night. Another theory was to light bonfires. Hoping to capitalize on the fear, one city business advertised their baths for only 37.5 cents. Animal waste was considered a possibility for spreading the disease and wagon loads of excrement were removed from city streets.

Decades later it was determined that the cause was intestinal bacteria that passed out of the body in feces. People who did not clean their hands well could pass it on by handling food that others ate. The most frequent way, though, was by contaminating drinking water. About 80 percent of healthy individuals exposed to it did not exhibit symptoms but could pass it to others. Of those who did have symptoms, about 80 percent survived. People in ill health, children, and the elderly were most susceptible.

Thousands of immigrants were coming to Milwaukee, some to stay and some destined for other parts of Wisconsin. A number of them contracted cholera in the confines of incoming ships and were dead, or near death, when they arrived at the city's piers. The city's first fatalities occurred in early July and deaths continued until early September. Farmers were reluctant to come to town, fearing they would die, and the amount of produce in the city declined, as did its wheat exports. The Board of Health warned residents against eating green vegetables like cabbage and cucumbers. People avoided one another. When a victim died, the other inhabitants of their household were shunned. The Board of Health reported on August 9 that cholera had completely disappeared from the city, but that was premature; six more people would die the next day with many more to follow.

Proportionally, many more deaths occurred in Chicago, which had a population about forty percent larger than Milwaukee's. Chicago had a reputation as a filthy city, prompting some of its residents to come to Milwaukee, which was considered cleaner and safer.

Determining an accurate number of 1849 cholera deaths in Milwaukee is difficult. At the end of August, newspapers reported that there had been 104 fatalities since July. There were more deaths in early September. Deaths were undoubtedly underreported because there was a reluctance to publicize them for fear of hurting the city's economy by scaring immigrants from coming, and a desire not to cause panic among residents. There were charges that neither the Board of Health nor physicians were reporting all cholera cases. Burial permits and death registrations were not required at that time so there are no official records of the deaths.

The federal mortality schedules related to the 1850 census show that 92 city residents died of cholera during July and August 1849. This figure does not include those who died with the diagnosis of diarrhea but were actually victims of cholera. Nor does the figure include the German, Norwegian, Welsh, Scottish, and Irish immigrants who were dying or dead upon reaching the city. The names of 52 other victims, who were not named in mortality schedules, were reported by newspapers and other sources, bringing the names of known victims to 144. The total number of victims was probably over 200.

The Third Ward was the hardest hit, especially those who lived close to the piers where immigrants entered the city. Their drinking water was taken directly from Lake Michigan, which undoubtedly was contaminated by waste from boats and by the immigrants themselves as they were washed at a bathing house on the shore built for that purpose. Cholera generally was most intense among poor people in urban areas due to crowding and a lack of sanitary systems, conditions prevalent in the Third Ward at the time.

About one-third of the known victims were Irish, a much higher proportion than their one-fifth of the population. With about 200 total dead, the number of Irish victims was probably between 65 and 75. Among the Irish who died were Alderman Richard Murphy and Bridget Furlong, the wife of one of the city's leading Irish citizens, John Furlong. Julius Patricius Bolivar McCabe, a native of County Armagh, who produced city directories in Ireland and who compiled Milwaukee's first city directory in 1847, also died in the epidemic.

Education

There were no public schools in Milwaukee in 1842, but Irish boys and girls had their first formal educational opportunity when St. Peter's School was opened. That year 25 boys were taught in a classroom in the basement of the church on E. State and N. Jackson streets by Joseph Murray, "a scholarly Irish gentleman."[26] The German boys were taught in another classroom by Mister Englehardt. Two young women, Catherine Shea and Miss Murray, were the first teachers for girls in a nearby building on N. Jefferson Street. The children of Irish laborers were more likely to attend school than the offspring of German laborers, an indication of the importance that the Irish placed on education as a means of improving themselves economically.[27]

In 1843, Thomas Keogh, 32, replaced Joseph Murray. Keogh and his wife, Ann Boylan, had left County Cavan for the United States in 1841. He had an education and a moderate amount of savings when he came to Milwaukee two years later. Keogh soon found a job at St. Peter's School, where he worked for a year before opening a private school in the Third Ward. The Keoghs would lose two of their five children, Margaret and Agnes, in the sinking of the *Lady Elgin*. Another private school was founded at the time by another Irishman identified as Mister Finnegan.

1846 brought about some major changes when St. Peter's became the First Ward Public School and Thomas Keogh's private school became Third Ward Public School. Milwaukee became a city that year and a public school system was needed. St. Peter's was enlarged and more classrooms were added as the student count climbed to 80.[28] Since religion could not be taught during classes in a public school, the Catholic students stayed after regular classes to be instructed in their religion by the pastor, Peter McLaughlin. Thomas Keogh was hired by the school commissioners to run the Third Ward Public School.

1846 also brought three Sisters of Charity from Maryland to establish St. Joseph's Academy as the girls' school at St. Peter's parish, as well as founding a Catholic girls' orphanage that would be known as St. Rose's. The school's enrollment of 30 pupils increased as orphans were added to the student body. Most of the orphans, like the orphanage's first occupant, Katie Colfer, were Irish. Two-year-old Katie and her parents, Michael and Catherine Colfer, had come from County Wexford to Milwaukee, where the parents died of smallpox in a barracks on Jones Island. St. Peter's pastor, Peter McLaughlin, promised them that Katie would be cared for and kept his promise by placing her with the Sisters of Charity. Katie grew up at St. Rose's and later entered the convent in Maryland.

Originally called St. Luke's, the church was later known as the Cathedral of St. Peter. It was the forerunner of the Cathedral of St. John the Evangelist. (*Fifty Years at St. John's Cathedral*, David J. O'Hearn, 1897)

She came back to Milwaukee to teach and was known as Sister Martha.

St. Aemilian's Orphanage for Catholic boys was founded by John Henni in 1849 and was located on N. Jackson Street across from Cathedral Square. In 1854, it was moved to the St. Francis Seminary grounds in St. Francis and was run by the Sisters of St. Francis of Assisi, a German religious order.

Chapter 3

1850–1859

By 1850, the number of Irish-born in Milwaukee was up to 3,000 and that number does not include children born after the parents left Ireland. With the total population of the city at 20,000, Irish immigrants made up somewhat over 15 percent of its residents and, when their children were included, the city was probably about 20 percent Irish and Irish American.[1] The number of Germans was nearly double that of the Irish, and with immigrants from other countries, Milwaukee's population was more foreign than native born.

The Third Ward's 4,200 inhabitants included almost 1,400 Irish-born plus their children. The other Irish neighborhood, Tory Hill, had a smaller number of Irish than the Third Ward, but since it covered a smaller area with no official borders within the Fourth Ward, it is more difficult to determine its population. But we do know that there were nearly 500 Irish residents living in the Fourth Ward and the majority lived in Tory Hill. An analysis of the 1850 Fourth Ward census sheets that include Irish families shows few non-Irish people on those pages and indicate a greater density of Irish in Tory Hill than that of the Third Ward.

There were about 700 Irish living north of the Third Ward, most of them on the Lower East Side. Another 265 Hibernians lived in Walker's Point on the South Side. Only about 150 Irish resided in the Second Ward, west of the Milwaukee River and north of W. Kilbourn Avenue, which was predominately German.

In 1850, the Third Ward School's enrollment of 200 children was the largest of the city's 5 wards and the mostly Irish school had the highest average attendance.[2] A study of 1850 census data shows that the 68 percent attendance rate of Irish boys 5 to 17 years old exceeded the British and German rates and was second only to Yankee boys. The Irish girls' attendance was only 54 percent, indicating a lower interest in educating girls and a desire to send young girls into domestic service to learn the various aspects of running a household, as well as to help with their families' incomes.[3]

Irish Class Distinctions

By the early 1850s, the school situation had stabilized. The First Ward Public School was moved to N. Broadway and E. State Street. The German Catholic students were attending the school at Old St. Mary's, the German church. Most of the Irish boys attended the Catholic schools at St. Peter's (soon to be renamed St. John's) or St. Gall's, or the public school in the Third Ward. The girls had three choices—the public schools or one of the two girls' schools at St. Peter's. One was St. Joseph's Academy, in a stand-alone building, where classes were taught by the Sisters of Charity and a tuition of about $4 per quarter was charged. The other option was the school in the basement of St. Peter's, where orphans and poor girls were taught by less qualified teachers and the education was free.

There was criticism of this two-tiered system that allowed girls of families with more money to receive a better education than their poorer neighbors. There is no doubt that Irish class distinctions existed. Those with money tended to live in Yankee Hill or the Lower East Side rather than Tory Hill or the Third Ward. It was not just wealth that separated the two classes; it was also social, cultural, and educational differences.

The marriage between Robert Blosse Lynch and Catherine Gill exemplified the gulf between the two classes. Lynch was born in Headford, County Galway, about 1818.[4] He was well-educated and worked in Dublin as a clerk in the Bureau of Charities. While in his early 20s, Robert, his brother, Peter, and his sisters and their families emigrated to the United States, where they lived in St. Louis before coming to Milwaukee in the summer of 1847. Catherine Gill was born in Ireland around 1830 and came to Milwaukee without an education and worked in Peter Lynch's Yankee Hill household as a servant.

Under normal conditions the two would not have married, according to Robert Lynch. He married Gill in 1851 but kept the marriage by a justice of the peace a secret. During later divorce proceedings, his attorney stated that Lynch "was intoxicated and so completely under the influence of liquor" and "he never would have made promise to marry . . . had he been in his right mind and free from the influence of intoxicating liquors."[5]

They lived as husband and wife for three weeks before he left and refused to recognize her as his wife or support her. Lynch was quoted as saying she was "an ignorant servant girl with whom in a social relation he could not happily live."[6] In a letter to his brother, he added, "I slept with her a half dozen times and I think I highly honored her."[7]

Recruiting and Aiding Irish Immigrants

In 1849, two Irish immigrants, John Gregory and David Power, set up a business called the Irish Emigration Society to induce Irish immigrants to come to Wisconsin and Milwaukee, and to help them travel here from Eastern seaports without being swindled. It was not unusual for immigrants to be taken advantage of in their journeys west. The *Milwaukee Sentinel* reported an example of an Irish group of five adults and one child who had just reached the city. They were sold tickets in New York that would supposedly take them to Milwaukee via railroad from Albany to Buffalo, then by boat to Milwaukee, with all expenses covered. Instead of going by train from Albany, they had to take a canal boat, were charged extra for their luggage, and had to pay for their berths and meals during the nine-day trip on the Erie Canal. When they reached the ship at Buffalo, they were told that they needed to pay for a second cabin for their voyage to Milwaukee. In total, the trip cost a third more than the original payment.

Gregory, from County Kerry, was 66 years old, while Power was 40 years younger. Both were surveyors. Gregory was also a civil engineer, astronomer, teacher, and author. As immigration agents, they offered a variety of services. For a commission, they would arrange travel from New York or Boston, both cities with surplus Irish, to Milwaukee—with no surprise expenses. Gregory and Power would also help Irish residents who sent for relatives in Ireland for an agreed upon amount of money. They were successful in bringing a woman named Bridget Kelly to Milwaukee, but they had problems getting Thomas Holloran's two young children from

Limerick to Milwaukee via the port of New York. The European agent they worked with sent the children to Quebec instead, probably because the cost of passage to Canada, which was within the British Empire, was only one-third of the cost of travel to New York. The children eventually made it to Milwaukee and were united with their Tory Hill family. The Society would arrange for jobs for clerks, mechanics, and laborers, and would also purchase land outside of Milwaukee for potential farmers.

The business advertised its services locally as well as in the *Boston Pilot*, the leading Irish-Catholic newspaper in the country, and claimed that it had helped bring 200 immigrants to Milwaukee during the previous year.[8] Gregory published a book that compared the climate, features, and natural resources of Wisconsin to Ireland's, and concluded that since so many people in Ireland were poor, Wisconsin was a better place to live because it offered more opportunities. He also warned that the immigrant was likely to be taken advantage of every step of the way to Milwaukee, and that he should be careful to deal with only honest, respectable people when arriving in the city. The book, over 300 pages long, was of limited help since so many Irishmen were illiterate.[9]

Gregory and Power's business was dissolved after a few years. Gregory, who was elected Milwaukee County Surveyor ten times from 1850 to 1859, also sold real estate with his son George. In his early 70s, after

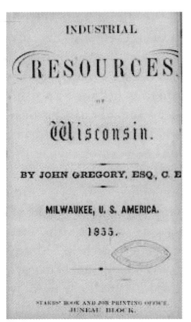

Engineer John Gregory compared the resources of Ireland and Wisconsin. (*Industrial Resources of Wisconsin*, John Gregory, 1855)

being widowed, he married English immigrant Elizabeth Goadby, 26, in 1855 at St. Paul's Episcopal Church. The marriage ended in divorce after producing three sons. Gregory died at St. Mary's Hospital at the age of 96 in 1880 and was buried in Calvary Cemetery. His son, John Goadby Gregory, became a Milwaukee newspaperman and local historian. David Power continued his career as a surveyor, real estate agent, and inventor. He died in the Newhall House fire in 1883 and was also buried in Calvary Cemetery.

The state also recruited immigrants. It set up an office in New York City in 1852 called the Wisconsin State Emigrant Agency. The organization distributed information to those arriving on ships, staying at hotels, and frequenting taverns in that city. Europeans were targeted, especially citizens of England, Ireland, Germany, and Holland, with advertisements appearing in those countries' newspapers. The agency estimated that 4,000 to 5,000 Irish immigrants came to the state the following year. An office opened in Quebec City the next year also drew Irish to Wisconsin, and other societies in the United States and Ireland helped direct Irishmen to Milwaukee and Wisconsin.[10]

John White Elected Sheriff

John White, a Democrat who lost in his bid to become County Sheriff in 1846, was elected to that position in November 1850. The flamboyant White, a tall, energetic man from Ulster with a resonant brogue, was called the "White Irishman" because he dressed all in white, including a white stovepipe hat. White, a grocer, was one of the leading Irishmen in the city at the time.

Then, as now, the city usually voted Democratic, and so did the county. During Milwaukee's first quarter century as a city, a Democrat held the position of mayor 24 of the 25 years. Politics were part of the Irish culture. The Irish knew how to make their constituents happy and how to make deals. They would often work together with the Germans to get their men named as candidates. For example, each time Edward O'Neill was elected mayor, a German held a high position on the ticket and was also elected.

The Third Ward was the center of Irish political influence. When Irishmen from the southern part of the county decided they wanted their own candidate for their state senate district, which included the Third

Ward, "they were no more successful against the third ward bosses than an isolated group of Irishmen could have been in defying Tammany Hall in New York."[11]

Occupations

Milwaukee was rapidly expanding and required many workers to continue its citymaking. Irish laborers found employment, but had a difficult time making ends meet due to sporadic seasonal labor and low wages. Laborers were paid about a dollar a day and worked six days a week when work was available. When the temperatures were too low or, on occasion, too high to work, they lost wages. The same was true when rain, snow, or other factors prevented them from working. Often their families had to pitch in to put food on the table. Mothers took in laundry or sewing. Some teenage sons had to forego an education to earn money, and 10- and 12-year-old daughters were sent out to work as servants to augment family finances. Older girls and young women also worked in domestic service, usually for Yankees, which helped them learn to run a household and become familiar with the ways of Americans. A few younger women worked as teachers or nurses.

Men worked at docks, piers, warehouses, brick yards, meatpacking houses, and stables. They continued to grade streets, fill in marshes, and reduce steep bluffs to manageable hills. Some worked in foundries or small factories or as peddlers or shingle makers. Others worked as porters, waiters, and bartenders.

Smaller numbers owned animals that they used to pull wagons and carts as they worked as the teamsters of their day. Some Irish immigrants gained skills before arriving in Milwaukee and worked as tailors, shoemakers, masons, carpenters, painters, wheelwrights, and coopers. Lake Michigan provided livelihoods for sailors and fishermen. Nearby farmland could be rented, and some Irish grew produce for sale to urban neighbors.

Not all the Irish were laboring men. A few immigrants were boardinghouse operators, tavernkeepers, or small-scale grocers. Others worked as clerks in stores, shops, and other businesses. There was also a handful of professionals among the Irish immigrants. Irish physicians of the day included James Johnson, who was educated in Massachusetts and became a leader in the Irish community, and Martin Burke. There were

Physician James Johnson was one of the most influential Irishmen in early Milwaukee. (*Medical History of Milwaukee*, Louis Frank, 1915)

also a few Irish lawyers and engineers. John Rooney probably had the most unusual occupation for a Milwaukee Irishman; he was an auctioneer. Rooney was born in Ireland in 1828 and lived in Ohio before coming to Milwaukee about 1846. Both Johnson and Rooney would lose sons in the *Lady Elgin* disaster.

Irish merchants dealt in lumber, real estate, wool, and other products, but they favored the grocery and liquor business. Many of the leading Irishmen in the city at the time, including John Furlong, John White, John McManman, Garrett Barry, and Richard Murphy, became grocery merchants, with some of them also dealing in spirits. These middle-class men made up about ten percent of Milwaukee's Irish workforce, which was about the same ratio as New York City's Irish and twice that of Boston's. In both Detroit and St. Louis about 20 percent of the Irish were non-laborers.[12]

Animals

Right from the beginning, Irish neighborhoods were alive with animals. Teamsters and carters depended on their horses, donkeys, mules, and oxen for their livelihoods. Goats and cows provided families with milk and butter. A wide range of fowl produced eggs and meat. Some Irish people let their animals run freely, a practice that angered their non-Irish neighbors, who objected to the roaming pigs, goats, and cows and complained that "you were sure to meet one or more of those filthy animals sauntering along the streets and sidewalks."[13] The animals

45

uprooted gardens, left their excrement on sidewalks, and filled the city with unpleasant odors. At a meeting to discuss citizen concerns and a ban on straying animals, one man complained that a pig went into a store downtown, stuck his head in a container of butter, and ate ten pounds of it. When another said that he had to drive two hogs out of his yard, Pat McGinnis of the Third Ward responded:

> Well, now thin, if yees don't want to oppriss the poor, what the divil would yees be after doing the loikes of this for, be jabers. For sure what is a poor man or a widdy to do wid her cow or pig, and she not the schmell av a pin to kape them in. Why couldn't yees get a shilling's worth av nails and a boord and fix up yees' old gate, and not be makin' sich a sphlatter as this?[14]

The town did not accept McGinnis's argument and passed an ordinance in 1840 that prohibited hogs from running through the streets and "great was the wrath of the Third Warders."[15] The owner of a captured hog could be fined one dollar and would have to pay another dollar to the person who caught the pig. Or the captured swine could be killed and eaten by its captor without liability.

By 1854, things had not improved much. One observer described N. Water Street between E. Buffalo and E. Chicago streets in the Third Ward as "heaps of manure, hundreds of dogs running at large, hogs on the sidewalk, swill carts crowding the ladies into the street..."[16] One ferocious old sow attacked a girl who had just left a store carrying a basket of food. The girl was shaken but not injured, however her food was trampled and ruined. Complaints to City Marshal Tim O'Brien fell on deaf ears. O'Brien declared "that he would be damned if he would interfere or deny the liberty of the streets to any hog."[17] Complaints were still coming in six years later when parents refused to allow their children to play in Cathedral Square because of the manure left by cows and hogs.

Large animals were eventually required to be kept in pens, but small animals still ran at large. Near the end of the century, a Fourth Ward alderman resolved to prohibit Tory Hill chickens, ducks, geese, swans, and other barnyard fowl from running at large in adjacent neighborhoods. His ordinance was passed, allowing these animals in the streets of Tory Hill but not on the streets north of W. Clybourn Street.

Cholera, 1850

During the summer of 1850, there was a recrudescence of cholera. Its progress north toward Milwaukee was noted in newspaper reports of cholera deaths in New Orleans, St. Louis, Detroit, and Cincinnati. When the disease reached the city, it caused more deaths than it had in 1849. The Board of Health did not report the names of victims in 1850 as it had the previous year, but only the number who died in each ward, pointing out that the number in the Third Ward was inflated by immigrant passengers who were dead on or shortly after arrival. Newspapers reported 167 deaths for that year's epidemic, but many felt the number was closer to 300, with some estimates doubling that. Once again, the Irish probably died in larger numbers than their percentage of the city's population.

The president of the Board of Health was the recently elected City Marshal, Timothy O'Brien, 38. O'Brien was born in County Limerick and came to Milwaukee in 1842 after spending 11 years in New York and Detroit. Known as "Father Tim," a contemporary described him as "one of the most aggressive men who ever lived here."[18] He was loyal to his friends, never forgave his enemies, and always spoke his mind freely. He was a leader in the Irish community and served in many elected posts over the decades. Another contemporary said O'Brien was a master of fabrication, while a third said "he was honest, upright, and reliable. What he said he would do, he did. They tell great stories about Tim but many are not true. His friends were ever ready to tell a story at his expense."[19]

O'Brien became a legend for his service during the epidemic. He carried the dead and dying off the ships coming into the harbor, carted corpses to cemeteries (the Catholics to the cemetery near N. 22nd Street and W. Wisconsin Avenue), and helped bury them. People worshiped him for his bravery. He contracted cholera but recovered, and he received $125 for his work during the epidemic.

There were no cases of cholera in the city in 1851, but there were a few deaths in the period from 1852 through 1854, although cholera would not be the killer that it was in 1849 and 1850. When the Catholic cemetery on W. Wisconsin Avenue was closed in 1857, the bodies were moved to the newly created Calvary Cemetery at N. 55th Street and W. Blue Mound Road.

The City Guard, the Kenosha Wheat Riot, and Potawatomi Removal

In April of 1850, the City Guard saw its first out-of-the-ordinary action. It was in Kenosha and the task was to keep order after that city's "Wheat Riot." After the bankruptcy of a Kenosha wheat agent, 40,000 to 60,000 bushels of wheat were found to be missing from his warehouse. The farmers who produced the wheat had placed it on consignment with the agent and stood to lose their crop with nothing to show for it; they were not happy and a disturbance followed. The City Guard, as a state militia filling the role of the future National Guard, went to Kenosha and did their job; there was no more rioting. The Guard returned home, and the farmers took the agent to bankruptcy court. There was one problem before the company had left for Kenosha, though. Guard member Patrick Phennessy, fearing active duty, deserted. Some claimed that the stout, five-foot, four-inch Phennessy was found under his bed by those searching for him. He faced a court martial by City Guard officers and the story of his desertion elicited laughter and amusement among his comrades for many years to come.

In 1851, the federal government broke another of its treaties with Native Americans, in this case the Potawatomi tribe, and said its members must be moved to Kansas, where the government had so generously purchased land for them. In July, nearly 1,000 members of the tribe massed near the village of Theresa in Dodge County. Some of their leaders encouraged them to refuse to leave their homes. Major McManman led members of the Milwaukee Battalion, including the City Guard, to Theresa to talk with the leaders. The Potawatomi decision makers gave in and agreed to leave. City Guard Lieutenant "Father Tim" O'Brien was ordered to stay behind and, in the event that the Potawatomi reneged on the deal, to ride his horse as fast as he could back to Milwaukee to report the problem. But there were no problems and about 600 Potawatomi were transported to Kansas. The rest, refusing to leave, scattered throughout the state.

The Leahey Riot

Between 1850 and 1861 there were seven significant riots or mob actions in Milwaukee. The "Leahey Riot," the "Voting Riot," and the "Lynching of Marshall Clark" were actions conducted by Irish mobs

48

against, respectively, Protestants, Germans, and an African American. The "Liquor Law Riot," the "Railroad Riot," and the "Bank Riot" were German actions against Yankees, with an Irish militia involved in quelling the latter two. "The Rescue of Joshua Glover," an African American, was carried out by a mixed mob.

Edward Leahey was made-to-order for the anti-Catholic groups that were growing around the country in response to the large number of Irish and German Catholic immigrants. Leahey was an Irish immigrant who was no longer a Catholic. He claimed that as a former monk of La Trappe, France, he had seen the Church close up and was willing to tell all—for a price.

Leahey was born in Ireland about 1808, and while nothing much is known of his time in Europe, there is no evidence that he was ever a Trappist monk. He arrived in this country when he was about 30 years old, and by the time he was 40, he had decided to make his living by lecturing. He advertised himself as the "ex-Monk of La Trappe" and dressed in monastic garb (which concealed a pistol), and claimed he would reveal the secrets of the confessional and other subjects of "priestcraft." No women or youths were allowed entrance; each man paid 25 cents to attend.

Leahey was described by one observer as having "a fine figure, easy manner and a good voice."[20] He gave his "lectures" in Boston, New York, Philadelphia, and other East Coast cities throughout 1847 and 1848 without problems. His programs were well attended and in Baltimore drew overflow crowds.

Leahey's performance included the reading of sexual references from religious texts, and he read them with "lascivious innuendo and leering insinuation" as he attempted to excite his audience.[21] He also told stories about priests impregnating nuns and murdering and burying the infants to cover their misdeeds. Of special delight were the stories of how priests asked probing questions of females in the confessional which, of course, led to the seduction of the repentant sinners.

An observer said the audience "seemed to enjoy his lewd jokes hugely, and the filthier his style and the lewder his indecent innuendo, the more they seemed to be refreshed in spirit. It was as if a kindred saint stood up before them, and the unclean drippings of his tongue were to them like heavenly manna."[22]

As his success grew, so did the animosity towards him by many

A LECTURE

On the Treatment of Females in the
Confessional, by Popish Priests,

ACCORDING to the standard of Popish Theology,
sold in this country, to answer the use of members of the Roman Catholic Church, will be delivered this

Wednesday Afternoon, April 9th,

AT 3 O'CLOCK,

In the Free Congregational Church,

By Rev. E. LEAHEY, D. D.,

Late a Monk of La Trappe.

I cordially invite any Roman Catholic Priest to be present at my Lecture, and then it will be shown whether
the reading of the standard Catholic Books, published
under the sanction of the Right Reverend Bishops among
us, is bearing false witness against them.

EDWARD LEAHEY.

Gentlemen ONLY admitted at 25 Cents.

☞ The proceeds of the Lecture will go to the pro-
pagation of the Gospel among Catholics.   Ap. 9.-lt-

Leahey advertised that he would tell about priests
seducing women in the confessional. (*Milwaukee
Daily Sentinel and Gazette*, April 1851)

Catholics, particularly Irish Catholics. In December 1849, Leahey was
beaten by a mob of Irish Catholics in Sandusky, Ohio, as he tried to enter
the lecture hall. An angry crowd in St. Louis tried unsuccessfully to stop
him from lecturing. Leahey then moved with his wife and daughter from
Ohio to Racine, Wisconsin, where he was prevented from speaking when
German Catholics helped the Irish stop him. Where his performances
were not banned as obscene, or stopped by mobs, Leahey's notoriety
assured him of large crowds and full pockets.

In early April 1851, local newspapers announced that Leahey, who
now lived on a farm near Portage, Wisconsin, would come to Milwaukee
and give several sermons at local churches on Sunday, April 6, and on
Monday he would give one of his "Secrets of the Confessional" lectures.

Catholics criticized the Protestants who would allow a known scoundrel

50

like Leahey to defile their churches by telling his filthy, lying stories from their pulpits. Protestants said the principle of free speech overrode Catholic objections. Irish Catholics were embarrassed and humiliated by the traitor Leahey going into the dens of Protestants and bolstering time-honored stories that they had been telling about the "whore of Babylon," as they referred to the Catholic Church.

Comments in local newspapers heightened emotions. Moderate Catholics encouraged everyone to ignore Leahey's performance. Expecting that there would be security for the lecture but not for the sermons, those ready to chase Leahey out of town attacked while he was giving a Sunday evening sermon in the Methodist Church on the corner of W. Wisconsin Avenue and N. Second Street.

The church was filled with men and women expecting to see Leahey and hear his sermon. He opened by mentioning that some Irishmen had attacked him earlier that day and wanted to kill him, and someone from the back of the church said, "They were right, kill him."[23] The rioters entered the church swinging clubs "right and left." Most of the women escaped through windows, which were 12 feet from the ground, by sliding down a plank to a cart below. The intruders, who included a few Germans, tore up pews, broke windows, and smashed the chandelier in the center of the nave to smithereens.

Leahey's adversaries managed to make it to the front of the church, but the knowledge that Leahey was armed prevented them from advancing further. At this point, one of the church trustees promised that Leahey would leave the city before the sun rose again. When the mayor, Don Upham, arrived at the church, which was totally under the control of the rioters, he agreed that Leahey would be sent away without speaking. Meanwhile, John White, the Irish sheriff, and others calmed the crowd outside. When Upham told them that Leahey would leave town and would not be allowed to speak in Milwaukee, they gave three cheers for Upham and three cheers for the Third Ward. While Leahey was escorted to the United States Hotel, some of the crowd jeered and threw stones, though none hit him. No one was killed during the riot, but some teeth were lost and more than 20 people were injured. The Irish community suffered a black eye that would linger for many years for attacking innocent churchgoers and ignoring the basic American principal of free speech.

But the city was not through with Leahey yet. The next morning, a letter from the Catholic clergy and some influential Catholics condemning the attack was printed in the newspapers. Protestants criticized the mayor for caving in to the rioters and demanded that Leahey be allowed to give his lecture. A committee was set up to make a decision, and it did, unanimously; Leahey would be allowed to speak. On Tuesday and Wednesday nights he gave his talk in the Free Congregational Church on N. Broadway, with security provided by ward constables stationed inside and firemen and other citizens outside.

In June, four men were charged in court with inciting the riot: Alderman Edward McGarry; City Engineer Michael McDermott; Michael Walsh, a grocer; and Daniel Kennedy, who ran a boardinghouse. Protestants complained of too many Third Warders on the jury, but the *Milwaukee Sentinel*, a conservative newspaper, reported that "Some half dozen witnesses were examined but nothing elicited which seems to implicate the parties directly."[24] All four men were acquitted.

In the aftermath of the Leahey Riot, the Yankee population of the city was alarmed that there was inadequate security for their protection. The city marshal and ward constables were not enough, and they did not

The Methodist church on N. Second Street and W. Wisconsin Avenue was the site of the Leahey Riot. (Author's collection)

think that they could count on the foreign militias. They decided that "a strictly American military organization" was necessary for their safety, and a plan for a volunteer militia company, the Milwaukee Light Guard, free of all foreigners, was born.[25] This company could be called up by authorities to help quell disturbances. Both the Light Guard and the city police department were founded four years later in 1855.

Leahey continued his lecture tour, which was often marred by violence. He claimed to audiences that a priest had seduced his wife in the confessional. The next winter, though, it was a nearby farmer who seduced Leahey's wife. Mary Leahey wrote to him on his Eastern tour that she wanted to leave their home near Portage and go to California with Bernard Manley, the neighboring farmer.

Leahey, not accepting his wife's affair, wrote to her from Norfolk, Virginia, "Remember you are a married woman and have two little children, and a respectable husband." He continued, "I have good confidence in God, my savior, that you have kept yourself, as I have done since I left you, free from the wicked ways of this deceitful world."[26] After Leahey returned home, Manley forced Leahey to accept his wife's infidelity by taunting him with details of their relationship. Leahey sued Manley for alienation of affection, and when Leahey lost the verdict, he pulled his pistol in the Columbia County courtroom and shot and killed Manley and shot and injured Manley's attorney.

In September of 1852, Leahey was convicted of the murder and sentenced to Waupun State Prison, where he repented and re-entered the Catholic Church in 1856. He was pardoned on July 16, 1860, by the governor and the next day he advertised in the Milwaukee newspapers, promising to recite the speech he had made to the jury that convicted him, for 25 cents—to men only. The lecture failed to attract even a dozen people and was cancelled. Leahey offered other subjects for his lectures: his wife's seduction, his trial (which he said was unfair), the murder itself, and his return to the Church. None drew any crowds in Wisconsin. It was said that he travelled to the East for a lecture tour but, if so, he was no more successful there. There was talk that he would be the Republican Party candidate against Judge Larrabee, the Democrat who presided over his trial, but it turned out to be just talk. Leahey returned to his farm near Portage, where he died in 1868.

Capital Punishment

In February 1852, the City Guard was scheduled to go to Kenosha again, this time to provide security at the hanging of John McCaffary, convicted of drowning his wife. The plan to use the City Guard was scrapped when it was decided the Kenosha Guard could keep the peace less expensively. The Kenosha man dangled on the end of his rope for a long time before he died in front of 2,000 to 3,000 spectators, horrifying residents throughout Wisconsin.

On N. Milwaukee Street in 1851, John Gullen was murdered in his Third Ward home. His killers, Patrick McDonald and James Connaughty, were convicted of first degree murder, a crime that required the death penalty. The execution was scheduled for November 15, 1852, and would be the second state-sponsored hanging since Wisconsin became a state in 1848. In the time leading up to Milwaukee's first planned execution, defense lawyer James Mallory filed for a new trial because of errors in conducting the initial trial. The Supreme Court agreed, but through a

A gallows was built near the jail at the left end of Cathedral Square. The Cathedral of St. John is shown with its original tower, 1854. The tower was removed in 1880 due to safety concerns and a new tower replaced it in 1893. (Author's collection)

series of miscommunications the information did not reach Governor Farwell immediately. Farwell had said that if a new trial were granted he would stop the execution, but when he was finally notified, he did not respond.

Less than 48 hours before the scheduled deaths, Mallory rode a horse through the night to Madison to plead with Farwell. The next afternoon the gallows was being built in the jail yard at the north end of Cathedral Square, which was crowded with citizens, some protesting capital punishment and others hoping to see a hanging. When word came by telegram that Mallory had been successful in convincing the governor to cancel the executions, the crowd went home, and the gallows was disassembled. Capital punishment was abolished in Wisconsin eight months later. McDonald was freed for his new trial, but he skedaddled to Canada. Connaughty was convicted of third degree murder and sentenced to Waupun State prison for ten years.

The City Guard Fire and the Railroad Riot

The City Guard suffered a setback in March of 1852, when a fire in Doctor Johnson's building on N. Water Street consumed the third floor, the site of the Guard's armory, destroying their arms and equipment. They were unarmed only briefly before the state re-equipped them. Their headquarters was moved to Treat's Block near Johnson's damaged building. Showing how it appreciated the Guard, the city presented them with a new flag of white silk depicting the "Goddess of Liberty," along with a female figure representing America with the motto, "Welcome to our shores," and another female representing Ireland stating, "Where liberty dwells, there is my country."[27]

In 1853, the Guard's drill and parade routine was interrupted by the Railroad Riot in Milwaukee. They were now captained by John Jennings, a 30-year-old Irish wool dealer who replaced John White when he was elected as County Sheriff. Four hundred workers on the La Crosse and Milwaukee Railroad, mostly Germans, were owed back pay, and they demanded their due, loudly and vehemently. Constables, firemen, and the City Guard were called on to put down any threat to the peace. They were met with missiles of stones and brickbat, but fire hoses cleared the Germans from the field. The railroad workers did eventually receive their pay, and the City Guard's coffers grew by $94 for their part in the action.

The Voting Riot

There were two occasions, the Leahey Riot and the Voting Riot, when the City Guard was not called out to help, because the unrest included Irish residents and there was a fear that the Guard would just make the situation worse by joining the rioters, if they hadn't already.

On Tuesday, March 7, 1854, Milwaukee residents went to the polls to elect city officials. At the time, challenging the right of a fellow Milwaukeean to vote was a common practice. Usually, it involved a German challenging the right of an Irishman to vote. On this day though, it seems that an Irishman questioned a German's right to vote at the First Ward's polling site at City Hall on N. Water Street. The German was upset by the challenge and issued a challenge of his own, daring the Irishman to fight.[28] The Irishman, and many of his countrymen, took up the challenge and began a donnybrook that involved hundreds of Irish and Germans.

The Hibernians immediately took the strategic advantage of the higher ground up E. Wells Street toward N. Broadway. From there they could shower the Germans below with bricks, stones, and anything else they could throw. The small security force of constables and sheriff's deputies was powerless against so many rioters. Hundreds of spectators watched from a safe distance but many windows, not at a safe distance, were smashed. In less than an hour, the battered Teutons left the glass-littered battlefield to the victorious Celts.

Dozens were bloodied and bruised, including Sheriff Page, who had been knocked down by a projectile. One German, John Fick, who had previously been arrested by Deputy Sheriff William Beck, got his revenge during the melee by throwing a rock at Beck, wounding him. Fick, fellow German Michael Trass, and Irishman Thomas Scott were arrested for their parts in the riot.[29] Newspapers blamed alcohol and a lack of police presence for the riot. None of the city's militia companies had been called to quell the riot, as they were either German or Irish and the fear was that rather than put down the disturbance, they might escalate it.

Rescue of Joshua Glover

John Jennings was the captain of the City Guard when it was called upon to assist in preventing a jailbreak. Due to Jennings's actions, the Guard did not respond, which ultimately led to the breakup of the company.

On the morning of March 11, 1854, Joshua Glover, a slave who had escaped from his Missouri "owner" and was captured at Racine the previous day by a U.S. Marshal, was brought to Milwaukee and detained in the jail on Cathedral Square. Glover was to be returned to Missouri in accordance with the Fugitive Slave Law, but several thousand Milwaukeeans, led by newspaperman Sherman Booth, had a different idea. Throughout that morning, Booth rode his horse through the town, calling on Milwaukeeans to meet at the jail in the afternoon.

The U.S. Marshal ordered John Jennings to call out the City Guard to assist him in preventing a jailbreak, an order he also gave to one of the German companies, the Milwaukee Riflemen. The city's fire companies were also called on to help. Jennings was reluctant to call out his company, so he went to Milwaukee Battalion Major John McManman for advice. McManman, who would be appointed to the state's highest military position, Adjutant General, the next month, counseled Jennings to get the order in writing. After receiving the written order, Jennings continued to stall, but McManman showed him the law covering the situation and recommended that he obey it.

As the mob grew, Jennings was still hesitant to comply with the order. When he said he wanted assurances that his men would be paid, the U.S. Attorney's office assured him they would be. Jennings then said that the Guard had been "badly used" by the United States in the past and he did not know if they would turn out if called.[30] When he finally ordered them to meet at their armory, he heard that the jailbreak had already taken place, so he dismissed the company while Glover was beginning his trip on the Underground Railroad to freedom in Canada.

Because the City Guard was sent home, its members did not receive pay. Because the 50 or so members of the Milwaukee Riflemen reported to, and remained in their armory, they were paid even though they did not try to stop the jailbreak. Like the City Guard, all fire companies ignored the order and went unpaid.

Jennings's actions seemed to be those of a man who wanted Glover to escape, which was at variance with the attitudes of most of the Irish, who were not supporters of emancipation. Freed slaves would mean four million more people competing with the Irish for low paying jobs. In a similar situation in Boston four months later, a runaway slave, Anthony

Joshua Glover marker in Cathedral Square.
(Photograph by the author)

Burns, was escorted to a boat, and back to captivity, by an Irish militia company.

The U.S. Marshal was furious that his orders were not obeyed, and the City Guard was accused of being a mercenary band that only fought for pay and plunder, a charge they denied. Jennings's actions caused a split in the company. A month later, Jennings claimed that the City Guard's terms of enlistment were over and that a reorganization was necessary. The Sarsfield Guard, named for Irish patriot Patrick Sarsfield, was organized and included some members of the City Guard, with Jennings as captain of the new company. The Sarsfield name was short-lived however. Throughout the summer, a series of newspaper announcements listed among the city's militia companies, John Jennings, Captain of the Carroll Corps, and Patrick Kelly, Captain of the City Guard.[31] The new company, whether called the Sarsfield Guard or the Carroll Corps, did not prosper. In court proceedings in May 1855, he was described as "Captain Jennings, of the defunct military company."[32] Kelly's City Guard marched in the Fourth of July parade of 1855, but with reduced numbers, as that company was now also languishing.

The Union Guard and the Montgomery Guard

By the end of 1855, all Milwaukee Irish militiamen were united in one company, called the Union Guard, with Edward O'Neill elected captain and John White and Edward McGarry as his lieutenants. The first militia company of Yankees or, as they liked to call themselves, Americans, was also organized in 1855, and called the Light Guard.

The Union Guard's Hall and headquarters were located in Furlong's Block on the southeast corner of N. Water and E. Clybourn streets. Furlong's Block was built by John Furlong, a contractor and merchant and one of city's best-known Irishmen. He was born in County Cork in 1813 and came to Milwaukee in 1836 with his father, George. The hall was the site of balls, dinners, and other fundraisers to pay for furniture, furnishings, and fittings for the Guard's new headquarters. Money from fundraisers bought uniforms and musical instruments valued at about $7,000.

The hall also served as an Irish cultural center where St. Patrick's Day festivals and other Irish events were held. Traveling Irish entertainers performed there, playing Irish music, singing Irish songs, and reading Irish poetry. Important Irish figures, such as William Smith O'Brien, who participated in the Young Irelander Rebellion of 1848, were fêted at the hall.

O'Neill quickly brought the Union Guard to respectability with impressive parading and drilling routines. As the City Guard had, they paraded on special days with other companies, some of them from other cities and sometimes, in other cities. Perhaps the company's oddest task took place at the Waupun State Prison. Prison guards were called to Madison for an official inquiry, so the Union Guard was ordered to the prison to guard the inmates.

In 1857, John Jennings was involved in forming another Irish company, the Montgomery Guard, with Jennings elected captain. Their armory was in Treat's Block, the former City Guard's armory, across N. Water Street from the Union Guard's headquarters. The two companies would often march together and support each other's activities, and although the larger Union Guard always received more press and praise, the Montgomery Guard would outlive them.

When Edward O'Neill was not available to lead the Union Guard, Garrett Barry took over. Early in 1858, O'Neill resigned after being promoted to Lieutenant Colonel of the Wisconsin Militia, and Barry was elected captain. A short time later, John Jennings resigned from the

Montgomery Guard to give more time to his sheepskin business and John L. Doran replaced him as captain.

While most of the Union Guard lived in the Third Ward, their captain, Garrett Barry, was of the Irish merchant class and, like most of that class, lived in the more desirable area north of the Ward in the Yankee Hill neighborhood on N. Jefferson Street near E. Knapp Street. Barry was born of an Irish father and Spanish mother in Baltimore in 1814. His father was a successful merchant who could afford to provide Barry with an education at St. Charles College in Baltimore. Barry's intelligence propelled him to an appointment to the United States Military Academy at West Point. He graduated in the summer of 1839 as a second lieutenant. That summer, while spending time at a Hudson River resort, he met his future wife, Mary A. Atwater, of Connecticut. They were married in 1842 in an Episcopalian ceremony in New Haven but raised their children as Roman Catholics.

Three years later, Barry was transferred to Fort Crawford at Prairie du Chien, Wisconsin, where his duties included convoying for government surveyors who were continuing to draw the maps that divided the state into townships, sections, and acres. In his travels he purchased land in several counties, including Milwaukee, where he had business contacts. The United States' invasion of Mexico in 1846 came next for Barry. After a year of fighting, he resigned his position as a first lieutenant and moved to Milwaukee.

Barry and his wife were financially comfortable. In addition to their city home, they had a farm on the edge of town and he dabbled in several businesses over the next ten years, none for very long and none very successfully. He was in the drug and medicine business with physician Martin J. Burke for a short time. That was followed by two short-term partnerships as a grocer and commission merchant, and his career as a forwarding agent was also brief. In the community though, he was highly respected. He helped raise funds for St. Rose's Orphanage, a hospital, and other charitable causes, as well as being involved in Irish activities.

There is no known roster of Union Guard members, but the city directory for 1859–60 tells us that the Union Guard had 70 members. And we know who the 20 company officers were because their names were printed in *The Daily Milwaukee News* when it listed the results of the election of officers in April 1860. Other sources mention eight other

Garrett Barry, captain of the Union Guard. (*The Lady Elgin Disaster*, Charles Scanlan, 1928)

members. Unlike the majority of Milwaukee's Irish who were laborers or servants, these 28 members were professional, skilled, or clerical workers. They were tailors, carpenters, mechanics, deputies, policemen, shoemakers, clerks, and agents. They included a harbormaster, a teacher, a liquor dealer, and three draymen.

Under Barry's guidance, the guardsmen maintained their high level of drilling and maneuvering skills and were often seen parading on Milwaukee streets, and sometimes on the streets of Buffalo, Detroit, Chicago, or other Midwest cities. On each trip, the Union Guard was met at their destination by local companies, with whom they would parade, dine, and celebrate before being escorted back to the boat or train that would take them home. The *Milwaukee Sentinel* said they "were great favorites with both the military and civilians."[33] They paraded with the Montgomery Guard on St. Patrick's Day and other occasions. On the Fourth of July, all the city's companies would march—the Irish, the Yankee, and the German companies along with marching brass bands.

As the Civil War approached, the militia companies grew more impressive and would draw crowds wherever they went. The companies never missed an opportunity to attract attention and one of the surest ways was to escort each other. If the Union Guard took a trip, the Milwaukee Light Guard would escort them to the boat. If an out of town company came to the city, local companies would march to greet them and take them to their destination. When the Guard went target shooting at Barry's farm west of the city, no one along the route could miss them because of the music being played by the marching band that had been hired by the company. Target practice included food, fun, and prizes for the best shooters of the day.

Third Ward Gets a New Border

In 1858, the piers into Lake Michigan at the foot of E. Clybourn Street were made obsolete when the Federal Government opened a channel from the river to the lake at the southeast end of E. Erie Street. This canal, called the "Straight Cut," allowed ships to reach Downtown directly from the lake. It also separated the Third Ward from Jones Island.

The Straight Cut, beneath the Hoan Bridge, allows large vessels to enter the inner harbor. (Photograph by the author)

Chapter 4
1860–1869

By 1860, Milwaukee's population of 45,463 included about 4,400 people born in Ireland. Counting their North American–born children, the Irish probably were still making up about 15 percent of Milwaukee's population.[1]

The 1860 census enumerator for the city's Fourth Ward, which included Tory Hill, went above and beyond the call of duty when he listed the county of birth of those born in Ireland, rather than just listing Ireland as their birthplace. Counties Galway, Clare, and Tipperary each gave the Fourth Ward more than ten percent of its Irish. Cork and Kilkenny ranked next highest and these five counties provided over half of the Irish immigrants to the Fourth Ward. Kerry, Limerick, and Meath each added about five percent. Except for Meath, these counties are all in south and west Ireland.[2] The Third Ward's Irish most likely had a similar background.

As the Third Ward's marshes were filled in, its population swelled from 4,200 in 1850 to 7,700 in 1860. The number of Irish rose by 900 during those years, but the Irish presence in the Third Ward dropped from 50 percent to about 36 percent, though it was higher when Irish-American children were included, and much higher in the residential section bordered by E. Clybourn, E. Erie, N. Van Buren, and N. Milwaukee streets. Their neighbors in the Ward included Germans, English, Welsh, and other nationalities. Tory Hill's population also increased and became even more densely Irish. The rest of the city's Irish lived mainly east of the Milwaukee River north of the Third Ward, or along the north and south sides of the Menomonee River Valley.

Occupations

The largest segment of the Irish workforce was employed as laborers, but some Irish were able to start climbing the economic ladder. The gas works that was built in the Third Ward provided better paying jobs for residents, but it also emitted very unpleasant odors. Irish men and their sons were learning trades that moved them from unskilled and semi-skilled occupations to skilled jobs like stone cutting, bricklaying, cabinet making, and plumbing. Some young men were serving as apprentices, learning paperhanging, cabinetmaking, and even the architectural trades; and a few were training as lawyers. They also held the stereotypical Irish-American occupations of policemen, constables, and sheriff's deputies. Those acting as firemen were volunteers.

Irishmen started businesses in boiler making, wagon making, contracting, distilling, clothing manufacturing, and house moving. People had houses moved for two reasons: they built a better house on their property and sold the old home, which was then relocated, or they simply moved their house to a more desirable area. Third Ward resident Owen Goss came to Milwaukee from County Louth in 1850 and started his house moving business that over the next 50 years would relocate more than 8,000 buildings.[3]

Irish women were also becoming more active in the community, serving as teachers, nurses, governesses, milliners, and salespeople in addition to their traditional positions as housekeepers, seamstresses, and washerwomen. Based on the 1856 Milwaukee County jail registers, prostitution was not a major source of income for Irish women; of the 20 women arrested for prostitution that year, only two were Irish.

But the city's Irish were jailed for other types of crimes in greater numbers than other nationalities. The jail records showed that 45 percent of those arrested for crimes were Irish, a proportion three times higher than their percent of the population.

The *Lady Elgin* Disaster

In 1860, six years after the rescue of Joshua Glover, the Fugitive Slave Law was still an issue. Sherman Booth, the newsman who had riled up the mob that freed Glover, had been arrested for thwarting the law and was tried, convicted, sentenced, and incarcerated for his part in the jailbreak. However, the Wisconsin Supreme Court ruled the federal Fugitive Slave Law illegal and released Booth. In 1860, the United States Supreme Court ruled that the law was legal and ordered that Booth be sent back to jail. Then Republican abolitionists introduced legislation in Madison to have Wisconsin secede from the Union and declare war on the United States. The legislation got nowhere but inspired much heated debate and led to the disbanding of the Union Guard.

The Republican governor, Alexander Randall, said that he had received a report that Union Guard Captain Garrett Barry would side with the United States if Wisconsin declared war on it. Randall wanted to know if the report was true. Barry responded, in a letter printed in several newspapers, that he had told no one that he would side with his country, but it would make him and his men guilty of treason to take up arms against their adopted land, as many of them had taken oaths of loyalty to the United States as part of the citizenship process. Not liking that answer, Randall not only relieved Barry of his commission, but also disbanded the entire Union Guard, whose members were Democrats, "in the interests of the militia of this state."[4] Neither Barry nor any member of the company was given an opportunity to defend themselves.

Some later claimed that militia leaders around the state had been polled, and presumably Barry was the only one to object to warring on America. That was not the case however, as one newspaper of the day asked, "Why was not the same question asked of any other companies?"[5] Certainly, if John L. Doran, Captain of the Montgomery Guard, was asked, he would have responded as Barry did. The captains of other Irish military companies in the state would have answered Randall the same way, and probably some of the German companies would have too.

Randall required that the Union Guard turn in its state-owned muskets. Being disbanded did not put them out of action though; they just reorganized as the Milwaukee Independent Union Guard and passed a resolution supporting Barry's stance. In June, Barry purchased 80 new muskets at two dollars each from the U.S Armory in St. Louis and the militia company received them in time for the Fourth of July parade. It was decided that a fundraiser was necessary to pay the $160 debt for the arms, so an excursion to Chicago was advertised. For one dollar, supporters would be able to take the *Lady Elgin*, a magnificent side-

Alexander Randall disbanded the Union Guard because they would not support him in warring against the United States of America. (Wikimedia Commons)

wheeled luxury steamship, to Chicago on Thursday evening, September 6, 1860. On Friday, they could experience the sights of the Windy City and hear Stephen Douglas, the Democratic candidate for president, speak. Friday evening, they would return to the *Lady Elgin*, which would get them home in time for work on Saturday morning.

Several hundred excursionists met on a dock on the Milwaukee River near E. Erie and N. Water streets and waited with anticipation and excitement for the arrival of the *Lady Elgin*. But everything did not go according to plan. First, there was disappointment as word spread that Stephen Douglas would not be in Chicago. Second, the steamship was very late in arriving, and third, while the *Lady Elgin* did eventually take them to Chicago, it would never bring them back.

The excursionists on that warm September 6th evening had to wait on the dock for almost five hours, until nearly midnight, due to the late arrival of the 252-foot-long *Lady Elgin*, under the command of Captain Jack Wilson. The vessel was on a circuit that included Chicago at its southern end and the port of Superior on Lake Superior at the other end. The tired and restless crowd was composed of Union Guard members and their families and other supporters: members of the Montgomery Guard; a few members of the Milwaukee Riflemen and another German company, the Black Jägers Rifles; some members of the Milwaukee Light Guard; and two marching brass bands, the American Cornet Band and the private City Band. There were also many fire department members from the Rough and Ready and the Fillmore companies, both dominated by Irishmen.

Some of the excursionists tired of waiting, gave up, and went home. One was Guard member John Rossiter, a 26-year-old teamster, who lived two blocks from the dock and went home to bed. His friends later woke him and talked him into going back and waiting some more. Another who left the dock was Eliza Curtin, 21, a seamstress who also lived nearby. Curtin went home tired and discouraged but her mother, Bridget, was afraid Eliza was going to miss out on a good time with her friends and encouraged her to go back. She did, but with tragic results for both mother and daughter. Others, who left the dock and stayed away, were more fortunate.

Other Milwaukeeans, who were not necessarily supporters of the Union Guard, took advantage of the excursion rate to ride the impressive steamship to Chicago. After the *Lady Elgin* left Milwaukee, some of the passengers partied in the main lounge while others tried to rest, a few of them in private staterooms. By the time they reached Chicago on Friday morning, the sky was beginning to lighten. Normally, there would be at least one Irish militia company in Chicago on hand to escort the Union Guard but due to the early hour, that did not happen. The eager Milwaukeeans spent the day exploring a city that was twice the size of their own and had many attractions, most of them new to the visitors.

About a dozen excursionists rented rooms at the Tremont House, Chicago's equivalent to Milwaukee's luxurious Newhall House. This would allow them to rest before starting the day's activities and return for rest breaks during the day. Shopping, a fair, theatres, and a huge diorama on Ireland that included singing and music were among the attractions. The Union Guard wowed the crowds on Chicago streets in the afternoon with their intricate maneuvers. In the evening, there was a four-hour banquet including speeches, music, and song, and all was right with the world as they headed back to the *Lady Elgin*. But Margaret Burke, 23, so

The *Lady Elgin* at the dock in Chicago during its
last day above water. (*History of Milwaukee, City and
County*, William Bruce, 1922)

enjoyed herself throughout the day that she felt guilty and worried that
something bad was going to happen. She wanted to go back home by
train but her husband, Edward, 33, a contractor, insisted they stick with
their plan.

As the excursionists returned to the *Lady Elgin*, there were already
about 50 passengers on board who were going to ports north of Milwaukee
on Lake Michigan and Lake Superior. These included a British Member
of Parliament and his son, nine well-to-do members of a touring group
from the South, and two Mineral Point, Wisconsin, mothers and their six
children who were on their way to visit the families' breadwinners, who
were working at a copper mine near Lake Superior.

John Herbert, a surviving Union Guard member, later testified that
there were 31 guardsmen on board. It would have been unusual if the
full complement of 70 members had taken the excursion. Because almost
everyone worked a six-day workweek, all members could not participate
in every activity. On a previous trip to Chicago for example, 36 members
went. On another occasion, 45 members were able to take off work on a
Monday to practice. Many of the rank and file could not afford to spend

a day's pay on the one-dollar ticket or lose a day's pay to attend the event. But with family, friends, and other supporters, the excursionists numbered a little over 300.

There were others bound for Milwaukee, including some members of the extremist Wide Awake Club, a paramilitary arm of the Republican Party, who had attended a large Republican rally in Chicago on Thursday. When the *Lady Elgin* steamed out of Chicago late that warm, muggy Friday night, with the excursionists, the crew, the through passengers, and others going to Milwaukee, there were about 400 people aboard, 100 over its rated capacity but well below its actual capacity. The vessel also carried almost 200 head of cattle and a wide range of equipment, including cast iron stoves and other items, as well as the mail bound for ports on Lakes Michigan and Superior.

A storm that had been roaring down the length of Lake Michigan for many hours was on its way to Chicago as the *Lady Elgin* steamed north toward Milwaukee. Passengers bound for points farther north were in their rooms for the night and some Milwaukeeans who had taken rooms were sleeping or getting ready for bed. Most, though, were in the large common area, some lounging or trying to sleep, others drinking and dancing to the music being played by the musicians from the marching bands. The bands could play more than martial music and they often hired out for balls, weddings, and funerals. Third Ward fiddler Johnny Coughlin, a disabled man, was onboard and must have played some Irish tunes.

Revelers were still trying to dance three hours later but the rolling of the side-wheeled steamboat made it impossible. The *Lady Elgin* was in a full-blown storm, with pouring rain, lightning, and thunder, when it was rammed by the lumber-carrying schooner *Augusta* at about 2:15 a.m. At the moment of collision, waves held the ships at odd angles to each other, resulting in the *Augusta* ramming a large hole below the *Lady Elgin's* waterline at the larboard, or port, sidewheel. The crew of the *Augusta* did not think there had been any significant damage to the much larger steamboat, and there was nothing they could do anyway as the storm took them southward toward Chicago.

Lady Elgin Captain Jack Wilson ordered the crew to lower a lifeboat into the water to try to plug the hole with mattresses and blankets. There was a rush to get into the boat as it was lowered. Six crew members and six passengers, all men, jumped into it, while many others pressed forward in an attempt to get in. Afraid that too many people would sink their vessel, the crew pushed off before it was full but pulled in a crew member who jumped into the water after them. The boat had only one oar and by the time another was thrown to them, the storm had taken the lifeboat too far away from the ship to help. Over the next few hours, the wind took the lifeboat, which could have comfortably carried another seven people, close to shore near the small community of Winnetka, Illinois, about seventy miles south of Milwaukee, where the thirteen men were saved.

Within minutes of the collision the severity of the ship's condition became clear and the 40-year-old Captain Wilson ordered the *Lady Elgin* to head toward shore. He encouraged everyone to go to the top deck, commonly referred to as the hurricane deck, but a significant number remained below. Wilson then told the crew to begin chopping at the hurricane deck's supports, so the deck could break free from the *Lady Elgin* as the ship sank and not go down with it. He was hoping it would become a raft for hundreds of people. He also told some passengers to take the doors off the staterooms to provide something to float on.

After the failure of the lifeboat to plug the leak, Wilson ordered the first and second mates and three crew members to lower another small boat off the larboard side to try to plug the gaping hole. When the boat hit water, it was immediately swamped by the surging waves. The five men had almost no control of the water-filled vessel, but they were able to push it away from the larger vessel where there were dozens of people eager to jump into the small boat. The gap between the boat and the mother ship widened and, like the lifeboat, this boat was underused. It could have carried twice as many people as it did. The small boat made it to shore but only three of the five survived the breakers.

A huge wave snapped the supports of the towering smokestacks and one stack fell, killing several people on the deck. When the engine broke through the hull and dropped to the lake floor, water rushed in and the ship sank lower in the water. People jumped into the ever-growing waves, many of them holding anything they hoped would keep them from drowning. About twenty minutes after the collision, the steamship sank. People still on the ship below the hurricane deck, and many in the water near it, were pulled under. A few moments later, dozens of heads broke the water's surface, but many, including Garrett Barry's, did not.

70

The 200-foot-long hurricane deck broke off just as Wilson had hoped, but it meant death to most of those who rose to the surface beneath it. The deck broke in two almost immediately, at the holes where the smokestacks had been, leaving two huge rafts, one over one hundred feet long, supporting hundreds of people. The building waves immediately began to break the rafts into smaller sections. Two small boats, each with a capacity of ten to twelve persons, were stored on the hurricane deck, and they were launched. One carried eight people but only half of them survived. The other boat had just five people in it and only one, Martin Eviston, 30, who ran a Third Ward boardinghouse, survived. There were a large number of life preservers, which were wooden planks with two

FRIGHTFUL CATASTROPHE.

Collision of the Steamer Lady Elgin and
a Schooner on Lake Michigan.

Sinking of the Steamer and Loss of
Over Three Hundred Lives.

The Clerk's Statement of the
Disaster.

HEROISM OF THE LADIES.

Names of Persons Known to be
on Board.

The sinking of the *Lady Elgin* made headlines throughout the country, like this one in the *New York Herald*. (*New York Herald*, September 9, 1860)

holes provided for hand holds. They required strength and stamina to hold onto in the raging water and were mostly ineffective.

With every lightning flash, those in the water could see fellow passengers struggling to stay afloat, using anything they could to keep them from sinking. They held onto dead cattle, stateroom doors, a drum, timber, a raft, anything to hold them above water.

The blowing wind was cold on the skin and caused joints to cramp and fingers to stiffen, but the water had been warming up throughout the summer and some people kept warm by staying in the water. Fortunately, the northeast wind carried people toward the Illinois shore three miles away. The normal westerly winds would have pushed anything in the water away from the Illinois shore on a long journey towards Michigan, 75 miles away.

Martin Eviston's brothers and their wives were also aboard. The last Martin saw of his brother Thomas, the head of Milwaukee's volunteer fire department, and his wife, Bridget, was on the ship, Thomas decked out in his stovepipe hat. Neither husband nor wife survived. Martin's other brother, John, who owned a boiler works, and his wife, Ellen, survived by climbing into the floating pilot's house. They rode it toward shore where the breakers forced them into the water. With hundreds watching from the bluffs, John held on to Ellen as they made it closer to shore, where a group of students from the nearby Garrett Biblical Institute, led by Edward Spenser, pulled them from the crashing waves.

The storm continued to build. Trees were uprooted and fences flattened in Milwaukee and, over the lake, the winds were driving the huge waves even higher. People weakened by the struggle were washed off rafts, and some clinging to floating debris became too exhausted to hold on. The wave motion nauseated many, and vomiting and retching sapped their precious strength, causing more deaths. Many who went under had started the evening already nearly exhausted due to lack of sleep and many hours of activity and partying.

Garrett Barry's 12-year-old son, Willie, clung to a raft for hours before his strength gave out and he was washed off. His 15-year-old friend, Willie Pomeroy, the son of Third Ward School principal Fennimore Cooper Pomeroy, was washed off the raft just before it reached the breakers. The young did not fare well. They lacked strength and there was no one strong enough to take care of them through the long, grueling trip to

**John Eviston and his wife, Ellen Reddy, were
survivors of the *Lady Elgin* disaster.** (*History of
Milwaukee, Wisconsin: From Pre-Historic Times,*
Frank Flower, 1881)

shore. Terrence McDonough, a 13-year-old student, was the youngest to
survive. Twenty-one others his age and younger perished.

Widowed policeman Martin Delaney, 33, told student John Murray,
14, that if Murray made it to shore he should tell Delaney's brothers to
take care of his three children. Delaney was heard yelling for help as he
went under. Murray survived to deliver the message.

Seventeen-year-old newsboy Dennis Gilmore, born in County
Galway, was able to stay on a raft and make it to shore about nine hours
after the sinking. But being saved did not insure happiness. Gilmore went
insane while fighting in the Civil War and spent the rest of his life in
institutions, most of it in the National Soldiers' Home in Milwaukee.

Charles Beverung, 25, a German wagon maker in the City Band and
one of only two members of the band to survive, clung to his drum, which
carried him to shore and safety. The instruments of the other surviving

band member, Adelbert Doebert, floated to shore, but his violin was in pieces because the glue holding it together had dissolved. Patrick Maher, a 32-year-old fireman, and George Furlong, the 19-year-old son of the owner of the Union Guard's Hall, happened on a crate floating with a half dozen dead cattle inside. They climbed aboard and rode the crate to shore where the breakers did their best to break it up, but the two survived.

Captain Jack Wilson encouraged the passengers on his raft to hold blankets, doors, or anything else up to the wind as sails to take them to shore faster. Wilson was last seen near the shore when he was thrown off the raft, which then hit him and sent him under the water.

Over a period of 12 hours after the sinking, more than 200 people got close to shore, but the closer to land, the more dangerous the breakers became. The surf turned over rafts and tossed people to their deaths. Many of the exhausted people who reached within 15 or 20 feet of shore were thrown down by the crashing waves and dragged back out by the undertow. Aided by the heroic efforts of local residents on shore, almost 100 were saved.

With one exception, the rough seas meant no boats could enter the water for lifesaving efforts. The afternoon after the sinking, County Sligo–born John Prindeville took his tug, *McQueen*, out of Chicago to try to help those in the water. He said afterward that he was never so scared in his life and that he should not have gone out into the huge waves. His efforts resulted in spotting dead cattle and the recovery of the body of an infant. Prindeville went out again two days later for recovery operations and over the next six days picked up 108 bodies, including that of Captain Wilson. Later, when Milwaukee aldermen approved Prindeville's bill for recovery operations, he donated the money to the *Lady Elgin* Relief Fund.

When the 13 men in the lifeboat had reached shore, the news was immediately telegraphed to Chicago and Milwaukee. Railroad trains brought family members and a recovery committee from Milwaukee and authorities from Chicago. The scene in the Third Ward on Saturday afternoon "would be utterly impossible to convey...it seemed as though sounds of mourning proceeded from every third house."[6]

Similar to the chaos and confusion in the early reporting of the September 11, 2001, attacks regarding victim names and numbers, newspapers began printing lists of people who were on, or thought to be on, the *Lady Elgin*. These early lists included many errors in fact and spelling. There were people listed as passengers, but who were not, like Gurdon Hubbard, the owner of the *Lady Elgin*; Philip Best, leader of Milwaukee's recovery operations; and William and Margaret Kennedy, who were married a few hours before taking the *Lady Elgin* to Chicago but continued on from there to honeymoon in Vermont.

Many names were misspelled. Thomas Shea, a survivor, had his surname spelled in newspaper lists as Shea, Shay, and Chase, and Philip Aylward's last name was printed as Elywood, Elwood, Elward, Elmore, and Ellsworth. A week after the accident, survivor Ed Mellon wrote in a letter to his brother and sister, "...the newspapers and lists of the lost were very imperfect. In some newspapers they had me lost and saved in the same paper."[7] Mellon's name was also listed in newspapers as Mallen and Mullen.

If all the names printed as passengers in the newspapers were accumulated, errors and misspellings included, there would be over 700 names, which has led some to claim that there were 700 or more passengers on board the *Lady Elgin*.

Survivors' testimony named many people who were on the *Lady Elgin* and in some cases described their deaths. Family and friends gave authorities descriptions of those lost, including ages, physical features, clothing, and adornments. These descriptions helped in identifying many bodies, but some corpses were never identified due to decomposition or a lack of any unique identifying characteristics, clothing, or jewelry. Some bodies may never have been recovered. The final report issued seven weeks after the disaster concluded that there were about 400 on board and that about 300 of them died.[8] This fits with Captain Jack Wilson's estimate that there were about 400 people on the ship, according to survivor Fred Snyder.[9] Many months of research by this author, combing through probate records, church and cemetery burial records, funeral notices, city directories, tombstones, and a wide variety of other records, has provided evidence to support these numbers (see Appendix 2).

There was some confusion in identifying a few of the bodies. For example, one report was that a body was identified by Michael Murphy, a drayman, as James O'Brien's, by a mark in his shoe. Others identified the body as that of bookkeeper Richard Commerford. Friends of Daniel McAuliffe said the body was his, and friends of Andrew Pierce thought it was his body. The corpse was actually Michael Murphy's; it was identified by James O'Brien, a Third Ward shoemaker who had not been on the *Lady Elgin*, and recognized a mark that he had inscribed in Murphy's shoe.

The sinking of the *Lady Elgin* was the largest loss-of-life disaster in Milwaukee's history. A city of 45,000 had lost about 240 of its residents, 170 of them Irish, most of them from the Third Ward. In total, about 300 people perished, the largest loss of life due to a ship sinking in one of the Great Lakes. Of the nearly 100 who survived, about 70 were from Milwaukee.

Tuesday, September 11, 1860, was declared a day of fasting and prayer in Milwaukee. Schools and businesses were closed and draped in mourning, some from the rooftops to the sidewalk. Flags were flown at half-mast. The bells of churches and fire engine houses started ringing at 8 a.m. and continued for more than an hour. Thousands milled around St. John's Cathedral, which held the first 17 bodies to be buried. The requiem mass for the dead began at 10:30 a.m. The funeral procession that followed was more than a mile long and it was estimated that 10,000 people, almost a quarter of the city's population, participated. Military units, with arms reversed, marched slowly to the playing of funeral dirges. City officials, fire engine companies, religious organizations, countless carriages, and four Union Guard survivors were in the procession. The military units were dismissed near N. 10th Street and W. Wisconsin Avenue, while the rest proceeded to Calvary Cemetery on W. Blue Mound Road.

Many bodies were recovered in the following days and funerals in the city became the norm. The numbers diminished over the weeks, but bodies were still being found beyond the year's end. Garrett Barry's body was recovered in November, along with Thomas Neville's, a private in the Union Guard and coachman for a wealthy banker. The body of the 22-year-old, Irish-born Neville was identified because of his powerful build and the gold ring he wore. Their funeral procession was almost a mile long and concluded with volleys being fired at the gravesites by the Milwaukee Light Guard. The following August, Ellen Williams's body was found and identified by her ring. The last body recovered and identified, also by a ring worn on her finger, was Lydia Hopkins's in May of 1862.

Surprisingly, there was only one family in which all members died and that was Frank Lumsden, editor of the *New Orleans Picayune*, his

Many victims of the *Lady Elgin* sinking are buried in this section of Calvary Cemetery, which is dubbed Lady Elgin Hill. (Photograph by the author)

wife, and their two children, who were through passengers. Three Third Ward families, the Bohans, Kilroys, and Rices, were not totally wiped out, but only because in each case they had left their youngest child at home.

Women did not fare as well as men. Eighty women were lost and only nine survived. Ellen Eviston, 26, and Margaret Burke, 23, were both saved through the efforts of their husbands. Twenty-six-year-old Catherine O'Leary made shore on a plank but lost her husband, Daniel, and their six-year-old son, Jeremiah. The oldest woman to survive, 42-year-old Leopoldine Leverrenz, a mother of seven, and described as a poor woman from the Sixth Ward, made it to shore and safety, but her husband, Otto, did not.

Every Irish person in the Third Ward lost a neighbor, many lost an immediate family member, and most, because they all seemed to be related one way or another, lost an extended family member. Citywide, 54 women were widowed, 144 children were left with only one parent, and 39 children were orphaned, which was fortunately far less than the 1,000 orphans reported by the *Milwaukee Sentinel*.[10] Relatively few Catholic children went to orphanages. The population at St. Rose's orphanage increased by five girls between 1860 and 1861, while the boys' institution, St. Aemelian, saw an increase of only two children.[11] The Milwaukee Protestant Orphan Asylum took in fifteen children orphaned by the sinking of the *Lady Elgin*.[12] Most of the Irish orphans were cared for by relatives, like the three sons of Robert and Sarah Ring, who were raised by Robert's brother, or Thomas and Catherine Bohan's orphaned son, who was raised by Thomas's brother. It wasn't just children who depended on the perished. Nineteen-year-old Anne Fitzgerald and her seventeen-year-old brother, Patrick, left their widowed mother, Mary, without support after their deaths.

The *Lady Elgin* Relief Fund was set up and began receiving donations immediately. A benefit concert of Mozart's "Requiem" was performed at St. John's Cathedral by the Milwaukee Musical Society. The proceeds of a military picnic and ball were donated to the fund. Donations came from individuals and groups throughout the continent. The largest amount, $409, came from Philadelphia, the "City of Brotherly Love." The English Dramatic Society of Montreal sent $78. Mrs. Millard Fillmore of Buffalo, wife of the former president, added $50. But most of the money came in one- or two-dollar donations made by Milwaukeeans and Wisconsinites. The total collected was over $7,500, which did not last long in supporting over 200 people. And the amount paled when compared to the more than $1,000 collected in Chicago just for the family of Captain Jack Wilson. Milwaukee printers raised $175 for the family of fellow printer Alex Corbitt. Friends of the Komarick brothers from Bohemia, Franz, 23, Anton, 20, and Joseph, 17, who played in the marching band and were lost, took up a collection for their mother, the widow Catherine Komarick. There were other collections taken for specific families and individuals.

Edward Keogh, who lost two sisters and a cousin on the *Lady Elgin*, and who represented the Third Ward in the state assembly, introduced legislation that would provide $5,000 to the fund, which was rapidly being depleted. But the *Lady Elgin* Relief Bill did not pass. Donated funds helped 90 families initially, and 60 destitute families, mostly those of victims who were laborers, were helped for a few months before relief funds ran out.

On a Racine street corner, a Mrs. Williams tried to take advantage of the situation by claiming that she lost three relatives on the *Lady Elgin*.

When that didn't garner enough money, she upped the claim to five relatives. Newspapers gave her sympathy, but the public was not fooled.

The reputations of both Tim O'Brien and his son-in-law, James Hoye, were affected by the disaster, but in different ways. "Father Tim" O'Brien, 48-year-old Third Ward councilman and one of the best-known men in the city, was in the lifeboat of 13 survivors. O'Brien testified that he told his wife and daughter to stay below in their room and then, when he went to see what was happening, he was "forced" into the life boat. This started criticism of O'Brien and one newspaper ridiculed him, saying that he was a survivor by compulsion.[13] Mary Fitzgerald O'Brien, his 24-year-old wife; Hannah Hoye, his 24-year-old daughter; and 20-year-old Ann Fitzgerald, his sister-in-law, were all lost.

O'Brien's son-in-law's reputation improved after the disaster. James Hoye, a bridgetender, was born in Kells, County Meath, in 1831 and immigrated to Milwaukee, where he married Hannah O'Brien in 1854. Hoye had not made the trip to Chicago but was a member of the recovery

Most of the tombstones of *Lady Elgin* **victims at Calvary Cemetery are weathered and nearly illegible, but Mary Matthew's tombstone is easy to read.** (Photograph by the author)

committee from Milwaukee. After he spent several days searching for his wife's body along the beaches near Winnetka, a rumor started that he had stolen a watch. Hugh Horrigan, who lost his 19-year-old son, Michael, in the disaster, was also helping in the recovery operation and he jumped to Hoye's defense. Horrigan said that Hoye had been at the beach every day, often without eating, in search of Hannah's body. Horrigan continued, that whatever Hoye "had done in the past, he had not had a drop to drink and he had acted as a worthy man."[14] Others who had spent days searching at the beach also came to Hoye's defense. Hannah Hoye's body floated 80 miles over the next six weeks and was recovered 11 miles north of Milwaukee. James Hoye remarried several years later, and the Third Ward voters must have thought he was a "worthy man"; they elected him as the representative for the Third Ward in the state assembly almost continuously from 1869 through 1883.

There were other, later, victims of the disaster. One was Bridget Curtin, who had encouraged her daughter, Eliza, to go on the excursion and have a good time with her friends. After Eliza drowned, Bridget was never the same and she died a few years later, it was said, of a broken heart. College student Edward Spenser, who attended the Garrett Biblical Institute near Winnetka, was a hero who plunged into the waves 17 times with a rope tied around him, so those at the other end of the rope could pull him back in with each of the 17 people that he had saved from the water. Spenser's health was ruined by his exertions and he spent the rest of his life enfeebled. Bridget Keogh survived with help from John Herbert, but she never regained full strength, and shortly after her marriage to fellow survivor John Rossiter, her frail health led to her death.

One victim was Thomas Slaughter, a 32-year-old African-American saloonkeeper from Walker's Point, whose marriage to a 16-year-old Caucasian musician, Eliza Watson, the previous November in Detroit had created a stir. Interracial marriage was illegal in Michigan, so when a black Episcopal priest married them, he was fined $50. Neither Slaughter nor Watson was charged because they were both already married to someone else, rendering their marriage invalid.

Another victim was John Horan, 30, a Third Ward carpenter from County Galway, who was a member of both the Cathedral Literary Society and the Montgomery Guard and a former bodyguard for Sherman Booth. Horan was also the census enumerator for the Third Ward during the summer of 1860, and all census takers were sworn in as "assistant marshals" to give them the authority to carry out their enumeration duties. This title was exaggerated in lists of victims in newspapers, some listing Horan as a "Deputy Marshal," others as "U.S. Marshal," and one New York paper as "Deputy U.S. Marshal for Wisconsin."

On Friday, October 26, at 7:30 p.m., the remaining Union Guard members met at Lieutenant John Crilley's house to settle the affairs of the company. The catastrophe had done what Governor Randall could not do—permanently disband the Union Guard.

Ed Burke, who survived and saved his wife, Margaret, was arrested a few weeks after the sinking for throwing rocks at a Republican parade, but sympathy was on his side because of the disaster and he was released. Over the eight months following the disaster, at least eight children were born whose fathers were *Lady Elgin* victims, including Garrett Barry's daughter, Garretta, who was born the following May.

Over the years, there have been stories about victims' bodies floating back to the Third Ward. Union Guard member Cornelius O'Mahoney, 35, was a teacher at the Third Ward School on E. St. Paul Avenue. His body supposedly floated to the foot of that street, but in reality, his body was recovered off of Whitefish Bay. Another Guard member, Nicholas McGrath, 32, operated a saloon and distillery on E. Erie Street. His body was said to defy nature and float upriver to his saloon, but it did not; his remains were found off of Winnetka. Patrick Rooney, 17, was the son of auctioneer John Rooney, and his body, so the story goes, floated to shore near his father's Third Ward business. His body, if ever recovered, was not identified.

The most commonly uttered myth regarding the *Lady Elgin* disaster is that the loss of so many Irish residents prevented the Irish from garnering the significant political power that they would otherwise have had. But the Irish population of the city, counting the children of the immigrants, was no more than 20 percent and their influence was centered in the Third Ward, where they elected Irish politicians and received patronage work. Few Irish would be elected from German wards and German immigrants would continue to arrive in the city for decades, dwarfing the numbers of Irish.

The idea that the Irish would have controlled a political machine in Milwaukee, as they later did in Boston and Chicago, is unrealistic. Certainly, the political characters within the Ward could have been

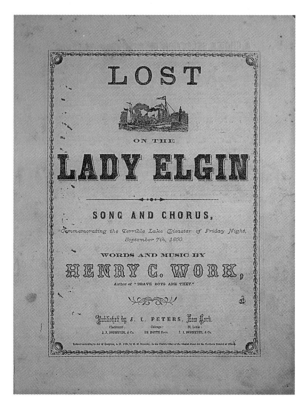

A song, "Lost on the Lady Elgin," was written by Henry C. Work shortly after the disaster. The song cover erroneously states the date of the catastrophe as September 7. (Library of Congress.)

different. If the very popular Frank McCormick, a 25-year-old councilman and a victim, had survived, there may not have been room in Third Ward politics for a James Hoye or a Cornelius Corcoran, and veterans like Tim O'Brien or John Crilley may have been pushed aside by others who were lost. Some may have had an impact on city politics. Garrett Barry, who had been elected the County Treasurer, could possibly have had a run as mayor, but then would Edward O'Neill have served as mayor for four one-year terms in the 1860s?

The disaster did have a major economic impact on the Third Ward, which was regarded as the city's poorest ward. Most of the adult males who were lost were better off financially and better educated than their neighbors. A few were professionals or proprietors, and many of the rest held clerical, skilled, or at least semi-skilled jobs, which meant that their above-average-income households would slide down the economic scale after their deaths. The composite income generated by Third Ward wage earners would be affected for decades.

In the years following the disaster, *Lady Elgin* survivors would attend an annual mass for the victims at the Cathedral, but in 1889, they decided to form an association that would meet annually to commemorate the tragedy. They numbered 26 members in 1890 and reached a high of 38 in 1891, with about a third of them no longer living in Milwaukee. The *Lady Elgin* Survivors Association, at least the members who were able, met at Marble Hall on N. Broadway, just south of E. Wisconsin Avenue. The hall was run by survivor Fred Snyder until his death in 1897. By 1906, the number of survivors had dwindled to a handful, all of them elderly and no longer able to meet. Margaret Hayes Crean was the last known survivor when she died in January of 1924 at age 83; her brother, William Hayes, had been a victim of the sinking ship. Margaret later married the brother of victim Mary Crean.

In 1892, to honor the victims of the *Lady Elgin* disaster, enough funds were raised to pay for an annual memorial mass "as long as St. John church exists in Milwaukee . . . and until the world shall come to an end."[15] The Cathedral of St. John still exists in Milwaukee and the world has not ended, but the *Lady Elgin* disaster receded in collective memory, and in 1946 the masses stopped.

In the years immediately after the sinking there was talk of a memorial for the *Lady Elgin* victims, but nothing came of it. After the Newhall House fire in 1883, there was a push for a combined memorial for the two disasters that took the lives of over 200 of the city's Irish. That effort ended with memorials in Calvary and Forest Home cemeteries for the Newhall House victims only. In 2008, a group formed to erect a monument to the *Lady Elgin* disaster, but that effort died.

In 1996, the nearest thing to a memorial, an historical marker, "Sinking of the *Lady Elgin*," was erected in the Third Ward. The marker could have been written by a supporter of Governor Randall in that it states that the Union Guard was decommissioned because it supported the Fugitive Slave Law, rather than that it was decommissioned because it would not support Randall's threat of treason, a crime for which Garrett Barry declared "I and my men would deserve to be hung."[16] The marker also inaccurately states that "there were more than 500 Union Guard

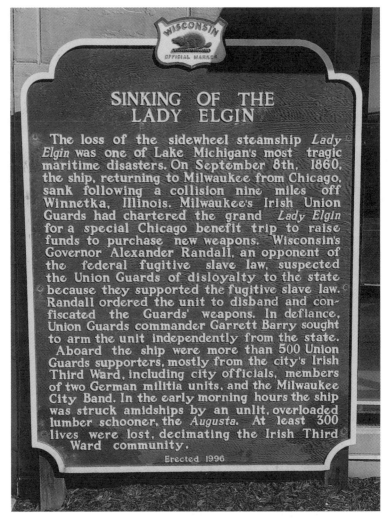

SINKING OF THE LADY ELGIN

The loss of the sidewheel steamship *Lady Elgin* was one of Lake Michigan's most tragic maritime disasters. On September 8th, 1860, the ship, returning to Milwaukee from Chicago, sank following a collision nine miles off Winnetka, Illinois. Milwaukee's Irish Union Guards had chartered the grand *Lady Elgin* for a special Chicago benefit trip to raise funds to purchase new weapons. Wisconsin's Governor Alexander Randall, an opponent of the federal fugitive slave law, suspected the Union Guards of disloyalty to the state because they supported the fugitive slave law. Randall ordered the unit to disband and confiscated the Guards' weapons. In defiance, Union Guards commander Garrett Barry sought to arm the unit independently from the state. Aboard the ship were more than 500 Union Guards supporters, mostly from the city's Irish Third Ward, including city officials, members of two German militia units, and the Milwaukee City Band. In the early morning hours the ship was struck amidships by an unlit, overloaded lumber schooner, the *Augusta*. At least 300 lives were lost, decimating the Irish Third Ward community.

Erected 1996

The Lady Elgin Historical Marker has errors. The ship sank three miles from shore, not nine miles. The Union Guard was disbanded because it would not fight against the United States, not because it supported the fugitive slave law. There was a total of about 400 people on board including crew and other passengers, not "more than 500 Union Guard supporters." (Photograph by the author)

supporters" on board. With crew and non-excursionists that would mean at least 600 on board when, in reality, there were about 400 people on the ship.

The 150th anniversary of the sinking of the *Lady Elgin*, which resulted in the largest loss-of-life disaster in Milwaukee's history, has now come and gone. Its victims are no longer remembered in an annual Mass, and their only monument is an inaccurate historical marker.

The search for the sunken *Lady Elgin* began in the 1940s but was not successful until 1989, when the latest underwater scanning technology provided a wide view of the lake floor. The wreck was strewn along a one-mile stretch in about fifty-five feet of water, three miles east of Highland Park, Illinois. Among the artifacts recovered were some of the muskets that led to the disastrous excursion.

The Civil War Begins

Two months after the *Lady Elgin* disaster, Americans voted to elect a new president. There was no doubt that the city's Irish would support the Democrat, Stephen Douglas. The opposition was the recently formed Republican Party, with its main goal of abolishing slavery or at least stopping its expansion. The new party was not going to be friendly to the Irish. It included remnants of the conservative anti-Catholic Whig Party and former anti-Catholic Know Nothings. There would be no reason to vote for these traditional political enemies except as a vote against slavery. Not too many Irish would vote to set slaves free because of the fear that there would be more competition for laborers' jobs as the market was flooded with former slaves. Electing abolitionists would very likely mean war, so Douglas won the majority of the votes cast in Milwaukee, including a landslide in the Irish precincts, but lost statewide and nationally to the Republican candidate, Abraham Lincoln.

The election of Lincoln did mean war. Before he took office in March 1861, seven slave states reacted by banding together to form the Confederate States of America. On April 12, Confederate forces fired on Union soldiers at Fort Sumter, South Carolina, and the Civil War began. When President Lincoln called on each Northern state to help put down the rebellion, four more Southern states joined the Confederacy.

With the Northern states' larger population and industrial superiority over the agricultural South, many thought the war would be decided quickly in the North's favor. The North was so confident that the war would soon be won, that the enlistment term for volunteer soldiers was only three months.

The desire to preserve the Union and its ideals was at a fever pitch, and with the added incentive of the chance for excitement, young men throughout the North were anxious to enlist. Farm boys would be able to leave their long hours of tedious labor and have an opportunity to socialize with others their age. City laborers could forget their daily grind of scratching out as many hours of labor as they could. Military service would give them shelter, clothing, and food, as well as monthly pay. Whether from city or countryside, all of them would look good in uniform and the young ladies were encouraged to be patriotic and give men in uniforms more attention. The young men had dreams of glory that would make their families and friends proud of them. For those who had served in militias, this would be an opportunity to use the skills they had been honing.

For the Irish militias in America, there was hope that service in the war would give them the experience necessary to eventually expel the English from Ireland. In Wisconsin, the Yankees did not want to give the Irish that experience. The prevailing thought was that Yankees alone would win the war and foreign-born were not only not needed, they were not wanted. When the Hibernian Guard, a Fond du Lac Irish militia company, volunteered to enlist, Wisconsin Quartermaster General S. E. Lefferts told them that "there are enough young Americans to put down the trouble inside of ninety days and we do not want any red-faced foreigners."[17]

With that kind of welcome, only two Irishmen from Milwaukee were among the nearly 800 men who filled the initial Wisconsin regiment, enlisting for three months. However, the war did not end in three months, and more than fifty Wisconsin regiments would be needed to fight the four-year-long war. Lefferts's opinion about the Union not needing any "red-faced" Irishmen changed very quickly. The state would accept many Irish militias into its service in the upcoming months, but not Fond du Lac's Hibernian Guard. After Lefferts's rejection, the Hibernian Guard voted to disband and was not involved in the war.

By the time the Second and Third regiments formed in the state, the enlistment period was up to three years, and Irish were welcomed. About a dozen of the city's Irish enlisted in these regiments, with hundreds more to follow in later regiments formed in both Wisconsin and other states.[18] Military experience for the fight for Ireland's freedom was a factor for many of them, but there were other reasons. Love of the United States and its opportunities for themselves and for Irish still to come led to genuine patriotism and a desire for the Republic to succeed and flourish. Pride in the "fighting Irish" traditions, and the chance to excel in the face of Yankee prejudice and prove themselves loyal citizens were also motivations. For those living in or near poverty, the army would be a step up. The various bounties and incentives that were paid could amount to a year's pay or more for a soldier's family. Some who were facing jail sentences, like Robert B. Lynch, a former Milwaukee City Clerk convicted of embezzlement, and Hugh Quinn, a "desperate character," chose enlistment rather than imprisonment.

The Montgomery Guard, the Bank Riot, and the Iron Brigade

With the outbreak of the Civil War, John L. Doran resigned as captain of the Montgomery Guard and joined the state militia as a colonel. His place was taken by John O'Rourke, a Third Ward bookkeeper and a sharp-shooting former member of the Union Guard. Business had taken O'Rourke from Milwaukee during the summer of 1860, which prevented him from taking the excursion on the *Lady Elgin*. Membership in the Montgomery Guard reached 48 men by the end of 1860 and it continued to grow throughout early 1861. By May, the company reached its capacity of 100 men. Many of the new recruits were not Irish, leaving the Irish with a thin majority. Slated to join Wisconsin's Sixth Regiment as Company D, the Guard went into training at Camp Scott, on the north side of W. Wisconsin Avenue between N. 12th and N. 14th streets.

The company saw its first action on June 24 without leaving the city. The Bank Riot took place when an association of banks voted to no longer recognize the scrip used as currency by some of its members. Several hundred German workers, upon learning that their money would be worthless, marched to the banking district on N. Water and E. Michigan streets demanding that their money retain its value. When they did not hear what they wanted to hear, they ransacked two banks, their contents feeding a bonfire in the street. A few people in the banks were attacked, as were other businesses along the block. A police force of 18 men was inadequate to quell the rioters, so the Montgomery Guard was called to restore order. There were only 37 members in Milwaukee at the time, and they were sent without ammunition or bayonets. The rioters backed up as John O'Rourke and the guardsmen approached, but their small numbers and lack of offensive capabilities soon became apparent to the mob, who began pelting the soldiers with anything they could throw. The company withdrew when Lieutenant John Nichols and three other guardsmen were hit in the head with projectiles and Nichols suffered the indignity of losing his sword to the crowd. Most of the rioters scattered when another company, the Zouaves, was called in and charged the mob with bayonets flashing. Water from a fire company's hoses took care of the rest. Reinforcements of several more companies brought calm to the city. The banks were back in business in a few days and the rioters got what they wanted; the banking association reversed course and promised to recognize their currency.

John O'Rourke and the Montgomery Guard soon joined the rest of the Sixth Regiment in Madison. At the end of July, the regiment was sent to protect the nation's capital, short about six men who had deserted before leaving Madison. The regiment stayed on the outskirts of Washington, D.C., until March of 1862, but then went on the offensive for the next three years.

As part of the "Iron Brigade of the West," along with Wisconsin's Second and Seventh regiments as well as a regiment each from Michigan and Indiana, they participated in 20 major battles at places like Bull Run, Antietam, and Gettysburg, and these engagements took their toll. No other brigade suffered as high a percentage of casualties as the Iron Brigade. There were other "Iron Brigades" in the war, but over the years the "of the West" was dropped as the Iron Brigade took its place in Civil War history as *the* Iron Brigade. Of those who did not die on the battlefield or in a hospital, most came home suffering from wounds or disease, some emotionally or physically disabled for life, and many died prematurely. Dozens of Milwaukee Irish served in the Brigade.

Neither John O'Rourke nor his lieutenants, John Nichols and Patrick McCauley, fought with the Iron Brigade though. In the tedium of Washington guard duty, politics became the pastime of the Yankee hierarchy of the Sixth Regiment and they decided a purge of company officers was necessary. The purge included anyone they deemed incompetent, incorrigible, or Irish.[19] In October 1861, after the three men were replaced as officers, they resigned. McCauley and Nichols joined Wisconsin's "Irish Brigade," then being organized by John L. Doran. Time proved the Yankee staff of the Sixth Regiment to be poor judges of leaders. By the end of the war, McCauley was a major and Nichols was

John O'Rourke, the "Johnny" in the Civil War song "When Johnny Comes Marching Home"? (Captain John O'Rourke House Collection.)

a lieutenant, demonstrating that being Irish was not the same as being incompetent or incorrigible.

John O'Rourke took a different path. He accepted command of the 11th Battery of Wisconsin's Light Artillery, which later was integrated into the First Regiment of the Illinois Light Artillery. As the war dragged on and casualties mounted, O'Rourke's future bride, Third Ward resident Annie Gilmore, like most of the rest of the country, was growing more anxious and worried. Her younger brother, Denny Gilmore, was serving in the Milwaukee Regiment, the 24th. He had survived the *Lady Elgin* disaster, but she worried about him surviving this conflict. And she worried about the fate of John O'Rourke. Her older brother, Patrick Sarsfield Gilmore, who lived in the East, was a nationally-known composer and bandleader. In July 1863, to cheer Annie, and the rest of the country, Patrick Gilmore published the upbeat song "When Johnny Comes Marching Home" with John O'Rourke in mind as "Johnny," according to the O'Rourke/Gilmore family oral history.[20]

It could not have helped Annie's emotional state when, six months later, O'Rourke was captured by the rebels and spent thirteen months in Confederate prisons. In March of 1865, he escaped and made it back to Union lines just in time to be discharged as the war ended. O'Rourke came back to Milwaukee after the war but opportunities in other places called. Annie stayed in Milwaukee. It took O'Rourke almost ten years to find the financial security he wanted as a banker in Plattsmouth, Nebraska. He finally came back to Milwaukee for Annie and they were married at the Cathedral of St. John in January 1875 in a wedding described by the *Sentinel* as "stylish." After the reception the couple boarded the train for Plattsmouth. Before O'Rourke's death seven years later, the couple had

Patrick Gilmore, John O'Rourke's brother-in-law, who wrote "When Johnny Comes Marching Home." (Library of Congress)

four children and John was twice elected as Plattsmouth's mayor.

One Milwaukee Irishman who was not affected by the Yankee purge of Irish officers in the Montgomery Guard was Thomas Kerr, and that was because Kerr was only a private, but he wouldn't be for long. Kerr was born in Ireland about 1830 and after his family moved to the United States, he joined the U.S. Army and fought in the Mexican War, where he had two fingers of his right hand shot off. Afterwards Kerr, a carpenter, moved to the Third Ward, where his popularity led to his election as foreman of the Third Ward volunteer fire company. He joined the Montgomery Guard when it was founded, and when John O'Rourke folded the company into the Sixth Regiment, Kerr went too. Kerr's fearlessness and leadership led to rapid promotion. He was a second lieutenant by the time he was shot in the left knee in 1862 at the Battle of South Mountain in Maryland. He was shot in the right side of his chest as a captain at Gettysburg, Pennsylvania, in 1863. The next year he was shot in the right leg and was wounded in the hip in the Battle of Cold Harbor, Virginia. In 1865, Kerr was shot in the right side at the Battle of Hatcher's Run, Virginia. When the war ended, Kerr was a lieutenant colonel in command of the Sixth Regiment, a regiment he had joined as a private. Until his death in Milwaukee in 1903, Kerr carried in his coin purse three of the bullets that had wounded him.

Darby Carney and the Lynching of Marshall Clark

Ten weeks after the city had gained experience in mob control by putting down the bank rioters with military companies stationed at Camp Scott, warning signs of another mob action appeared, one that was even predicted in one newspaper. Yet with troops still available at Camp Scott and plenty of time to stop it, the city did virtually nothing. Consequently, Milwaukee's only lynching took place in the Third Ward. It was one of 16 lynchings in Wisconsin history, and the only one in which the victim was an African American.

Just as it was getting dark on Friday evening, September 6, 1861, a confrontation between two black men, James Shelton and Marshall Clark, and two Irishmen, Darby Carney and John Brady, occurred on the corner of E. Michigan and N. Milwaukee streets. Carney and Brady, claiming that Shelton and Clark insulted two white women walking by, started arguing with the two African Americans. Carney was recognized by his adversaries and one of them said, "We know you, Darby Carney, we are as good as any damned Irishman, anytime, or any Yankee either."[21] Shelton then stabbed both Carney and Brady and, as he and Clark were running from the scene, he also stabbed John Ellis, an English lamplighter who was carrying his ladder home after lighting the street lamps.

Shelton and Clark next went to the park at N. Third and W. Michigan streets (now Zeidler Union Square), where there was a tent show featuring Dan Rice, one of the most popular entertainers of the nineteenth century, who was performing with his circus. Shortly after the show, both men were arrested and jailed.

Irish-born, 36-year-old Darby Carney owned a boardinghouse on the southeast corner of E. Clybourn and N. Milwaukee streets. He named it the Emmet House in honor of Robert Emmet, a leader of the abortive Irish rebellion of 1803 who was hanged, drawn, and quartered by the English for his efforts. Carney was well known in the city, mostly for his drunk and disorderly arrests, as well as for assault and battery charges both by and against him. His friends said that he was not troublesome unless he was drinking, but drunk he often was. After Shelton slashed his belly open, Carney was carried to his home.

John Brady lived in Muskego and was visiting his brother who lived in Milwaukee. Hours after the stabbings, he was found wandering out of the E. St. Paul Avenue marsh, wet, muddy, and delirious. He had been stabbed in the shoulder and was taken into a nearby home and cared for. The lamplighter, John Ellis, was stabbed in the hip and arm, but was up and about the next day.

James Shelton, a 28-year-old Virginian, was a waiter at Anderson's ice cream establishment on N. Broadway near the Newhall House. Shelton was described as a person "of a quiet, orderly disposition" who "hardly ever drinks anything."[22]

George Marshall Clark, a 22-year-old born in Pennsylvania, was a barber, a trade he learned from his father, George, who ran his business on W. Wisconsin Avenue. George Sr. was considered a "very respectable man; but his son . . . was an ugly, dissipated and worthless fellow."[23] Shelton and Clark lived together near N. Fifth and W. State streets.

Relations between Irish and blacks were seldom good. Both were on the bottom of the job ladder, fighting for the same places on the lowest rungs. The Irish were Democrats, and the Democratic Party was anti-emancipation and pro-immigrant, as were most Catholic Church leaders and many Irish. Not surprisingly, blacks generally despised the Democratic Irish Catholics.

The morning after the stabbings, Shelton and Clark admitted their guilt but excused themselves for it by saying they had been drunk. Darby Carney was still alive but, with his intestines coming out of his body, it did not look like he was going to survive. There was enough angry talk throughout the Third Ward all day that the evening *Daily Milwaukee* warned that it would not be surprised to learn of an attempt to "rescue the prisoners and bring them before Judge Lynch's Court."[24] The newspaper was prophetic and the actions of the authorities were pathetic. When fire bells in the Third Ward signaled Carney's death about 11 o'clock Saturday night, a mob formed, growing as it moved north and numbering about 50 with as many as 300 onlookers. It was midnight when they reached the jail at the north end of Cathedral Square. Several pistol shots rang out, warning the jailors of the mob's arrival.

Fearing that all prisoners might escape if the mob were successful, the jailors had prepared by separating Clark and Shelton from the rest of the prisoners and locking them in a back room of the jail. Police Chief William Beck did not seem well prepared at all, as he stood in front of the jail door with only two Irish policemen. They were not much of an impediment to the crowd trying to reach Darby Carney's attackers; Beck was hit in the head with a stone and the two policemen were easily pushed aside. William Kendrick, the jailor, had a pistol, but after the mob used a heavy timber to ram the door open and burst into the jail, he put it down. At the same time, the back door of the jail was forced open by the mob. The keys were taken from Kendrick's assistant and used to unlock the room where Clark and Shelton were held. Clark was grabbed and taken out the front of the jail while Shelton, unnoticed behind a door, snuck out the back exit and escaped. He ran west and entered Camp Scott, the Civil War camp at N. 12th Street and W. Wisconsin Avenue. The soldiers there had no idea who Shelton was and told him to keep moving, so he kept going west.

Marshall Clark was dragged, beaten, and pushed down N. Jefferson Street to E. St. Paul Avenue and then west to the Fillmore Engine House on the river. He was held in the fire station for an hour while the mob leaders tried to determine whether the man they had was really Clark or, as he claimed, George Marshall, who had been jailed as a pickpocket. Incredibly, during that time there was virtually no interference by authorities. When Sheriff Charles Larkin, a Yankee, made no attempt to enter the firehouse but tried to reason with the mob outside, he was told, "Go to Hell, you damned old fool."[25] Edward Keogh was only 25 years old but already a leader in the community. He cleared the crowd from the firehouse by warning the occupants that the fire company would be held responsible, their engine could be taken away and the company disbanded and, unlike the Union Guard of a year earlier, would not be able to reorganize independently. Most of the crowd left.

The few men who remained determined that the prisoner was Marshall Clark and not George Marshall, the pickpocket. Clark was taken a block south to E. Buffalo Street where, a little east of N. Water Street, the mob spotted a pile driver where they ended Clark's life by hanging him from it. His death occurred at approximately 2 a.m., September 8, 1861, one year to the hour after the sinking of the *Lady Elgin*. His body was taken down about 20 minutes later by Policemen John McCarty and *Lady Elgin* survivor, Martin Eviston, and taken to the morgue at the police station.[26]

Later Sunday morning, crowds gathered throughout the city, some to visit the gallows, some to exclaim their horror, and some to discuss more lynchings. The previous night a German fireman had been injured by John Quinn, one of the mob, who was arrested. A rumor circulated that the German had died, and a German mob threatened to storm the jail to hang Quinn. The Irish mob believed that Shelton was still in the jail and they wanted to lynch him too. Sheriff Larkin proposed that a few members of the Irish mob inspect the jail and see for themselves that Shelton was gone.

Finally, 24 hours after they should have, the mayor and the police chief called in the military, who were only a few minutes away at Camp Scott. By Sunday evening, cannons were in position near the jail on both N. Jackson and N. Jefferson streets and manned by the Washington Artillery. The Home Guard and the Wisconsin Rangers camped in Cathedral Square and pickets were set up for several blocks around the courthouse jail. There was no more trouble.

Then the finger-pointing began. One newspaper reported that, "[t]he police are mostly Irish and did not oppose the mob much,"[27] which was partially true. The police did not "oppose the mob much," because as policeman John McCarty said, the police "thought it was no use."[28] But the police force was not mostly Irish, it was only about one-third Irish, so why didn't Chief Beck call out more than two Irish

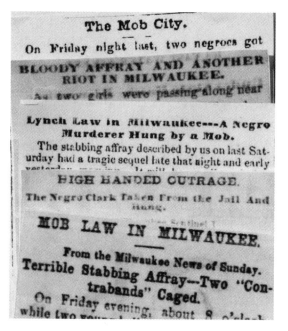

Newspapers were critical of the mob mentality in Milwaukee after the lynching of Marshall Clark.

- *Whitewater Register, September 13, 1861*
- *Watertown Republican, September 13, 1861*
- *Madison Wisconsin Daily State Journal, September 9, 1861*
- *Indianapolis Indiana State Sentinel, September 25, 1861*
- *The Manitowoc Pilot, September 13, 1861*

police officers? Others blamed Mayor James Brown, who said he did not want to be mayor anyway and that he counted on Police Chief Beck to take care of police matters. Beck resigned. A petition was circulated to have Governor Randall remove Sheriff Larkin from his position. Some forgave the slow response to the quickly developing Bank Riot ten weeks earlier, but pointed out that lynching talk began almost 24 hours before it occurred, and the recent experience in putting down the Bank Riot should have stopped the lynching, especially with the military in camp nearby. Certainly, of the major mob actions of the years 1850 to 1861 (Liquor Law Riot, Leahey Riot, Railroad Riot, Voting Riot, Rescue of Joshua Glover, Bank Riot), the Lynching of Marshall Clark was the worst; the only one where someone had died, and the only one where there was both the time and manpower to easily prevent it.

On Monday, September 11, James Shelton was captured a few miles south of Waukesha by policemen Thomas Shaughnessy and Peter Smith and brought back to Milwaukee. In October, he was tried for the murder of Darby Carney and acquitted, probably because Marshall Clark had already given his life for the crime. Immediately after the trial, Shelton was secreted away from the city, some say to Chicago.

In November, John McCormick, a 26-year-old shoemaker; James O'Brien, 35, a tavern keeper; Patrick McLaughlin, 21, a shingle maker; John Devine, a 25-year-old drayman; and Dennis Delury, 20, a laborer, were tried for the murder of Marshall Clark. During the trial, the charges against Delury were dropped for lack of any evidence. The jury could not agree on a verdict for the other four, so they were freed. The defendants were tried again the following January and acquitted.

The Irish Brigade and Mutiny at Camp Randall

After the Montgomery Guard's officers were shoved aside by the Yankee officers of the Sixth Regiment, Patrick McCauley and John Nichols joined John L. Doran in recruiting for the "Irish Brigade" (17th Regiment) in late 1861 and early 1862. The term "Irish Brigade" was a bit of a misnomer since this was only one regiment and a brigade generally consists of multiple regiments. A more accurate name would be the "Irish Regiment," but this would not be accurate either as it was not exclusively Irish. When enough Irishmen could not be coaxed to fill the ranks, Native Americans and French mountaineers of the Green Bay area were recruited along with Germans and Yankees. The full 17th Regiment numbered about 1,000 soldiers.

The youngest Irish recruit was John Phelan Jr. Phelan was born in Milwaukee on June 2, 1847, to a Third Ward shoemaker who died when John was 13 years old. John Sr. was a friend of John Doran and when Doran organized the Irish Brigade, he brought John Jr., age 14 and a half, with him as a drummer boy. Phelan was mustered out at the end of the war and died at the Milwaukee National Soldiers' Home in 1913. Doran, a defense attorney who was born in County Mayo about 1820 and came to Milwaukee at age 24, was one of the framers of the state constitution.

The green regimental flag included a harp and an eagle, the flags of the United States and Wisconsin, and the words "Wisconsin Irish Brigade" and "Faug A Balac" (Irish for "Clear the Way" and more commonly spelled "Faugh A Ballagh"). Patrick McCauley was made captain of Company A, the Emmet Guards of Dodge County, and John Nichols, a lieutenant in the Native American company K.

The Irish Brigade went into training at Camp Randall in Madison in early 1862. The training went along smoothly until the day after St. Patrick's Day, Tuesday, March 18, when it was announced that the regiment would leave the state for St. Louis, Missouri, the next day. The men were told that because of this haste in leaving, the normal procedure of pay before departure was impossible. The men, who were counting on the pay to support their families in their absence, demanded their due in a variety of languages, and said they would not leave without it. Many had families who had come to Madison to see their men off and collect the enlistment bonuses that they would need to live on.

To make matters worse, in spite of snow and a strong wind, and with no provision for shelter for the night, the men were ordered to take down their tents and pack them so they could be loaded on the trains. The reactions of the men varied from sullen to enraged. Many refused to take down their shelters, but their officers reasoned, pleaded, and threatened until all the tents were ready for shipment. Then the men were told to assemble; they were going to be addressed by the new governor, Louis Harvey. It took over an hour to assemble, with nearly 1,000 men standing with weapons on their shoulders, in the snow and cold, getting angrier and angrier and demanding that they get relief from the weather, saying they wouldn't treat a dog the way they were being treated. Standing on a horse-drawn buggy, Colonel Doran introduced the governor, who apologized to the men for not being paid before leaving and explained that they would be paid when they got to St. Louis. Then Doran told the men that everyone who was willing to accept this should remove their weapons from their shoulders and place the rifle butts on the ground. Very few rifles butts touched earth. Doran, and many of his officers, sympathized with them.

When they were dismissed, half frozen, the men began to seek shelter. In camp, they found dilapidated barracks and shanties which kept out most of the wind and snow. In an effort to get a warm night's sleep, stoves were set up in the wooden structures. Before midnight, a fire started in one of the buildings, which, with the strong wind aiding it, sent hundreds of men out into the night. The fire burned so quickly that two men were unable to escape and burned to death. Many of those who did get out lost clothing, equipment, and personal possessions.

The next morning, Wednesday, the men were cold, tired, and depressed by their losses, and their anger and bitterness grew. They again assembled and were told that they would board one of two trains for St. Louis that day. Company A said they would go along with whatever Captain McCauley decided. He said he chose to obey the order and, by the way, he would shoot any man in his company who did not get on board.

Other companies followed suit and after regimental officers, government officials, and others had begged and threatened, about 500 men had been persuaded to board the train that left the depot around noon. Four companies, including Company H, the Milwaukee Badgers, refused to board the second train. Many of those who refused scattered around town to find a good place to drink, while others left Madison for their homes. There were rumors that drunken soldiers would shoot up the town, but the men had no ammunition and the only injuries suffered were to soldiers fighting among themselves.

On Thursday, about 200 more soldiers were persuaded, some with loans of $5 or $10 from their officers, to board a train for St. Louis. That left about 250 men unaccounted for and still on the loose. Most were back at Camp Randall, which they had to themselves since all other regiments had shipped out. But they were not alone for long. One hundred and fifty veterans from the Illinois Irish Brigade were sent from Chicago to

Irish Brigade Flag. (Photograph by the author)

gather up the inexperienced remnants of Wisconsin's Irish Brigade. After reaching Madison, the Chicagoans had a leisurely meal before they broke into squads and went to find the men they would put on trains for St. Louis. They found them in drinking establishments, in camp, and on the streets. Some put up a fight, but it was useless; 200 more members of the Irish Regiment were going to St. Louis. But there were still some who did not go; records show that 40 men deserted the regiment between March 19 and March 21.[29]

As part of the Army of the Mississippi, the 17th Regiment spent the summer and early autumn in Corinth, Mississippi, joining an army of 22,000 men in holding the critical rail juncture that had been captured during the spring. Confederate forces of equal strength were sent to get it back. On October 1, the rebels sent out a force to tear up rail lines, but were totally routed by Patrick McCauley and Company A, who captured rebel horses and equipment and sent the survivors scattering. Two days later, the southern army attacked in a battle that lasted two days. On the second day of fighting, the Irish Brigade "fought gloriously."[30] As the enemy tried to outflank them, the 17th was ordered to "charge bayonets." Led by John Doran, with a deafening battle cry of "Faugh A Ballagh," the Brigade "cleared the way" of rebels. Soon the entire Confederate line began retreating, resulting in one of the few Union victories up to that time. General John McArthur praised the Irish Brigade, saying they "made the most glorious charge of the campaign."[31] John Nichols and his Native

American company received particular thanks for their skirmishing and scouting skills.

John Doran left the regiment in November and few were sorry to see him go. The men thought him insulting, oppressive, and abusive of his authority. McArthur must have agreed because he had Doran arrested, but instead of facing charges, Doran resigned and moved to Chicago. When the very popular Adam Malloy, a 32-year-old Irishman, was named to replace Doran, the men held a boisterous celebration. Malloy led the Irish Brigade through many battles in the South, ending with Sherman's March to the Sea.

Drafts and the 24th Regiment, aka the Milwaukee Regiment

In June of 1862, President Lincoln called for 300,000 more volunteers. Each state had a quota that was to be filled with volunteers by August 15 or the state would be required to conduct a draft, which was universally despised. There was a stigma attached to the draft. For a man to be forced to serve was a social taboo; it reflected on his manhood. Conscription was the reason many immigrants left Europe and they in particular were against a draft. With the war plodding on and casualty lists growing, and the increasing likelihood that the labor pool would expand with the freeing of the slaves, not to mention that the wealthy could buy their way out of the danger of war, the Irish were less than enthused about serving. But the most common way to avoid the draft was to volunteer. The volunteer received a $100 enlistment bonus from the United States and additional bonuses from his state and local districts, with the latter sometimes including land grants.

With only about six weeks to recruit roughly 12,000 Wisconsin men, the efforts were frantic. It took a few weeks for the state to come up with a plan and put it into action. Communities competed for volunteers by offering higher bonuses. Some Milwaukee Irishmen were recruited by wealthier municipalities that offered more compensation. This practice reduced the quota of men required from the wealthy community, but no credit was given to the volunteer's hometown. It also increased the number of poor men in the army.

Recruiting for the Milwaukee Regiment of 1,000 men began in late July 1862, with the intent that the entire regiment would be filled with volunteers. The city had fundraisers to provide volunteers with money in addition to any federal or state enlistment bounties. There were special incentives, such as the offer that the first two married men who enlisted in the John Nazro Guard would split eighty acres of land out in the country, or that the first six volunteers in the John Plankinton Rangers would each get four barrels of kerosene.

Fundraisers were also held to help enlistees' families. John Rooney, the Third Ward auctioneer, used patriotic music to get the most he could for a donated cow and calf. When bids stalled at $19, the band played "Yankee Doodle" and the offer jumped to $30, and "Hail Columbia" brought it up to $40. The promise of being serenaded home by the band got the winning bid of $50. A Third Ward saloonkeeper held a raffle for a drayman's horse and wagon, which raised $200 to help support the teamster's family while he served.

After the Montgomery Guard left the city in the summer of 1861, Milwaukee was briefly without an Irish militia company, a situation remedied by William Kennedy, a former Union Guard lieutenant. Kennedy, who lost several relatives and many friends in the *Lady Elgin* disaster, organized the Barry Guard in memory of his lost captain, Garrett Barry. Now, a year later, the city was again without an Irish militia when the Barry Guard, or about two dozen of them, became part of the Milwaukee Regiment as Company G.

The city's Irish could have filled an entire company in the Milwaukee Regiment, as the Germans did, but instead many enlisted in companies organized along occupational lines. Employees of the La Crosse and Milwaukee Railroad filled Company F, while those of the Milwaukee and

William Kennedy organized the Barry Guard in honor of Garrett Barry after the *Lady Elgin* disaster. (Ancestry.com, Family Trees GGuy0001)

Prairie du Chien Railroad completed Company D, with about a dozen Irish in each. Other Irishmen, employed as clerks or bookkeepers, joined the Merchant Guard of Company I. Since Yankees were not enlisting in the Merchant Guard as quickly as the Irish and Germans were, the company's recruiting efforts were directed at shaming them:

Ye Americans – don't permit the foreign population to surpass you in patriotism.

Ye native-born citizens – leave not to foreign hands the duty you owe your native land.

Ye Yankees – your country calls.[32]

All companies of the Milwaukee Regiment were filled with volunteers by mid-August of 1862 and trained at Camp Sigel, located on the East Side on land bordered by N. Prospect and N. Bartlett avenues, between E. LaFayette and E. Royall places. On Friday, September 5, the regiment left town for Kentucky. Unlike those in the Irish Brigade, the new soldiers were paid before they left the city. There were always big send-offs for the regiments that trained in the city as they left for the battlefront, but the hometown regiment drew the largest crowds ever, as thousands of family and friends cheered them along the streets as they marched to the station for a train to the South.

A month later, the Milwaukee Regiment celebrated its first victory in the Battle of Perryville, Kentucky, but suffered its first man killed. The regiment fought in many battles in Tennessee and Georgia over the course of the war. They lost men in victory and defeat; their numbers diminished by deaths on the battlefield and deaths due to wounds and from disease and accidents. The regiment had a total of 157 men taken prisoner during the war. Most were later swapped for Confederate prisoners, but a dozen or so, including Irish-born Franklin schoolteacher James Mangan, died while confined at the infamous Andersonville Prison in Georgia.

When the Milwaukee Regiment left the city to join the war, the Wisconsin quota of 12,000 men was still not fulfilled. Forty-five hundred soldiers short of the goal, a draft by lottery was scheduled for November 1862. There were several ways to avoid the draft besides volunteering. One was to become unfit by self-mutilation and another was to flee to Canada. A man of means could pay $300 instead of serving, or pay a substitute to take his place. A middle-class man could join a sort of insurance group of 10 or 20 others, with each man paying from $15 to $30, to be used as the $300 buyout if any one of the group were drafted. When draft day came, there was a draft riot by Germans in Port Washington, and Ninth Ward German protesters interrupted the draft proceedings in that ward, but there was no draft to complain about in the Third Ward; it had met its quota through volunteers, as had Tory Hill's Fourth Ward.

The city's Irish did not fare so well in the next draft. In March 1863, Congress passed the Enrollment Act, which required the registration of all male citizens, and all immigrants who had filed for citizenship, between 20 and 45 years of age. The Irish support of the war had continued to dwindle. The Emancipation Proclamation, freeing the slaves, was now a fact, and the Irish were not happy about it. Continued high casualties among Irish soldiers in the Union Army was defeating the purpose of gaining military training to fight for Ireland's independence; they couldn't use the training if they were dead or maimed. The draft was still repugnant and so was the ability of those better off financially to buy their way out. Workers were reaping the rewards of wartime prosperity, which gave them steady wages, so receiving a bounty or being supported by the army became less appealing. But they quietly registered for the draft during the summer, while their brethren's draft riots in New York were the worst insurrection in the country's history, except for the Civil War itself. On draft day, November 10, 1863, dozens of Irish were drafted in Milwaukee without incident.

By the time of the presidential election of November 1864, support for the conflict in much of Wisconsin had increased with Union victories, but enthusiasm remained low among Milwaukee's Irish and German populations. While Lincoln won Wisconsin, Milwaukee residents voted overwhelmingly for the Democrat, General George McClellan. And though most Wisconsin regiments strongly supported Lincoln, the Irish Brigade voted for McClellan.

The Civil War Ends

Six months after Lincoln's re-election, the war ended and the survivors returned to their homes. Tory Hill resident Thomas Toohey, an employee of the La Crosse and Milwaukee Railroad (later known as the Milwaukee Road), was one of only three Milwaukee men to be awarded the Medal of Honor for valor during the Civil War. The award citation for Toohey, a member of the Milwaukee Regiment, reads:

> For gallantry in action on 30 November 1864, while serving with
> Company F, 24th Wisconsin Infantry, in action at Franklin, Tennessee.
> Sergeant Toohey voluntarily assisting in working guns of battery near
> right of the regiment after nearly every man had left them, the fire of
> the enemy being hotter at this than at any other point on the line.[33]

Toohey, a locomotive engineer, was born in New York of Irish
immigrants in 1835. After the war he returned to Tory Hill, but later his
railroad career took him to St. Louis and then to Kansas City, Missouri,
where he died in 1918.

Another Milwaukee Irishman who received the Medal of Honor was
Michael McCormick. Born in Ireland in 1833, McCormick was a Walker's
Point sailor who served in the U.S. Navy. His citation reads:

> Michael McCormick, serving as Boatswain's Mate on board the U.S.S.
> Signal, Red River, Louisiana, 5 May 1864. Proceeding up the Red
> River, the U.S.S. Signal engaged a large force of enemy field batteries
> and sharpshooters, returning the fire until the ship was totally disabled,
> at which time the white flag was raised. Serving as Gun Captain and
> wounded early in the battle, Boatswain's Mate McCormick bravely stood
> by his gun in the face of the enemy fire until ordered to withdraw.[34]

McCormick died in Milwaukee a month after the war ended and is
buried at the National Soldiers' Home Cemetery. The third Milwaukeean
to win a Civil War Medal of Honor, and the second from the Milwaukee
Regiment, was Arthur MacArthur, father of future general, Douglas
MacArthur.

Medal of Honor winner
Michael McCormick's
tombstone in Wood National
Cemetery in Milwaukee.
(FindaGrave.com, Wood
National Cemetery)

Milwaukee and the Fenian Invasion of Canada

Rifle shots echoed throughout downtown Milwaukee on the first day of June 1866. The Fenian invasion of Canada had sparked celebrations within the city's Irish community. Enthusiasm was high as some local Fenians participated in the invasion, and more prepared to go to Buffalo, New York, to help out in the conquest of British Canada. But one Milwaukeean, Robert B. Lynch, was not celebrating. He was captured and arrested for his part in the invasion and taken to a military prison in Toronto. During the coming months his trial would be front page news in the United States and Canada. By the end of the year, the reluctant martyr would be convicted and sentenced to be hanged.

Milwaukee's Irish were ecstatic about the invasion. An extra edition of 2,500 copies of the June 1 edition of the *Daily Wisconsin*, reporting the events, sold out in the Third, Fourth, and Fifth wards of the city. The next day's edition of the paper described the Irish as "congregated in squads upon the corners, in stores, in houses, hotels and saloons ...You could see in the heaving breasts, in the quivering tremble of their voices as they spoke, that a fearful power was at work within them..."[35]

What was this all about? Who were the Fenians (fē-nē-əns or fēn'yəns)? Why were they invading Canada? And why was Robert B. Lynch, a convicted embezzler, a man who rejected his wife after three weeks of marriage, and a man whose schemes brought financial ruin upon himself and his brother, going to become a poster child for the Fenian cause?

The Fenian Brotherhood, the forerunner of the Irish Republican Army, was formed on St. Patrick's Day in 1858 in Dublin, and named for the mythical band of ancient Irish warriors whose leader was Fionn mac Cumhaill (Finn McCool). It was an avowed secret society in both Ireland and America, with the objective of overthrowing English rule in Ireland. Fenian leaders had encouraged Irishmen to come to America to fight in the Civil War to gain military experience that would help them in their fight for Ireland's freedom, and help gain the support of the United States for an independent Ireland.

The Fenians were organized into military companies called "circles," and the head of each circle was called the "center." In 1863, during the Civil War, over 100 circles were formed in the United States, four of them in Milwaukee, with Jeremiah Quin as center of one of them. Quin, 33,

Jeremiah Quin was the leader of Wisconsin's Fenians and managed the Plankinton estate. Here he stands in front of the statue of John Plankinton. (*History of Milwaukee, Wisconsin*, John J. Gregory, 1931)

who was born in Kilfinane, County Limerick, and came to Milwaukee in 1852, was also the head center for the state of Wisconsin. He would later serve as president of the Milwaukee School Board and was a fierce advocate for public schools. Civil War veteran Patrick H. McCauley, a major in the Irish Brigade, was the center of the Wolfe Tone Circle, named for a leader of the Irish insurrection of 1798. It was supported by the Matilda Tone Circle of the Fenian Sisterhood, named for Tone's wife. The other Milwaukee circles, the O'Mahony and Sweeney circles, were named for national Fenian leaders in the United States. The Irish community in Greenfield also formed a circle, with Patrick Walsh as its center.

Each Fenian took the Fenian pledge:

I solemnly pledge my sacred word of honour, as a truthful and honest man, that I will labor with earnest zeal for the liberation of Ireland from the yoke of England, and for the establishment of a free and independent government on the Irish soil.[36]

The Catholic bishops in Ireland, and many Irish bishops in America, condemned the Fenians as a secret society. Milwaukee's archbishop, John Henni, chose not to issue a ban on local Fenian activity as the bishops of Chicago, St. Louis, St. Paul, and other U.S. cities had done. Henni felt that pressuring leaders privately was the best course of action and even claimed early success with this strategy, but he, like the banning bishops, was ultimately ineffective.[37] Six thousand Wisconsin men became Fenians.[38]

During the Civil War, Fenians helped raise money for the Irish Relief Fund for people in Ireland who were suffering from hunger. After the war, there were many meetings and fundraisers to arm and supply the Fenians. One picnic to raise funds in September 1865, said to be the largest picnic in the city up to that time, was held at Hawley's Grove on N. 24th Street and W. Wisconsin Avenue. It was estimated to have drawn 5,000 to 6,000 supporters who danced to Irish music, watched or participated in sporting events, and enjoyed ample food and drink.[39] It was a great success, but as author Finley Peter Dunne's bartending character, Mr. Dooley, would point out, "If Ireland could be freed by a picnic, it would not only be free today, but an empire."[40]

With circles now organized throughout the United States, American Fenian leadership was faced with a quandary: How were they to free Ireland? With between 150,000 and 175,000 battle-hardened Irish veterans of the Union forces, not counting thousands of Irish Confederate veterans, the leaders felt that the time to act was soon, before the Fenian enthusiasm diminished.[41]

An attack in Ireland was not feasible. Because the English in Ireland were able to put down any Fenian uprising there, Fenianism in Ireland was largely ineffective. So, a plan was hatched by American Fenian leaders to strike the nearest British possession, Canada. A conquered Canada could be traded back to England for Ireland's freedom. After capturing Canada, the Fenians would set up an Irish Republic in exile and then make the exchange to free Ireland.

Anti-English feeling was strong throughout the northern United States. The British had supported the Confederates during the war with ships and supplies. A group of Confederate soldiers had found sanctuary in Canada during the war and had attacked a Vermont border community. The United States had already cancelled a trade agreement that was favorable to Canada, and President Andrew Johnson was intent on extracting a settlement from England for their aid to the Southerners. Many in the United States government turned a blind eye to Fenian preparations for an invasion and Fenian leaders thought they had Johnson's tacit approval for their plans. The Fenians were armed with weapons purchased from the United States military.

While the Fenians were accused of being a secret society, their invasion plans were far from secret. For months, newspapers in both the United States and Canada speculated on when and where the attack would take place. Canadian militia and British troops were on alert but did not know where on the Canadian border the invasion would occur.

During the spring of 1866, Milwaukee newspapers reported that Fenian enlistments were increasing and that the men were armed and drilling. Fenians were parading on streets in Tory Hill and the Third Ward. About half were veterans and the papers speculated that they "will probably be quite a formidable foe to meet on the field of battle."[42] They were told to be ready at a moment's notice. Ships in Milwaukee, Sheboygan, and Manitowoc were ready to carry the troops to Buffalo. The May 12 *Milwaukee Sentinel* reported that the Fenian invasion would begin within two weeks. Irish-born former Wisconsin Adjutant General, John McManman, a Milwaukee liquor dealer, predicted that the Fenians would be slaughtered.[43] Nevertheless, a contingent of about 30 local Fenians left town for Buffalo, where the invasion would begin. Over 800 Wisconsin Fenians traveled to Chicago to join Fenians there in preparation for their journey to the battlefront.[44] The plan was to draw British troops west from Toronto, allowing other Fenians to attack places in eastern Canada.

In the early hours of Friday, June 1, the invasion began. Between 1,000 and 1,300 Fenians, including veterans from both the Union and Confederate ranks, most from the Midwest, and at least half from Chicago, crossed the Niagara River on barges from Buffalo to Canada, led by John O'Neill of Nashville, Tennessee. They captured Fort Erie, an old and mostly unused fort, without much effort. Fenian members of the crew of the Navy's *USS Michigan* had temporarily sabotaged the ship so it could not stop the Fenians from crossing, but in twelve hours it was operational again and patrolling the river, cutting off reinforcements and supplies for O'Neill.

The next day, with a small guard left at Fort Erie, which included Milwaukeean Robert Lynch, the Fenians marched west seven miles to Lime Ridge, deploying men along the way. The Canadian forces of about 1,000 men had travelled all night and planned to repulse the invaders.

But the Fenians had the experience of fighting during the Civil War and most Canadians had never seen battle. They met, and after two hours of shooting at each other, the Fenians routed their foe with a bayonet charge.

Other thousands of British and Canadian forces were mobilized and headed for Lime Ridge and Fort Erie. O'Neill needed some of the 3,000 Fenians still on the other side of the Niagara River in Buffalo, and he needed more arms and supplies. But with the *USS Michigan* preventing any river traffic and keeping Fenian reinforcements in Buffalo, O'Neill had no choice but to return to Buffalo. Canadian forces had already arrived at Fort Erie from the north and captured some Fenians there, including Lynch. O'Neill's army had to fight through the Canadians to reach the river and safety. After they crossed the river to the New York shore, they were arrested by United States authorities for violating the Neutrality Act. They were told that if they promised to abandon their expedition against Canada and go home and not come back, they could leave. Twenty-nine Milwaukeeans agreed to this and returned home.[45]

Fenians from Watertown, Fond du Lac, Oshkosh, La Crosse, and other parts of the state were still streaming into Milwaukee as preparations to join the invasion continued. Over 400 men met at Fenian headquarters, most of them Civil War veterans, armed, equipped, and uniformed in "dark blue blouse coat, light blue pants, and a blue military hat with a green band around it."[46] Included were several men over 60 years old as well as many teens. One 16-year-old girl, Molly Mahan, who had nursed her father's injuries during the Civil War, was to be the regimental nurse. She was declared a "Daughter of the Regiment" and the regiment took an oath "that she should be protected from harm and insult, as long as a breath of life remained in their bodies."[47]

Even as word of the end of the invasion reached them, some women sold their jewelry and family heirlooms to finance their husbands' transport to the field of action. Head center of all the city's Fenian circles, as well as the center of Sweeney-Roberts Circle, Edmund D. Burke, talked local authorities into releasing three of his soldiers who had been jailed for drunk and disorderly conduct, so they could join the expedition. Burke was born in County Tipperary in 1830 and emigrated to the U.S at the height of the potato famine. A stone mason, he lived in the North Point neighborhood and had been elected a city councilor the previous year. Burke claimed that he served as a captain during the Civil War in the

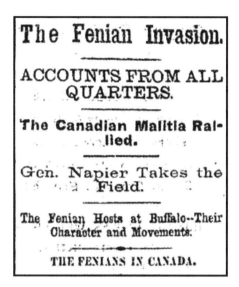

The Fenian Invasion.

ACCOUNTS FROM ALL
QUARTERS.

The Canadian Militia Rallied.

Gen. Napier Takes the Field.

The Fenian Hosts at Buffalo--Their Character and Movements.

THE FENIANS IN CANADA.

Headlines for the Fenian invasion
of Canada. (*Milwaukee Sentinel*,
June 4, 1866)

famous "Fighting Irish" 69th Regiment from New York, but if he did, it must have been under an alias since his name does not appear in that regiment's roster.[48]

Over the next few days, Wisconsin Fenians left for Buffalo, some by boat and others by train. Some hoped that President Johnson would have a change of heart and allow the invasion to continue, and all were looking forward to the trip. As one Buffalo-bound ship left a Milwaukee dock, its passengers were heard singing "The Wearing of the Green." Some 15- and 16-year-old boys, without their parents' permission, left to join the invasion by train, but they got only as far as Chicago before being sent back home by the police. Thousands of Fenians from other parts of the country descended on Buffalo, but the invasion was over.

During the following weeks, mass meetings were held in Milwaukee, and Andrew Johnson and other politicians were denounced for their treachery. Temporarily, the fight for Irish freedom was over. The invasion had cost the lives of thirteen Canadians and eight Fenians. Robert B. Lynch's trial in Toronto, along with several other alleged Fenians, was on the front page of newspapers throughout North America during the rest of the year.

Robert Blosse Lynch was born in County Galway about 1818.[49] He came to Milwaukee with his brother, Peter, in the summer of 1847. Milwaukee city directories from that time show that Peter was a grocer in the Yankee Hill neighborhood. The directories give no clue to Robert's occupation, only that he lived with his brother. Civil Court cases involving Robert are more informative.

The brothers were frequently in legal trouble for not repaying loans on time, a failure that Peter blamed on Robert. Their business in St. Louis failed, as did the Milwaukee businesses and those that Robert started in Janesville, Wisconsin, and Louisville, Kentucky. Peter complained that "I have had all the capital, he never has" and it was because of "his neglect of himself that I lost all."[50] Robert admitted, "Like all my misdeeds, liquor was the whole cause of it."[51]

In 1857, after he was elected to the position of City Clerk by the Common Council, things were looking up for Lynch. His new position paid an annual salary of $2,000, about five times the average worker's wages (although he was ordered to pay $400 to his ex-wife in their divorce decree). An excellent singer, Lynch was asked to sing the "Star Spangled Banner" at the city's Fourth of July celebration. The *Sentinel*, not always kind to Irishmen, supported Lynch's re-election, calling him a "competent and industrious officer."[52]

This success was not enough for Lynch and, in March 1860, he and the city comptroller were arrested and charged with embezzling city funds. In spite of Lynch's claim that his nationality was being held against him, he was tried and convicted. He ultimately avoided prison time by agreeing to serve in the Union Army during the Civil War. He was assigned as a private to the position of clerk for the 24th Wisconsin Infantry, the Milwaukee Regiment, in Louisville, but was discharged after only one year, most of which was spent absent while in the hospital.[53]

When he was captured by Canadian forces at Fort Erie, the 5-foot, 8-inch, grey-eyed, dark-haired Lynch was in his late 40s and wore a Napoleon III Imperial moustache. His defense was that he was not a Fenian but that he was there as a reporter for a Louisville newspaper. Because they would be arrested if they entered Canada, Fenian leaders could not testify in person that Lynch was not a Fenian. But influential Milwaukeeans attested to that fact, as did Secretary of State Seward. The Canadian court decided that since Lynch was born in Ireland he could be charged with treason because "once a British subject, always a British

Depiction of the Battle of Ridgeway fought between Fenians and Canadians. (Buffalo Lithographers Sage, Sons & Co., Library of Congress)

subject."[54] In late October, Lynch was convicted and sentenced to be hung on December 13, 1866. From his prison cell he wrote to his family in Milwaukee that he had no connection to the Fenians, "but if it is a crime to love my native land, then I am willing to suffer death, for I am guilty of that crime."[55] Lynch was being dramatic as he undoubtedly knew at this time that he was not to be executed.

When it was announced that Lynch's sentence would be commuted to life imprisonment, Fenian leader William Roberts was disappointed. In a letter to Lynch, Roberts said, "I regret to tell you that you are not to be hanged. So great a crime upon a non combatant like yourself would make every Irishman a Fenian."[56] Lynch served nearly four years of his sentence before being released in 1871. He died in Washington, D.C., in 1884 while working as a clerk at the U.S. Census Bureau. Lynch's former wife, Catherine Gill, never remarried and died in Milwaukee two years after Lynch's death. She is buried in Calvary Cemetery, along with Lynch's brother, Peter, and his family, including his son, also named Robert B. Lynch, who died at the age of 19 in the *Lady Elgin* disaster.

Mayor Edward O'Neill

Milwaukee elected its first Irish Catholic mayor, Edward O'Neill, in 1863 and re-elected him in 1867, 1868, and 1869. O'Neill was born in County Kilkenny in 1820 and at the age of 17 immigrated to Vermont where he learned the tailor's trade. He came to Milwaukee in 1850 and opened a clothing store. His intelligence and thoughtfulness quickly impressed his Third Ward neighbors and they elected him to represent them in the State Assembly and then the State Senate. O'Neill was a champion of disadvantaged youth and his bill to establish the Wisconsin Industrial School for Boys became reality.

He served many terms as a school commissioner and donated liberally to city orphanages. His business interests widened to include investments in coal and banking, and he became president of the Merchants' Exchange Bank. After serving four terms as mayor he retired from public life. When he died at the age of 70, much of his wealth was distributed to Catholic schools, orphanages, religious groups, and churches. His funeral was held at Holy Rosary Church with an estimated 100 orphans in attendance. O'Neill was buried at Calvary Cemetery.

With the rising popularity of the Republican Party after the Civil War, the influence of the Democrats decreased, not only nationally and at the state level, but locally as well. The near complete hold that the Democrats had on the mayor's position before the war weakened, as about

Edward O'Neill, Milwaukee's first Irish-Catholic mayor. (*Yenowine's News*, April 7, 1889)

half of the mayor's races during the rest of the century were won by Republicans.

Chapter 5

1870–1879

Based on 1870 census data, the number of city dwellers born in Ireland decreased by nearly 600 between 1860 and 1870. But in 1870 there was an undercounting of the number of city residents by census takers, who did not enumerate any business owners and their families who lived above or behind their businesses. There were more than 50 Irish business owners and their households who were not documented, so the decrease in Irish-born was less than census data suggests.[1]

During this time, Milwaukee's population increased from about 45,000 to over 70,000. The percent of Irish-born in the city dropped to about 5.3 percent of the total but, while figures for their Irish-American offspring are not available, their numbers would certainly bring the Irish community's population to well over 10 percent of the city's total. While the percent of the population of Irish-born in the city in 1870 dropped from the three previous decades, based on the number of Irish Catholic churches that opened during the 1870s, the Irish-American population of the city was growing significantly, a fact that would be confirmed by 1880 census data, which showed the nativity of the parents of those counted.

During this same period, the number of Irish-born in the United States increased by 27 percent, but the newcomers were not coming to Wisconsin. In addition to the decrease in Milwaukee, the number of those born in Ireland dropped in Racine, Kenosha, Sheboygan, and La Crosse, but nearly doubled in Chicago and Cleveland. The Irish also increased the population of developing cities to the west, like Omaha, St. Paul, and Kansas City.

Migrations

After the Civil War, and for the rest of the century, many Americans were on the move. One trend was migration from the North to the South. Some northern Republicans, taking advantage of the Union victory, went to southern states to exploit the political and economic situations there. One such "carpetbagger" was Milwaukee Irishman Thomas Bernard Keogh, who had survived the sinking of the *Lady Elgin* as a 19-year-old law student. He was appointed Register of Bankruptcy in North Carolina when he was 26, and by the time he was 30, he was a wealthy man. A few years later he began a six-year run as Chairman of the Republican State Committee of North Carolina. He died there in 1921.

Much more common was the move from Milwaukee to the West. Moving west was made easy by the opening of the transcontinental railroad and the many miles of track laid during the following decades. Among those leaving Milwaukee was railroad engineer and Medal of Honor recipient Thomas Toohey, who left Tory Hill for St. Louis and eventually settled in Kansas City. *Lady Elgin* survivor John Jarvis worked for the Milwaukee Road and became yardmaster in the company's St. Paul facilities. The widow and a daughter of Captain Garrett Barry, a victim of the same disaster, also relocated to St. Paul. New towns opened by the Milwaukee Road's expansion to the West Coast provided opportunities for other Milwaukee Irish.

While Milwaukee was no longer a significant destination for Irish immigrants, it was a magnet for young Irish Americans coming from Wisconsin farms. By the 1870s, much of the state's prime farmland was under cultivation, so there was little chance of creating new farms for the generation of children born in rural areas, and most existing farms could not support the many families that this new generation would produce. Milwaukee was an alternative to the boredom of farm life and it offered better educational prospects, vastly wider social possibilities, and more varied lifestyles. Most importantly, there were employment opportunities in Milwaukee's factories, businesses, professions, and government.

Among those coming to the city from the countryside was future Milwaukee mayor Peter Somers. His parents had emigrated from County Roscommon and established a farm in Waukesha County. In 1872, Somers came to the city to study law under County Meath native Edward G. Ryan, a future Chief Justice of the Wisconsin Supreme Court. Thomas

Edward G. Ryan, Chief Justice of the Wisconsin Supreme Court. (Wikimedia Commons)

A. Clancy was another young man from a Waukesha farm who made it big in the city. His father was from County Cavan and his mother was born in County Cork. At age 18, Clancy moved to Milwaukee and in his early twenties began working for the Milwaukee Fire Department. Twenty years later he became its chief, a position he held for two decades.

These Irish Americans were much better educated than their immigrant parents and some of them joined the ranks of the city's lawyers, doctors, and businessmen. Railroads employed the newcomers as unskilled and skilled workers, and as engineers and conductors. Many worked in factories, shops, and other businesses, and they moved higher up the economic ladder than their parents had. Young women came to the city to be employed as servants in middle- and upper-class households, while others acquired positions in the service industry and in shops. Disaster would befall a dozen of these young women in 1883 when they perished in a fire at the Newhall House, where they worked in housekeeping, laundry, kitchen, and dining room positions at the hotel.

Chicago was a draw for Milwaukeeans. The Windy City had a large Irish community and the bigger city offered more opportunities. The movement between Milwaukee and Chicago was not one way though. Some Chicagoans found prospects in the Cream City. Others came from the eastern United States and Canada, and some from farms and small towns in the Midwest. When Irish newcomers came to the city they tended to settle where there were other Irish people and avoided the German and other ethnic neighborhoods.

New Irish Churches

In 1855, Jesuit priests began the administration of St. Gall's Parish. In 1870, they built a new, much larger brick structure on N. Third and W. Michigan streets, just to the west of the older wooden building. The huge new church seated 1,000 people but was not adequate to serve the growing Irish population in the area.

In 1875, the Jesuits and some members of St. Gall's from north of Tory Hill opened another Irish Church, Holy Name, this one a wooden building at N. 10th and W. State streets that accommodated about 600

St. Gall's was the second Irish church in the city. (From the Digital Library at Villanova University, Collection of Church Lithographs, Packard, Butler and Partridge Lithographs)

people. A school was also opened on the grounds. Holy Name merged with St. Gall's to create Gesu parish in 1894.

In 1876, members of St. Gall's Church from Walker's Point, south of the Menomonee Valley, built a new wooden church at S. Seventh and W. Washington streets and named it St. Patrick. It seated about 600 people with a school located in the lower level.

The Irish of Bay View

In 1866, the Village of the Milwaukee Iron Company, later known as Bay View, was founded along Lake Michigan, a little over a mile south of the Milwaukee city limit of W. Burnham Street. The company produced iron rails for the bourgeoning railroad industry. Workers from Great Britain and Ireland formed the core of the new company town. The largest immigrant group was from England, followed by the Irish, the Welsh, and the Scots. By 1870, the population of the village had reached 400 people, about 12 percent of whom were born in Ireland. The company donated land at E. Russell and S. Kinnickinnic avenues for the Irish Catholic church, Immaculate Conception. The building was completed in November 1871 and eliminated the need for Catholic residents to make the trip north into Milwaukee for church services, baptisms, marriages, and funerals.

Religious conflict between the Irish and their neighbors arose in 1876 when the predominantly Protestant school board determined that the Bible could be read in the public school. The decision caused resentment throughout the community, particularly among the Irish, who objected to the Protestant King James version of the book that was being used. James McIver, born in County Armagh, an employee at the mills and recently elected as Justice of the Peace as well as a state legislator representing the village, led the successful fight to eliminate the reading of the religious book in Bay View schools.

The 1880 census shows that nearly 20 percent of the Bay View population of more than 2,800 was either born in Ireland or of Irish parentage. That same year, Thomas Russell, a rail straightener at the mills, was elected a village trustee and St. Lawrence Street was renamed E. Russell Avenue. Russell, born in County Cork in 1843, was brought to the United States as a child and came to Bay View in 1871.

In 1887, with Milwaukee expanding southward, residents voted to have their community become part of the city. However, the neighborhood kept its identity by holding St. Patrick's Day and other celebrations separate from those in the rest of the city.

The Death of a Hero, Patsy McLaughlin

When Fire Chief Patsy McLaughlin died on Tuesday, June 27, 1871, Milwaukeeans who heard the tolling of the bells announcing his death were filled with sorrow. Even though he was a city official, residents around the county grieved. Little boys, who hero-worshipped him and had run after him on the streets, cried. Fire insurance agents were saddened. City offices closed until after his funeral the following Sunday and were draped in mourning for 30 days. Thousands of citizens visited his open casket at City Hall, and thousands more solemnly watched the long procession from the Cathedral of St. John to Calvary Cemetery.

Patrick McLaughlin was born in New York in 1839, the first child of immigrants Henry and Ellen McLaughlin. Ten years later the family of seven moved to the Third Ward, where Henry worked as a laborer and the family grew to eight members. Henry and Ellen died during the 1850s and Patsy was left to take care of his siblings. At the age of 15 he volunteered at the Third Ward firehouse and worked his way up through the ranks and gained a reputation for being daring while maintaining a cool head. He was always the first man to enter a building on fire and his face was described as being perpetually red and blistered. By the time he was 28, Patsy was held in such high regard by businessmen, who had seen how effective the firefighters were under his leadership, that they petitioned the mayor to appoint him Fire Chief. The Common Council felt he was too young for the position and refused to appoint him.

In addition to being young, Pasty was small. He was called "Little Patsy" and described as a man in a boy's body. The next year, in 1867, Mayor Edward O'Neill again nominated him for the chief's position, and this time the Council agreed, making Patsy the second head of the Fire Department of Irish descent. (Thomas Eviston, who died in the *Lady Elgin* disaster, was the first.)

Even as chief, McLaughlin was usually the first man to go into a burning structure. He learned the new fire-alarm telegraph system and the inventor gave McLaughlin credit for using it more effectively than any other department in America. His organizational skills were superb;

the fire department he ran was very effective, and he had the loyalty and affection of his men.

Patsy died four years after his appointment as chief from the effects that firefighting had on his lungs. He had gone to most of the fires that occurred in the city when fires were an everyday occurrence. Insurance agents were so impressed with his results that they formed a unit in his funeral procession.

His skills and valor were not the only reasons he was so beloved. He despised anything low and mean and was kind and gentle. According to his mourners, "We shall not look upon his like again."[2]

The Sheridan Guard

During the years after the 1866 invasion of Canada, Fenianism in the United States began to fade. There were a few small raids on Canada, and Milwaukee Fenians continued to drill, but there was little direction for the movement. The city's Irish military leaders shifted their focus to fill a void created by the loss of the Union Guard in the sinking of the *Lady Elgin*, and the assimilation of the Montgomery Guard into the Sixth Regiment during the Civil War.

In June of 1869, the Sheridan Guard was born. It would be the longest lasting and best-known military company in the city after the Civil War. The Guard was named for Irish-American Civil War hero and general, Philip Sheridan, whose parents emigrated from County Cavan. Among Sheridan's military accomplishments were defeating Southern forces in the Shenandoah Valley and helping to force the surrender of Robert E. Lee. Sheridan, who was not a Milwaukeean, was pleased to have the new company named for him and he became an honorary member. On many occasions over the years, someone would recite the famous poem, "Sheridan's Ride," at a Guard activity. The poem told of Sheridan's heroic ride to rally his troops on the battlefield and was memorized by school children throughout the North for decades.

The first man elected captain of the Guard was Patrick H. McCauley, merchant and contractor, who had risen to the rank of major in the Irish Brigade during the war and had served as a center of one of the city's Fenian circles after the war. But McCauley instead chose to retain his position as major on the staff of the Wisconsin State Militia, a group that coordinated militia companies throughout the state. Richard Rooney was then elected the company's first captain. He had served in both the Union Guard and the Montgomery Guard, had captained a company in the Irish Brigade during the Civil War, and was later a Fenian. Rooney was born in Ireland in 1832, emigrated to the United States during the Famine, and settled in the Third Ward in 1854. He was employed as a cutter in a clothing store, eventually becoming the proprietor of a wholesale and retail men's clothing business. Like Garrett Barry and other Irish militia leaders, he was also elected to political office and served as county treasurer.

The new company's ranks were filled with Civil War veterans and it was not long before the Sheridan Guard was recognized as one of the state's finest. For nearly 30 years, the Guard would win many awards for their precision drilling and sharpshooting abilities and would be the premier militia company in the city, and the best known in the state.

Although the state provided the arms, each of the Guard's 60 to 70 members was expected to pay for his uniform and accouterments through dues of 50 cents per month (about a half day's pay for laborers), which could not have helped recruitment in a workingman's unit. Members drilled one or two evenings a week at their armory on N. Broadway between E. Clybourn Street and E. St. Paul Avenue. Other events on their agenda included annual balls, the first of which was held at the new Plankinton House hotel. Additionally, there were annual picnics and many other social activities throughout the year. The Guard marched in the city's parades and had target shooting in what is now Lake Park. They traveled to various Wisconsin cities for state and local drilling and shooting competitions. The time commitment was not easy for the rank and file when it cut into working hours. The other military companies in the city also found it difficult to recruit and retain members willing to spend the time and money to serve.

At the time of founding of the Sheridan Guard, there were a half dozen German and Yankee companies in the city, but over the next few years they all died out. New companies continued to be organized, but most did not last. Another Irish company, the Emmet Zouaves, was formed in 1872. It was named for the Irish rebel Robert Emmet, who was hanged by the English in 1803. The company's ranks were filled mostly by men from the Third Ward and Tory Hill. They shared the Sheridan Guard's armory, held balls and picnics, drilled, and practiced shooting, but it was hard to maintain the enthusiasm to keep the company going;

121

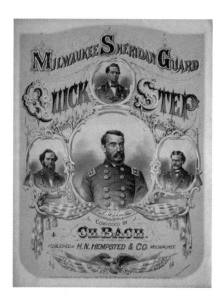

The cover of the score for the "Sheridan Guard Quickstep." (Library of Congress)

it marched in its last parade three years later.

The Sheridan Guard's Second Annual Ball in 1871, also held at the prestigious Plankinton House, was a pricey affair at five dollars per couple. The event included the first public performance of a newly composed and published march written for the company and entitled the "Milwaukee Sheridan Guard Quickstep." Christoph Bach, a German immigrant, band leader, and music director, wrote the march and incorporated the Irish tune, "The Harp That Once Through Tara's Walls," within it. The sheet music cover includes portraits of Philip Sheridan and the company's officers at the time; Richard Rooney, Patrick Connelly, and Andrew McCormick.

By the late 1870s, the officers of the Wisconsin State Militia began pushing for a more professional and disciplined militia. They wanted to appoint militia officers rather than having them elected by company members. They devised a set of rules to improve discipline, but the Sheridan Guard and other companies were not impressed. Company members wanted to elect their officers and said that having their officers appointed by the State Militia would ruin the *esprit de corps* cultivated by the company. Captain Rooney said the state was proposing enough laws "to hang a man from a fence post for disobedience."[3] Instead of more rules, what the Guard needed was more money to buy uniforms and equipment so volunteers did not have to shoulder the expense of belonging to the company. But this was the beginning of the end for the Sheridan Guard. Over the next two decades, the state would gain control of militia companies to the extent that the militia system would die out.

Knights of St. Patrick

The Knights of St. Patrick was a semi-military Irish fraternal organization serving Walker's Point and Bay View. It was formed in 1877 and was active for several decades. The group raised money for Irish causes, such as the Land League and Home Rule, and helped the needy in the community by sponsoring picnics, dances, concerts, and talent shows, and producing Irish plays like *Handy Andy: A Tale of Irish Life, Colleen Bawn,* and *Peep o' Day.* Members of the organization visited the sick and its uniformed members marched in local parades and sent delegates to Irish National Conventions. Patrick Mallon, a commission merchant born in Ireland, served as its first president.

Irish in the Police Department

When Marshall Clark was lynched in 1861, one newspaper, the *Daily Life*, put the responsibility on the Irish policemen, claiming that one half of the police force was Irish and that they made little attempt to prevent the hanging. It overstated the percent of Irish policemen, but the number of Irish on the police force did exceed their percent of the population. They comprised about one third of the department at the time of the lynching, about twice as many as would be expected as the Irish made up about sixteen percent of the population.[4] By 1870, Irishmen comprised nearly forty percent of the police force, a rate about four times their percent of the general population.[5]

Daniel Kennedy, the only Irishman to serve as Milwaukee Chief of Police during the nineteenth century, was appointed by Mayor John Black in 1878. Black, born in France, was a Democrat, as was Kennedy. One of Kennedy's first acts was to fire one quarter of the police force, 22 officers, for being Republicans. Only one of the fired policemen was Irish, while five of the new replacements were Celts. Kennedy's term was controversial and fraught with political fighting. His opponents demanded an investigation into Kennedy and his administration. The final report listed 18 charges against Kennedy, most of them that he drank too much and was loud, obnoxious, and profane. The primary accusation was that he had taken visitors to a well-known house of prostitution and remained there for an hour.[6]

Shortly after the report was made public, Mayor Black left town for the funeral of a relative. That gave Republican Thomas Brown, President of the Common Council, his chance to get rid of Kennedy and he fired him. A few days later Black returned and overrode Brown's action, reinstating Kennedy. But Kennedy did not stay long. The next month, Thomas Brown was elected mayor and he again fired Kennedy and appointed former chief William Beck to replace him. Beck fired half of the policemen on the force, 42 in total. Eighteen of the 33 Irish officers were fired, resulting in the department dropping from one-third to one-sixth Irish.

Daniel Kennedy, born in County Kerry in 1829, arrived in Milwaukee as a teenager and worked at jobs in a hotel, as a rail splitter, and in his father's business provisioning Lake Michigan steamers with milk, before being appointed to the police force when he was 29 years old. Two years after being replaced as police chief, Kennedy moved to Kansas City, where he ran a successful real estate business.[7] He died there in 1916.

Wholesale changes of police department personnel ended after Beck's term. In 1885, the authority to appoint the police chief was taken from the mayor and assigned to the new board of fire and police commissioners. This resulted in much longer regimes for police chiefs, as well as longer careers for policemen.

The Little Famine, the Land League, and Charles Stewart Parnell

The potato crop in Ireland was again attacked by blight in 1879. This crop failure lasted only one season, but with the eight-year-long Great Famine strong in memory there was widespread concern when it began. In the Irish language it became known as *An Gorta Beag* or "The Little Hunger." A variety of factors limited this famine to one of hunger rather than starvation. In contrast to its actions during the Great Hunger, the British government sent food to the affected areas, and the crop failure was ameliorated by improved food production techniques and a better transportation network.

Another significant factor was the support provided by America, where there were many more Irish than there had been in the 1840s, who could contribute financial help. Milwaukee was no exception. There were many small donations by the city's Irish as well as larger donations from wealthier residents. Major contributors included Milwaukee-born Thomas Shaughnessy, whose parents had come to the Third Ward from County Limerick in 1841. Shaughnessy would later become president of the Canadian Pacific Railway. Another was Jeremiah Quin, a former Fenian leader in the state and manager of the vast meatpacking and railroad holdings of the John Plankinton estate. Donor Michael Carpenter, born in Milwaukee of Irish parents in 1846, founded a Third Ward bakery that later became part of the National Biscuit Company (Nabisco).

Contributions to the Irish Relief Fund came not only from the Irish. Like the *New York Herald*, which raised large amounts of money for the needy, the *Milwaukee Sentinel* started its own fundraising efforts. It set a minimum donation of twenty-five cents from its readers. It wanted that amount from every employee of every business in the city and requested the same from all its readers outside the city. It encouraged beer drinkers to forego five beers and instead donate twenty-five cents.[8]

During this potato blight, the Irish National Land League was founded in Ireland to help tenant farmers gain ownership of the land they farmed. The League objected to farmers being evicted for not paying unjust rents and proposed that tenants obtain title to their lands by paying reasonable rents for a limited number of years. This highly successful and well-run organization provided a way for famine relief money to work its way to those who needed it most, and the thousands of dollars collected in Milwaukee were sent to Land League offices throughout Ireland.

Land League leaders Charles Stewart Parnell, Michael Davitt, and John Dillon toured the United States raising funds for the league. In February 1880, Parnell and Dillon arrived in Milwaukee at the North Western depot at the head of E. Wisconsin Avenue, and were greeted by cheering men, women, and children lining the sidewalks of the city's main street. Former mayor Edward O'Neill, Mayor John Black, and Andrew Mullen, who was born in County Mayo, joined Parnell in the entourage's first horse-drawn carriage. Dillon rode with Jeremiah Quin and Thomas Shea in the second vehicle, while others of the party followed. They were led by the Sheridan Guard and Clauder's band down E. Wisconsin Avenue to the Academy of Music on N. Milwaukee Street, where hundreds of spectators were turned away because the crowd of 1,600 filled the hall to its capacity.

Irish leader Charles Stewart Parnell. (Wikimedia Commons)

O'Neill spoke about the lack of civil rights of Irishmen in British-controlled Ireland. Parnell thanked Milwaukeeans for their support in relieving the hunger caused by the famine and talked of the need to disestablish the Protestant Church of Ireland, eliminate English landlordism, and stop England from gaining wealth on the backs of Irishmen. Dillon pronounced, "We would rather be called communists and save Irishmen from death than to see them dying and be called good citizens."[9]

Land League clubs soon were popping up throughout the country. Children and grandchildren of Irish immigrants were generally more enthusiastic in their support for Irish freedom than their fathers and grandfathers had been. Milwaukee leagues were formed on the East, West, and South sides and each raised money to support the cause in Ireland. In 1881, Parnell, Dillon, and other Land League executives were imprisoned in Kilmainham Gaol in Dublin, and British authorities outlawed the Land League, delaying its objectives for 20 years. The men were released in May 1882. Milwaukee's land leagues were consolidated in 1883, but they too soon died out.

Late in 1883, another Irish militia company was formed, this one called the Parnell Guard in honor of the Irish leader. Berkley Farrell, born in New Jersey of Irish parents and a veteran of the Milwaukee Regiment, was elected captain of the 50-member Parnell Guard. The company was just a few months old when there was a bitter split among its members, reflecting the turmoil in the Land League in Ireland. Farrell was out and former Sheridan Guard, Thomas McGrath, temporarily led the company in their drills until the dispute was resolved. It was finally settled by dividing the company into two factions, but with insufficient numbers neither was successful and nine months after its formation, the Parnell Guard disbanded.

Prejudice and Bigotry

Most of the Irish who came to Milwaukee were poor. With their poverty came alcoholism, domestic abuse, and other violence and crime. This helped set the Irish apart from their non-Irish neighbors, as did their miserable living conditions. Large families lived in one room shacks. Pigs, cows, goats, chickens, and other fowl ran freely through their neighborhoods and left excrement to foul the air and stick to shoes. Their homes were built on landfills and other less than desirable locations. The Gas Works located in the Third Ward produced odors so strong that residents became nauseous, and slaughterhouses and tanneries in the Menomonee River Valley stunk up Tory Hill.

Their lack of skills and literacy meant less work for Irish men and women in a city prejudiced against them. Signs in business windows and newspaper advertisements decreeing "No Irish need apply" hurt Irish job-seekers. The following advertisements appeared in the *Milwaukee Sentinel*:

Wanted - Female help. Neat and experienced girl to do second work; no Irish need apply. Mrs. P. McGeoch, near Soldiers Home.[10]

Widower. American and child, wants good sensible energetic woman of settled habits as working housekeeper; must work cheap and make good permanent home; no Irish need apply; must come well recommended.[11]

Perhaps as a justification for printing these advertisements, a *Sentinel* article claimed that the Irish in the Third Ward had hung out signs with the words "No German need apply." Patrick Donnelly, the Third Ward School principal and long-time Third Ward resident, disputed the statement, saying, "There has never been any such sign 'hung out' by any Hibernian in the Third Ward, not even in spirit." Donnelly maintained that the Germans and Irish in the Third Ward had always gotten along well, evidenced by some intermarriage, and that some petty politicians tried to turn race against race and creed against creed for their own benefit and that the *Sentinel* should not be "propagating so mean a principle."[12]

Newspapers carried Irish jokes, usually reflecting poorly on Irish

PAT TIES THE GOAT WITH FIFTY FEET OF NEW ROPE WITH DISASTROUS RESULTS.

"Pat Ties the Goat," an example of the depiction of Irishmen as monkey-like. (*Milwaukee Journal*, August 8, 1896)

intelligence and poking fun at them. Drawings and cartoons depicted Irish people as subhuman and ape-like. Irish jokes abounded in newspapers throughout the country. Most were not funny, or even understandable, by today's standards. Two examples that are comprehensible:

"No smoking allowed here" said the steward of the steamboat to the Irishman. "I'm not smoking aloud, your honor," said the Irishman.[13]

Pat O'Flaherty says his wife is ungrateful. "When I married her she hadn't a rag on her back, now she is covered with them."[14]

While notices that "No Irish need apply" were demoralizing and Irish jokes were demeaning, depictions of Irish as apelike were probably the most disgusting form of bigotry. In the 1870s, nationally known cartoonist Thomas Nast began drawing the Irish as subhuman and ape-like. Another artist, True Williams, the first man to illustrate *Tom Sawyer and Huckleberry Finn* for Mark Twain's novels, kept Nast's insulting Irish imagery alive when he portrayed Milwaukee's Third Ward residents as simian-like for one of George W. Peck's books.

In 1887, three years before Peck became Milwaukee's twenty-ninth mayor and four years before he became Wisconsin's seventeenth governor, he published one of his many humorous books, *Peck's Irish Friend, Phelan Geoheagan*. It is narrated by Phelan Geoheagan and written in an Irish

George W. Peck also wrote a series of Peck's Bad Boy books. The mean-spirited Bad Boy gloried in playing tricks on his father. In The Groceryman and Peck's Bad Boy, the subjects are the Fenians and St. Patrick's Day in the Third Ward.

Peck's Bad Boy and Milwaukee's Fenians

"O, that was only a Fenian scare. Nothing serious. You see Pa is a sort of half Englishman. He claims to be an American citizen when he wants office, but when they talk about a draft he claims to be a subject of Great Britain, and he says they can't touch him. Pa is a darned smart man, and don't you forget it. They don't any of them get ahead of Pa much. Well, Pa has said a good deal about the wicked Fenians, and that they ought to be pulled, and all that, and when I read the story in the papers about the explosion in the British Parliament, Pa was hot. He said the damnirish was ruining the whole world. He didn't dare to say it at the table, or our hired girl would have knocked him silly with a spoonful of mashed potatoes, 'cause she is a nirish girl, and she can lick any Englishman in this town. Pa said there ought to have been somebody there to have taken that bomb up and throwed it in the sewer before it exploded. He said that if he should ever see a bomb he would grab it right up and throw it away where it wouldn't hurt anybody. Pa has me read the papers to him nights, 'cause his eyes have got splinters in 'em, and after I had read all there was in the paper, I made up a lot more and pretended to read it, about how it was rumored that the Fenians here in Milwaukee were going to place dynamite bombs at every house where an Englishman lived, and at a given signal blow them all up. Pa looked pale around the gills, but he said he wasn't scared.

"Pa and Ma were going to call on a shedeacon that night, that has lots of money in the bank, to see if she didn't want to invest in a dead sure paying silver mine, and me and my chum concluded to give them a send-off. We got my big black injy rubber foot ball, and painted '*Dinymite*' in big white letters on it, and tied a piece of tarred rope to it for a fuse, and got a big firecracker, one of those old Fourth of July horse scarers, and a basket full of broken glass. We put the foot ball in front of the step and lit the tarred rope and got under the step with the firecrackers and the basket, where they go down into the basement. Pa and Ma came out of the front door and down the steps, and Pa saw the foot ball and the burning fuse, and he said 'Great God, Hanner, we are blowed up!' and he started to run, and Ma she stopped to look at it. Just as Pa started to run I touched off the firecracker and my chum arranged it to pour out the broken glass on the brick pavement just as the firecracker went off. Well, everything went just as we expected, except Ma. She had examined the foot ball and concluded it was not dangerous, and was just giving it a kick as the fire-cracker went off, and the glass fell, and the firecracker was so near her that it scared her, and when Pa looked around Ma was flying across the sidewalk, and Pa heard the noise and he thought the house was blown to atoms. O, you'd a dide to see him go around the corner. You could play crokay on his coattail, and his face was as pale as Ma's when she goes to a party. But Ma didn't scare much. As quick as she stopped against the hitching post she knew it was us boys, and she came down there, and maybe she didn't maul me. I cried and tried to gain her sympathy by telling her the firecracker went off before it was due, and burned my eyebrows off, but she didn't let up until I promised to go and find Pa.

"I tell you, my Ma ought to be engaged by the British government to hunt out the dynamite fiends. She would corral them in two minutes. If Pa had as much sand as Ma has got, it would be warm weather for me. Well, me and my chum went and headed Pa off or I guess he would be running yet. We got him up by the lake shore, and he wanted to know if the house fell down. He said he would leave it to me if he ever said anything against the Fenians, and I told him that he had always claimed that the Fenians were the nicest men in the world, and it seemed to relieve him very much. When he got home and found the house there he was tickled, and when Ma called him an old baldheaded coward, and said it was only a joke of the boys with a foot ball, he laughed right out, and said he knew it all the time, and he ran to see if Ma would be scared. And, then he wanted to hug me, but it wasn't my night to hug and I went down to the theater. Pa don't amount to much when there is trouble."[15]

Peck's Bad Boy and the Third Ward on St. Patrick's Day

"Hold on here," says the grocery man, feeling that he had been too harsh. "Come back here, and have some maple sugar. What did your Pa drive you away from home for?"

"O, it was on account of St. Patrick's Day," said the bad boy as he bit off half a pound of maple sugar, and dried his tears. "You see, Pa never sees Ma buy a new silk handkerchief, but he wants it. T'other day Ma got one of these orangecolored handkerchiefs, and Pa immediately had a sore throat and wanted to wear it, and Ma let him put it on. I thought I would break him of taking everything nice that Ma got, so when he went down town with the orange handkerchief on his neck, I told some of the St. Patrick boys in the Third ward, who had green ribbons on, that the old duffer that was putting on style was an orangeman, and he said he could whip any St. Patrick's Day man in town. The fellers laid for Pa, and when he came along one of them threw a barrel at Pa, and another pulled the yellow handkerchief off his neck, and they all yelled 'Hang him,' and one grabbed a rope that was on the sidewalk where they were moving a building, and Pa got up and dusted. You'd a dide to see Pa run. He met a policeman and said more'n a hundred men had tried to murder him, and they had mauled him, and stolen his yellow handkerchief. The policeman told Pa his life was not safe, and he better go home and lock himself in, and he did, and I was telling Ma about how I got the boys to scare Pa, and he heard it, and he told me that settled it. He said I had caused him to run more foot races than any champion pedestrian, and had made his life unbearable, and now I must go it alone."[16]

130

The Irish as ape-like. (*The Groceryman and Peck's Bad Boy*, George W. Peck, 1883)

dialect. Episodes deal with the shenanigans of Geoheagan, his wife Mary Ann, his uncle Old Man Dugan, the Widow McGucken, and others. All are illustrated by Williams as ape-like.

The *Milwaukee Journal* combined insults with cartoons depicting the Irish as lacking intelligence and more monkey-like than human. These caricatures persisted into the twentieth century, in spite of the success of many in the city's Irish population.

Sports

Irishmen in Milwaukee were into sports. It gave them a way to vent pent-up energy and escape from the monotony of everyday life. In a few cases, it provided a way for them to increase their incomes.

One sporting activity particularly popular with young Irishmen in early Milwaukee was fighting. It didn't cost anything, there was no equipment needed, and they didn't need to leave their neighborhood to do it. As William O'Connor, a priest born in the Third Ward explained, "With no tennis or golf at their disposal they took to fighting as a healthy outlet for surplus energy." He pointed out that there was no animosity behind the fights.[17]

Handball

Irish immigrants brought the game of handball to Milwaukee, and by 1860 the city had three handball courts, or alleys, as they were called then. Two were in the Third Ward and one served Tory Hill.[18] A combination of the sinking of the *Lady Elgin* and the Civil War decimated the city's young male Irish population and caused the local sport to wither temporarily.

In Ireland, handball in some form or another had been played for centuries. The game requires quickness, power, and stamina as a player hits the ball with his hand against a wall, with the goal of having the returning ball elude his opponent. In the early 1880s, when the best Irish players began competing against the best Irish-American players, the American public paid attention. Handball courts popped up in Irish communities throughout the country.

In Milwaukee, the old O'Byrne's Handball Alley on N. Broadway between E. Chicago and E. Buffalo streets was refurbished inside and out and renamed Farrell's Handball Court. At 60 feet deep, 24 feet wide, and 28 feet high, the wooden structure with a rear brick wall had a bar and a restaurant, and its gallery could accommodate more than 100 spectators.[19] No rowdyism was allowed and only respectable men were admitted. Players were generally of a higher economic status and included business proprietors, managers, and skilled craftsmen, but only a few laborers. No women, respectable or not, were permitted. The audience paid ten cents to watch Milwaukee's finest handball players compete with each other, as well as challengers from other Midwestern cities.

The popularity of the game spread to other residents. Baseball players of all ethnicities took up the game to keep in shape all year. It appealed to younger men and was played by students at St. Francis Seminary and gained many adherents on the campus of the University of Wisconsin.

The spaciousness of Farrell's Handball Court also provided a site for other activities, such as boxing matches and large meetings. After its destruction in the Third Ward Fire in 1892, handball was played in a facility a block south on N. Broadway, and at the Young Men's Christian Association at N. Fourth and W. Michigan streets. Although the sport appealed to many outside the Irish community, it continued to be dominated by Irish and Irish Americans for decades.[20] Today, it is most popular in Ireland and two of the countries that Irish immigrants brought the game to—Canada and the United States.

Baseball

Two of the five founders of Major League Baseball's American League were Milwaukee Irishmen. That was in 1901, but baseball, or a game like it, was played in Milwaukee as early as 1836, although it was not until after the Civil War that the sport became popular in the city. A Milwaukee team, the Cream City Baseball Club, was founded six months after the war ended, and in an era when team rosters were filled with amateurs, the club won three state championships in a row. One of the team's founders was Martin Larkin Jr., who was the captain and a star member of the team.[21]

Martin's parents, Martin Larkin Sr. and Ann Mehan, left County Kilkenny in the early 1830s and settled in New Jersey, where Martin Jr. was born in 1840. The family moved to Wisconsin in 1850 and to the Tory Hill area a year or two later. Martin Sr. was a laborer, but unlike many Irish laborers, he was literate, as displayed by his letters to the editor printed in the *Milwaukee Sentinel* during the 1850s. At age 18, Martin Jr. began his training to become a lawyer and four years later, in 1862, he was elected as the youngest member of the Wisconsin State Assembly.

Besides helping to establish the Cream City Baseball Club late in 1865, he was also a founding member of the St. Patrick Literary Society of St. Gall's parish. Before the baseball team began the 1866 season, Larkin was appointed the state organizer of the Fenian Brotherhood in preparation for the upcoming invasion of Canada. He traveled by railroad throughout the state recruiting for Fenian circles in Madison, Appleton, and Oshkosh. Whether Larkin participated in the June 1, 1866, Fenian invasion is not known, but three weeks after it, he was again traveling around the Midwest, not as an organizer but as a second baseman who "made some splendid runs and beautiful catches."[22]

From 1866 through 1868, the Cream City Club was state champion. After the 1868 season, Larkin retired from baseball and concentrated on Democratic Party politics, his law career, and his position as assistant editor of the *Star of Bethlehem*, a local Catholic newspaper. His mother died in 1870 and his father passed away in 1871. Soon after, Larkin moved to New York City, where he apparently was not very successful. He died there in 1878 and was buried in a pauper's grave.

Nationally, the popularity of baseball continued to rise. In 1869, the first completely professional baseball team was formed in Cincinnati,

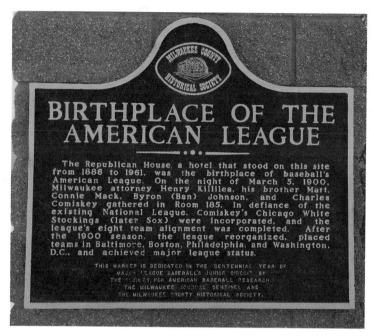

Milwaukee was the birthplace of the American League. (Photograph by the author)

but amateur baseball was still the rage in Milwaukee. Teams sprang up throughout the city and the Irish neighborhoods of the Third Ward and Tory Hill were no exceptions. Baseball was popular in Tory Hill, which fielded several baseball teams beginning in the 1870s. The Quicksteps, a Third Ward team led by flashy-fielding shortstop Cornelius L. Corcoran, played in the 1880s. It was considered one of the best amateur teams in the state and was the pride of the Third Ward.

After his baseball playing days were over, Cornelius Corcoran was elected a Third Ward alderman at age 27 and was still alderman when he died at 71. He served for nearly 44 years, a record for Milwaukee aldermen, and was Common Council president for 30 years, another record.

The Lees of the Third Ward were the best-known family of Irish ball players in the city. Tommy Lee pitched for Milwaukee's top-rated Maple Leafs and then turned professional, playing for teams in Chicago, Baltimore, and Memphis. He contracted malarial fever in the South and died in Milwaukee at the age of 23 in 1886.[23] His brother Johnny Lee played second base for the Maple Leafs and the youngest brother, Willie, was the Quicksteps' catcher. Willie Lee died before his twenty-second birthday, the year after Tommy's death. All three men were born in Milwaukee of Irish immigrant parents.

Henry and Matthew Killilea were two of the five founders of baseball's American League. They came to Milwaukee from the Irish community at Poygan, Wisconsin, as young men. Both were lawyers. Henry became a well-known trial attorney and Matthew was assistant district attorney, but baseball is where they made their names. Matthew was the president of the Western League's Milwaukee Brewers baseball team, while his older brother was a minor investor.

In 1900, the brothers, along with Cornelius McGillicuddy (aka Connie Mack, the Milwaukee Brewers manager), Charles Comiskey (another Irishman), and Ban Johnson re-created the Western League as the American League, which became a major league. Henry Killilea became known as the "Godfather of the American League." Milwaukee's entry in the league, the Brewers, lasted only one year before the team moved to St. Louis and was renamed the Browns (now the Baltimore Orioles). From 1902 to 1952, the Milwaukee Brewers were a minor league team in the American Association. Henry Killilea later became the owner of the Milwaukee Brewers and upon his death in 1929, his daughter Florence assumed control. Alderman Cornelius Corcoran, the old Quicksteps star,

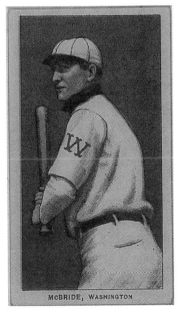

Shortstop George McBride's baseball card. McBride, born in the Third Ward, holds the Major League record for the lowest lifetime batting average based on over 5,000 at bats. (Library of Congress)

was a vice president and director of the team.

Shortstop George McBride was born in the Third Ward in 1880, the son of Peter McBride, a County Louth immigrant. George played for the Brewers the one year they were in the American League before they left for St. Louis. He apparently enjoyed playing in his hometown, because he turned down a contract to play for the major league St. Louis team, so he could play for the newly formed minor league Milwaukee Brewers. McBride did eventually go on to play in the majors for 15 years, and was the epitome of the "good field, no hit" player. While he led the American League in fielding four times, his lifetime batting average of .218 is the lowest in major league history for players with over 5,000 at bats.

Raymond Cannon was a man ahead of his time. Cannon, whose immigrant ancestors came from counties Donegal and Mayo, was orphaned when his parents died within two months of each other when he was one year old. A lawyer, he pitched sandlot ball and barnstormed with five of the Chicago "Blacksox" players, who were banned from professional baseball after being charged with throwing the 1919 World Series. Cannon represented some of the players, including Shoeless Joe Jackson, in trying to get their jobs back. He later represented Milwaukee as a congressman for three terms. His baseball claim to fame was that he founded a major league baseball players union in 1922. The union was unsuccessful, some think, because of his connections with the players involved in the scandal.[24] Major league players would have to wait until 1966 to have a union represent them.

Boxing

Although prize fighting was illegal because it was so brutal before cushioned gloves were used, a few Irish residents were paid to fight. Bouts were frequently broken up by the police in the Chicago and Milwaukee circuit when boxing promoters from those cities tried to circumvent the restrictions by claiming that they were offering "sparring tournaments." Authorities were usually not fooled. Another promoter tactic was to schedule bouts in buildings far from the city to avoid the police, but if sheriff's deputies got wind of a fight, they would stop it.

Sometimes the police would monitor the fights and only stop them if they became too brutal, like a bout in Bay View in 1898. Con O'Leary of Milwaukee was fighting James Davis of Racine. "O'Leary was driving

Davis around the ring with sledge-hammer blows delivered right and left and Davis was staggering when police stepped in."[25] O'Leary, a middleweight at 150 pounds, was a barkeeper in the Tory Hill area for many years.

Mickey Riley, born in the Third Ward in 1872 to County Kildare immigrants, also fought for money in the 1890s. He worked as a laborer and fought in the featherweight category at about 130 pounds. Riley had many of his fights end in draws, as fight judges would usually declare a fight a draw when it was broken up by police, and Riley had many of his fights stopped by the authorities. Riley's record was not sterling, but the money apparently was enough incentive to keep enticing him into the ring.

Winter Sports

Ice skating was popular in the Third Ward before the 1870s, when the marsh south of St. Paul Avenue and east of N. Jackson Street was filled in. Tory Hill was the place to be for sledding, with the steep hills on W. Clybourn Street. For Third Ward boys, the closest hill to "bob-sleigh" down was on N. Marshall Street from E. Wells Street down to E. Wisconsin Avenue. The police received many complaints about boys sledding in the streets and eventually banned the practice.

John Henni and His Successors

John Henni was the Roman Catholic bishop of the Milwaukee Diocese from 1843 until 1875, when Milwaukee became an Archdiocese and he its archbishop until his death in 1881. The Irish did not have much affection for him and he was not always a fan of the Irish. He favored Germans to such an extent that co-religionist critics said he was hurting the Catholic Church in Wisconsin.

Germans felt that the only proper way to practice their religion was in the German language. They certainly weren't going to learn English— they had no need. Many Milwaukee Germans, even those born in the city, spent their lives speaking only German. They spoke German in their daily activities, conversing with their neighbors, and dealing with employees and owners of local businesses, shops, and workplaces, while their children spoke and were taught their lessons in German in school.

Henni agreed with this practice. He wished all the priests in the state

John Henni, Milwaukee's
archbishop, was no friend
of the city's Irish. (*Fifty
Years at St. John's Cathedral,*
David J. O'Hearn, 1897)

were German-speakers. While there were many more Germans than Irish in the state, most Germans were not Catholic. In 1870, there were 120,000 Irish Catholics in Wisconsin compared to 117,00 German Catholics.[26] A major complaint of the Irish was that if there were one or two German families and one hundred or more Irish families in a congregation, it was a "mixed" church and needed a German priest.[27] By 1899, more than half of the St. Patrick churches in Wisconsin had German pastors. Henni installed German bishops in the cathedrals in La Crosse and Green Bay, where only German was spoken. This practice was said to turn away non-German speakers and inhibit converts to the religion.

St. Francis Seminary, that is, Henni's German seminary, was considered unfriendly to Irishmen, and some Milwaukee Irish who studied for the priesthood attended seminaries elsewhere. Those who did attend locally were discriminated against, even to the extent that they were charged more tuition than the German speakers. Since the faculty was predominately German, all students needed to learn German. By the end of the century, the seminary was not graduating Irish students. It was not that the Irish were bypassing higher education; most of the graduates from Marquette University at the time were Irish.

In 1879, Henni was ill and began to plan for his successor to be his friend and longtime associate, Michael Heiss. Local Irish and American priests objected to another German archbishop, but Henni forbade them to write articles against Heiss for publication. Heiss became the archdiocese's second archbishop in 1880. Ten years later, after Heiss died, another German was being considered to replace him. Again, non-German priests were unhappy, but this time some bishops joined them in opposing the naming of Frederick Katzer to the position. John Ireland, the Kilkenny-born archbishop of St. Paul, Minnesota, and John Keane, born in Donegal and bishop of Richmond, Virginia, fought against Katzer's nomination. They complained about the discrimination against non-Germans and wrote, "It is a common saying in America, that in going to Milwaukee one goes to Germany."[28] In spite of the opposition, Katzer was made archbishop in 1890, a position he held until 1903.

During Henni's administration he was quoted as stating that "No Irishman will ever sit upon my throne," and when Sebastian Messmer, another German speaker, was named Katzer's successor, it looked like Henni was prophetic.[29] But Samuel Stritch sat on Henni's throne from 1930 to 1939. Stritch's father was born in Dublin and his mother's parents were from Ireland. Moses Kiley occupied the same throne from 1940 to 1953. His Irish ancestors settled in Nova Scotia, where Kiley was born. William Cousins served as archbishop from 1958 to 1977, and like Kiley, he was descended from Irish Canadians. Timothy Dolan, archbishop from 2002 to 2009, was descended from Patrick Dolan of County Cavan and his wife Catherine of County Mayo.

Who Is Irish?

To try to determine the "Irishness" of groups of people, American researchers have often looked at lists of the surnames of the groups. They see names like McNamara, Cassidy, and Fitzpatrick and add them to the Irish group. But if they stop with the obvious Irish names, they are undercounting the Irish. There are many Irish names that are not common and may not be immediately recognized as Irish. For example, Milwaukeeans named Furlong, Powderly, Hussey, and Uniacke were all born in Ireland.

Some Irish names were Anglicized. Some MacAteers became Carpenters, McGlone has been changed to Monday, and some Monaghans changed their name to Monks. Other Irish took English names regardless of their own surname. These changes were made for convenience in an Anglo-dominated Ireland.

An analysis of the surnames of Fourth Ward Irishmen in the 1860 census shows that about 30 percent of them had English sounding names. Residents with names like Fox, Harrison, Hill, Kirby, and Layton were all born in Ireland. Researchers cursorily perusing the list would likely classify them as English, not Irish.

Mistakes can be made the other way, by classifying names as Irish when they may not be. Larkin is an example. It can be an Irish name but it is also English. Nineteenth century real estate developer and sheriff, Charles Larkin, has been identified as a Milwaukee Irishman.[30] His family, however, dates back many generations in the U.S. to English colonists in New England.

Since one out of ten Irishmen coming to Milwaukee in the nineteenth century was named Patrick, the name is a major clue in picking out the Irishmen in a list of names. The same ratio held true for the entire country. This is according to the author's analysis of census data from 1850 through 1940. Of males born in Ireland enumerated in Milwaukee during those decades, 10.77 percent were named Patrick. For the United States, Patricks comprised 10.98 percent of the Irish male population.[31]

Chapter 6
1880–1889

The city's population was 115,847 in 1880, and the number born in Ireland was 3,624, a slight decrease from 1870. The number of the city's Irish Americans who had one or more parents born in Ireland was 7,526, putting the percent of Irish and Irish Americans in the city at 9.6.[1] This does not include Irish Americans whose parents were not born in Ireland but whose grandparents were, so it's reasonable to conclude that those with Irish ancestry made up more than ten percent of the general population.

Ancient Order of Hibernians and Clan na Gael

The first of Milwaukee's five divisions of the Ancient Order of Hibernians (AOH) was founded in Bay View in early 1880. The AOH, a North American Irish Catholic organization, was founded to provide financial and social assistance for its members who were ill, and funeral benefits for those who died. It also supported Irish causes, and the Land League issue was a primary motivation for the organization of the city's divisions.

Membership dues and fundraisers like dances and picnics raised money for benefits, charities, and support of the Irish in their endeavors to gain civil rights and independence in Ireland. Committees of volunteers were appointed to visit the sick, and uniformed members marched in parades and funerals.

The rituals of the organization were secret, and members used passwords and signs in conducting business. This secrecy was looked on by some as being suspect. The Catholic Church was not happy with secret organizations and its normal procedure was to ban participation in them. But the AOH was supported by the local Irish clergy, and the German archbishop, Michael Heiss, had no problems with it and did not want any. He advocated a hands-off approach nationally.[2]

The second division was also founded in 1880 and it followed the same practices and functions of the Hibernian Benevolent Society that was founded in 1847, even meeting at St. Gall's and with most of the same officers. After seven years of parallel operations with the AOH, the Hibernian Benevolent Society disbanded in 1887 and distributed its assets to its members.

In 1895, a Ladies Auxiliary of the AOH was founded. All five divisions were consolidated in 1901 and continued their fraternal activities until World War II. The last known event of this version of the Milwaukee organization was a picnic fundraiser held in 1941.[3] The next version was born later in the twentieth century.

Five years after the city's Ancient Order of Hibernians was founded, a city branch of the Clan na Gael (Family of the Gaels), was organized. The national Irish-American organization was an offshoot of the Fenian Brotherhood that supported the Irish Republican Brotherhood, later known as the Irish Republican Army (IRA). As a secret society, it was condemned by the Catholic Church, and unlike the Fenians, it actually was secret. But like the Fenians, they held picnics to raise money.

During the summer of 1885, Clan na Gael members from Chicago and southeastern Wisconsin came to Milwaukee for the third annual Irish picnic and fundraiser, which was held at Schlitz Park on W. Walnut Street between N. Seventh and N. Ninth streets. The Committee of Reception was composed of dozens of Milwaukee's leading Irishmen.

The Sheridan Guard met Chicago's Clan na Gael Guard and visitors from other cities at the Milwaukee Road and the Chicago and North Western Railway stations. The 1,000 visitors and their escorts paraded through downtown and then to the park, where they joined about 8,000 local Irish for the festivities.[4] In addition to food and drink there was a variety of races and other athletic competitions. The tug of war was the most popular. There was dancing to jigs, hornpipes, and reels. Michael Egan, a fife player and local insurance agent born in County Kilkenny, led crowds in singing traditional Irish songs from his repertoire of over 200 tunes. The Clan na Gael Guard played airs like "Rory O'Moore,"

THIRD ANNUAL
IRISH PICNIC
—AT—
SCHLITZ PARK,
SATURDAY, JULY 25.

GAMES, COMPETITIVE PRIZE DRILL,
Eloquent Addresses
—AND—
GRAND BALL.

Excursion of OLAN NA GAEL GUARD and friends from Chicago; also the A. O. H. and Temperance Society of Janesville, and other uniformed Irish Societies from various parts of this state.
Excursion rates on all roads. Round-trip tickets one and one-fifth fare. Good to return on Monday, 27th inst., inclusive.

Milwaukee's Irish picnic included the Clan na Gael, the Ancient Order of Hibernians, and other Irish organizations. (*Milwaukee Daily Journal*, July 24, 1885)

"Wearing of the Green," and "Killarney." The picnic raised almost $4,000 and, after deducting expenses, the rest was sent to Ireland.[5]

There were two factions in the Clan na Gael. One backed using parliamentary efforts to gain Irish independence, while the other, the Sullivan-Egan faction, advocated using force and supposedly supported the bombing campaign that had been taking place in England. In 1886, the *New York Times* reported that there would be meetings of the two factions of the organization during that month. The parliamentary faction would convene in Chicago, while the Sullivan-Egan faction would meet in Milwaukee.[6] None of the leading Milwaukee Irishmen contacted by a *Milwaukee Sentinel* reporter professed to know anything about the subject, but speculation was that most favored the Sullivan-Egan branch. No details of the Milwaukee meeting, if there was one, were published. The Clan na Gael faded out for a time but was revived early in the next century.

The Newhall House Fire—
The Country's Deadliest Hotel Fire for
Over Six Decades

The temperature was in the single digits just before four o'clock in the morning on January 10, 1883, and it was snowing. As William McKenzie, the Newhall House night watchman, approached the sixth-floor elevator, he saw smoke coming from the shaft. McKenzie could have begun alerting the hotel's occupants and the building would likely have been safely evacuated in 10 or 15 minutes. Instead, he got into the elevator and descended into increasingly heavy smoke while those slumbering continued to sleep. For many of them, when they did awaken, it would be too late. The Newhall House Fire resulted in the deaths of at least 72 employees and guests in what was at the time by far the deadliest hotel fire in the United States, a dubious record that would hold until 1946. Nearly half of those lost were Irish, mostly women who lived and worked in the hotel as servers, maids, and laundry help.

The Newhall House hotel, designed by Edward Townsend Mix, had celebrated its twenty-fifth anniversary the previous August. The day it opened in 1857, every train arriving in the city was filled with people anxious to see the magnificent six-story structure clad in pale yellow brick. The new, luxurious 240-room hotel was helping to put Milwaukee on the map. Some thought there were a couple of hotels in New York on par with it, but that no hotel in between could compare. That may have been an exaggeration, but it was a large, first-rate hotel. Most of the city's 44,000 citizens were proud of it, and before it was even completed it was the best-known building in the city. Businesses advertised their location relative to it. Traffic on Broadway between E. Michigan Street and E. Wisconsin Avenue had increased throughout the summer, with people frequenting the offices and shops on the lower floors, which were open while work was still being done on the upper floors.

On opening day, 2,500 people dressed in their finest would inspect the building that fronted 180 feet on the west side of N. Broadway and 120 feet on the north side of E. Michigan Street. In the center of the rectangular building was another rectangle, a courtyard 80 feet long and 28 feet wide that provided light and ventilation to the interior rooms of the building.

The hotel's guests, and those who bought tickets to the Newhall House Festival, walked on the new white and black marble floors, and up and down two circular stairways that ran between the lobby on the second floor and the sixth story. They ate in the elegant dining room and listened to music played by a band on the second-floor balcony that ran the length of the building on N. Broadway. The band's music also entertained those on the street below who could not get in but were enjoying the spectacle. Another band played dance music in the ballroom of Albany Hall, which was reached through a covered walkway across E. Michigan Street from the Newhall House. At 11 p.m. the supper room opened and was jammed until 3 a.m. when the party finally ended. Well over 300 guests stayed at the Newhall House that night, while the disappointed overflow slept in other hotels and inns.

But the glorious future predicted for the Newhall House never materialized. Within weeks of the opening, the Financial Panic of 1857 struck and severely cut into the hotel's occupancy. The Civil War four years later ended the economic slump but did not provide much new business for the Newhall House. After the war, John Plankinton built an even more prestigious hotel, the Plankinton House, on the other side of the river and the Newhall House was no longer number one.

Over the following years, the Newhall House adjusted to new technologies and trends. Fire escapes were placed on both the N. Broadway and E. Michigan Street facades, but there were no signs on the inside indicating the doors that led to them. Nor was there a fire escape on the west side of the building on the alley, where most of the employees slept. In 1874, an elevator was installed near the south circular staircase, but when it ran, that portion of the building would shake and tremble. The oak wood lining the outside of the elevator car was greased twice a week with lard oil to reduce friction with the elevator shaft. Rooms near the elevator were not in high demand.

Near the E. Michigan Street end of the building, the construction of a skywalk across the 15-foot alley on the west side of the Newhall House connected its third and fourth floors to the Bank of Milwaukee on the other side (the marks on the bank building where the skywalk was connected can still be seen today). The Newhall House's proprietors, John Antisdel and his son, James, and their families lived in apartments

**Newhall House hotel at the corner of N. Broadway and
E. Michigan Street.** (Wikimedia Commons auf Deutsch)

in the bank building, as did some Newhall House boarders. Antisdel said
that some guests did not like to use the skywalk or the bank building's
rooms and that was why he lived there. Others said Antisdel did not want
his family to live in a firetrap and *that* was why he lived there. The roof of
the fourth-floor skywalk provided a bridge for anyone on the fifth floor
to cross over, and in an emergency those on the sixth floor could take a
ladder down to the skywalk roof to cross to the bank building. The hotel's
capacity increased to 300 rooms after a reconfiguration of some space
within the hotel and the addition of the apartments in the bank building.

However, two significant things did not change during this time. One
was that there were no fireproof walls partitioning the building to prevent
a fire from spreading; the partition walls were all wood. The other was
the use of water buckets. There was a bank of filled water buckets in each

corner of the upper four floors. They were there to put out fires, for the hotel had a history of fires. There had been at least 30 fires in the Newhall House since it opened. Most were small, but there was a big one in 1863 that destroyed nine rooms in the southeast part of the hotel. The water buckets were credited with preventing the fire from getting out of hand before the fire department arrived. There was fear that if the hotel burned it might start the whole downtown on fire. After the 1863 fire, legendary Fire Chief Patsy McLaughlin prophesized, "If that place ever burns, you will see some lives lost."[7]

In 1880, a fire that started in the northwest part of the building drove guests into a cold January morning. There was more damage from the water than there was from the fire, but the Newhall House was gaining a reputation as a fire hazard. In 1881, an arsonist started a fire in a basement wall near the elevator. The fire was noticed before it could do much damage and was put out, but it was evident that it was arson because someone had scraped away the plaster on the wall and stuffed papers between the laths. By 1882, the consensus was that the Newhall House was a firetrap.

On January 10, 1883, by the time Bill McKenzie reached the third floor, the smoke was so thick that he had to abandon the elevator. He had been told by John Antisdel that in the event of a fire, McKenzie should contact Antisdel and then use his own judgment to decide whether to warn the guests or not. Rather than doing either, McKenzie ran down the stairs to the main lobby on the second floor where Tom Delaney, the night clerk, was stationed. Delaney looked up as McKenzie approached and noticed smoke rising from the stairs next to the elevator. More time was wasted while the two men ran down the stairs to try to locate the source of the fire. The smoke was thick on the south end of the first floor, forcing them back upstairs, where Delaney called the fire department and McKenzie called down to the basement, where William Linehan, the engineer, was working on the furnaces in preparation for the day's activity. By this time, fire and smoke were roaring up the elevator shaft, rapidly spreading the fire to every floor because the shaft was not enclosed in brick or iron. The upper floors were filling with smoke.

Bill Linehan, who had been told by Antisdel to try to put out any fire rather than rouse the guests, ran up to the second-floor lobby and asked Delaney where the fire was coming from. When Delaney told him it was downstairs near the elevator, Linehan went to the first floor and pulled out a fire hose, but it kinked, and he had to spend time straightening it. By the time he finished, the fire was too close to the water valve to turn it on, so he ran up to the fifth floor to warn his sleeping sister, Kate, who was also a hotel employee. Most of the female employees slept in rooms on the west side of that floor above the alley.

McKenzie, meanwhile, went up to the third floor where he yelled, "Fire!" and knocked on several doors at the south end of the hallway, then crawled along the smoke-filled hall to the west, where he crossed the skywalk into the bank building and warned his employer, John Antisdel. McKenzie then went outside through the bank building.

Delaney, who had not been told what to do in the event of a fire, ran out on N. Broadway to direct firemen who had arrived on a horse-drawn ladder truck. He directed them to the source of the fire near the elevator, then went back up to the lobby as some people were fleeing down the stairs. One was John Antisdel Jr., 22, who came down from his room on the third floor, the only member of his family to sleep in the hotel. He and Delaney opened the safe and Antisdel shoved all the cash into his pockets while Delaney showed firefighters how to get to the second-floor balcony from inside the building. On the balcony they found a man who had landed after jumping from a floor above. Delaney and John Antisdel Jr. left the building when the ceiling of the second floor began collapsing.

When Engineer Linehan reached the fifth floor, he could not find his sister, but he saw 18-year-old Julia Burns lying unconscious on the floor. He picked her up and carried her down to the lobby and placed her on the stair landing, then went back up. He brought down a man this time, also unconscious. His third trip up the stairs saved the life of a dining room girl named Christina Hagen, and in three more trips he saved three more people before the fire and smoke prevented him from going up again. He then concentrated on carrying the people that he had brought down out of the hotel.

The firemen that Delaney had directed to the fire near the elevator saw the extent of the fire and determined that it could not be put out and that their efforts should be concentrated on saving lives. Unfortunately, because of a fire on N. 19th and W. Vliet streets, Fire Chief Lippert and five of the city's thirteen fire companies were occupied.

The first responders, six firemen on the ladder truck, decided to raise their extension ladder to the upper floors near the corner of the building

148

at N. Broadway and E. Michigan Street, where people were pleading for help. The huge ladder required eight trained men to raise it. In the past, the firemen were required to practice raising it once a week, but that exercise had ended over a year earlier, and now only three of the six men had worked with it before. Two policemen who had run to the fire assisted the firemen in raising the ladder, but immediately ran into a problem when it got tangled in the telegraph wires that extended over the sidewalk. After freeing it from the wires, they placed the ladder against the building and began to extend it. But it became jammed between two iron window caps, and in the attempt to extract it, the extension mechanism broke, and the ladder became useless.

Lewis Brown and his wife, Ann, were boarders on the fifth floor on the N. Broadway side, just north of the ladder-wielding firemen. They were awakened by the sound of the glass being blown out of their room's

The Newhall House on fire. (Wikimedia Commons)

transom window by the heat buildup in the hallway. Brown quickly tore up sheets and blankets and tied them together to make a rope. He told Ann to climb down the makeshift rope, but she refused, saying it would not hold her. He said he would go first so she could see that it would work, and he went out through the window. He was working his way down when something whizzed by him; it was his wife who had jumped and landed on the sidewalk. On the way to her death, she hit guest William Hall of La Porte, Indiana, who was also climbing down; he landed on the sidewalk, his legs broken. While being cared for at a nearby doctor's office later, Hall joked that he was going to have to cancel his plans to attend a dance the following week. He died of internal injuries the next day.

After the firemen laid the broken extension ladder aside, they pulled out the jumping canvas, an early form of safety net. It was square, 15 feet by 15 feet, with eight hand holds on each side. It was held, with help from policeman and bystanders, beneath the window of the Johnsons on the fifth floor. Allan Johnson, 58, and his wife, Martha, 53, lived in the corner room next to the fire escape door, so they knew what they would do in the event of a fire. But their room was also near the elevator and the flames were shooting through the broken transom window over their door, preventing access to the fire escape. Martha Johnson jumped first, but too close to the building and landed on the balcony railing before falling to the ground. Allan Johnson jumped further from the building but hit the telegraph wires, bounced off, and hit the edge of the canvas before landing on the sidewalk. Neither survived.

Judson Hough, from Peoria, Illinois, jumped from a room next to the Johnsons and fared no better. The canvas was not held properly and the force of a man jumping from the fifth floor was too much for the men holding the canvas, and Hough hit it as though it were not there. Broken bones and internal injuries led to his death a short time later.

This lack of success did not deter the canvas holders and they moved the canvas around to the E. Michigan Street side where the fire was at its worst. Irish inventor David Power and retired jeweler Thomas Van Loon were already lying dead on the sidewalk, both burned. They had jumped from the sixth floor, the floor with the fewest survivors. John Donahue, 25, with less than two hours of sleep after a night of heavy drinking, jumped from the fifth floor with his new wife in his arms. He and 22-year-old Gertrude Sutton had married two days earlier in Chicago. Donahue was born in Ireland but raised two blocks from the

Newhall House in the Third Ward, where he spent part of his youth selling peanuts to help his widowed mother support their family. He always had an ambition to entertain. Now living in Chicago, he was a comedian using the name John Gilbert and was a member of the Minnie Palmer Company, which was performing a play, *My Sweetheart*, at the Opera House. When the Donahues hit the ground, Gertrude was on the bottom. She died immediately but saved John's life by cushioning his fall. He was the only person who jumped from so high to survive.

Only one person took a chance on the jumping canvas on E. Michigan Street and that was Engineer Linehan's sister, Kate, who worked in the laundry. The canvas did not stop her from hitting the ground and dying, but it did stop others from jumping. Firemen yelled to William Busenbark, 29, to jump from his fourth-floor window to the canvas, but Busenbark had seen the others jump and decided to try for the telegraph wires. It worked. The wires broke his fall and he was battered and bruised, but he survived. Two men from Palmyra rejected pleas to jump to the canvas, instead they simply scaled down the façade from window cap to window sash to window sill from the fourth floor.

While firemen had been working with the extension ladder and canvas, Oscar Kleinsteuber, a 20-year-old electrician in charge of the police telegraph alarm system, was more effective than the firemen were. After hearing the alarm, he ran to the fire and went up to the second-floor balcony with a ladder, which he used to reach the fire escape. Rushing up the fire escape to the fourth floor, he opened the door and called for anyone in the smoke-filled hallway who could hear to come toward him to safety. Two women came out and went down the fire escape. Kleinsteuber went down with them to get a lantern so he could penetrate the hallway smoke. He went back up, yelling futilely for spectators to come up and help him, and found five more people whom he led down the escape. Four of those saved were members of the Madison Square Theatre Company, in town to present the play, *Esmeralda*, the following weekend at the Opera House. Kleinsteuber later said that if any firemen had gone up with him, many more people could have been saved.

There were only a few large suites on the second floor and the guests, with one exception, were able to simply walk down the stairs to the main entrance and out onto the sidewalk. The exception was the hotel's most famous guests, General Tom Thumb and his wife, Lavinia Warren. Their nationally-known troupe was in town performing at the Academy of

General Tom Thumb and his wife, Lavinia Warren, survived the Newhall House hotel fire. (Wikimedia Commons)

Music.

Thumb, born Charles Stratton, was a little person and comedian who impersonated famous people. He also sang and danced and was one of the best-known men in the country. His wife, also a little person, was a dancer and entertainer. As Tom Delaney was leaving the building, he pointed out the Thumb parlor on the E. Michigan Street side, beyond the burning elevator, to policeman John O'Brien. O'Brien ran past the fire to the room and knocked on the door, then went in and closed the door to shut out the fire. After opening the window, he called out for help and several men, including Bill McKenzie, placed a ladder at the window sill. The diminutive Thumb climbed down and was followed by O'Brien, carrying Mrs. Thumb. When they reached the safety of the express office across N. Broadway, Lavinia cried, "My jewels! My jewels! All my diamonds are gone! Oh! Oh!" General Thumb responded angrily, "My God! Woman, you howling about your diamonds! Look about you!"[8] Warren put her head down and said no more.

In the room above the Thumbs was their manager, Sylvester Groesbeck, 58, known professionally as Sylvester Bleeker, and his wife, Julia. When Groesbeck opened the door to his room, he was showered with burning cinders and his hair and eyebrows were burned. He slammed the door and worked to make a rope from sheets and blankets. He lowered the rope while his wife held on, but the 56-year-old woman lost her grasp and fell to the small balcony on the E. Michigan Street side. Groesbeck climbed down the rope, dropped to the balcony, and made it to the sidewalk down a ladder. Officer O'Brien helped to bring Julia to the ground from the balcony, away from the fire, but she later died from her injuries.

The canvas holders had now moved to the alley and what they saw horrified them. Eight or nine bodies were strewn on the cobblestones, all servants of the hotel, all had roomed on the fifth floor, and all were restricted to their rooms over the alley by the choking smoke and heat that filled the hallway. Seeing no way out, they jumped, and others would follow until there were twelve corpses in the alley. Two firemen, Edward Riemer and Herman Stauss, ran to the building north of the bank building with a ladder. Riemer left but Stauss, with the help of an employee in the building, George Wells, took the ladder to the roof of the building, which was on the same level as the fifth floor of the Newhall House across the alley. Mary Garvin and nine other women were in a room at the north end of the hallway. Mary McCauley, seeing no way out, had decided to jump but Garvin stopped her. The women decided to pray, and as they pled for a miracle, they saw Stauss's ladder poke through the window and into the room. It covered the 15-foot width of the alley and a little more. With the arrival of more firemen with another ladder, all ten women were able to crawl across the ladders to safety.

Other fire companies arrived at the scene, and after raising a ladder to the second-floor balcony, and from there another ladder to the balcony on the third floor, the firemen helped evacuate people. By now, Chief Lippert and his assistant, John Black, were on the scene. Black had been at the train station at the foot of E. Wisconsin Avenue ready to take a train to Chicago. He heard the fire alarm and went to the fire station a few blocks north of the Newhall House to change into his firefighting gear while Lippert had rushed by sleigh from the W. Vliet Street fire. But it was too late to do anyone at the Newhall House any good. Lippert feared the entire downtown area might burn so he telegraphed for help from fire departments in Racine, Chicago, and the National Soldiers' Home. Since nothing could be done to save the Newhall House, firefighters poured water on the surrounding buildings and were able to contain the fire. The calls for help were cancelled. Twenty-five minutes after the fire alarm

The ruins of the Newhall House. (Photo courtesy of Jeff Beutner)

was called in, the building began collapsing. It fell in parts, first the large cornice at the roofline, then the N. Broadway facade, then the E. Michigan Street side, and finally most of the west wall fell across the alley, leaving only parts of the west and north walls standing.

Twenty-four people who jumped were dead or dying, and burn victim Lizzie Anglim, a 22-year-old dining room employee, would only live a few days. Each of these 25 was buried in separate funeral services. The number of those who did not leave the building would not be known for days. A methodical search of the ruins began the next day but would be slowed by the massive amounts of water that turned to ice, record cold temperatures, snow, and unhappy workmen.

Irish-born contractor and Commissioner of Public Works, William P. O'Connor, 42, was chosen to supervise the digging of the ruins. With portions of the debris still smoldering, 120 men began digging along the N. Broadway side. The first day was spent in removing rubble and no bodies were found. On day two, a body was found in the southeast section and was assumed to be Libbie Chellis, who had been seen at her window above that area on the sixth floor during the fire. Her remains were placed in a box marked "1."

Workmen, who were paid $1.25 per day for ten hours of work, feared for their safety and threatened to strike on the second day until a partial back wall still standing was taken down. The wall was removed, and workmen uncovered five more remains. In many cases only a portion of a body was found. O'Connor left the site for a time in the morning to serve as a pallbearer for David Power at the Cathedral of St. John's.

On the third day, Saturday, the site was covered in white from a snowstorm on Friday night, but the workers made progress and uncovered ten more partial bodies. On Sunday, a reduced work crew found two more remains, and on Monday parts of ten more corpses were placed in boxes.

Fewer workers showed up each day because the unpleasant odors were making them sick and they were very squeamish about finding more body parts. Forty-two remains had been recovered after a week of sifting through the debris. The work finished on day 10, Saturday, January 20, with 48 boxes numbered. Some boxes held nearly complete bodies, while others contained only a few bones. On review, it was determined that the contents of boxes "15" and "16" contained the same person's remains and that box "3" did not contain anything human, but that box "30" contained parts of two different corpses. That meant that the number of bodies recovered was 47, not 48. Four of the 47 were identified, and they were buried by their families. Because some of the remains found were only a small part of the original, there was a belief that some bodies could have been totally incinerated and that the death count was higher than the 72 known victims.[9]

The city leaders decided to bury the 43 who were not identified in a large public ceremony, with interment in a special plot at Forest Home Cemetery. The Catholic clergy objected, saying Catholics should be buried from a Catholic church and in the sacred ground of Calvary Cemetery. A compromise allotted 20 remains to the Catholics and the Protestants buried the rest, though naturally it could not be assured that only Catholics were laid to rest in Calvary Cemetery or that no Catholics were interred in Forest Home Cemetery (see Appendix 3).

The morning of Thursday, January 25, dawned at two degrees below zero and it was not much warmer when the services began at 10 a.m. Businesses and public buildings were closed, and most were draped in mourning. The non-Catholic ceremony took place in the Exposition Building on N. Fifth and W. State streets, with the 10,000 people in attendance wearing coats and gloves in the frigid building. Sleighs brought the 23 caskets to the ceremony, which included remarks by city clergymen. The services ended abruptly when a steam pipe burst, sending steam into a section of the crowd. Someone yelled "fire" and many people stampeded, overturning tables and breaking windows to get out. The speakers assured the crowd that there was no fire, but the ceremony was over. The Protestant procession, led by Bach's Band, the Lincoln Guard, and other groups, moved east on W. State Street to N. Broadway, where they were scheduled to meet the Catholic contingent. But they were early and the services at the Cathedral had started late, so they had to stand and wait for half an hour in the frigid weather.

When the Cathedral services ended, the Catholic procession went to the meeting point, led by procession marshal Thomas Shea, a *Lady Elgin* survivor, followed by the Sheridan Guard, the Ancient Order of Hibernians, the Hibernian Benevolent Society, the Knights of St. Patrick, and many other groups. It was so cold that many of the musicians had a hard time playing their instruments. The combined marchers walked south on N. Broadway, past the Newhall House ruins and into Walker's Point, then west to S. Sixth and W. Florida streets, where the two processions diverged to their respective cemeteries.

After the funerals, Kate Connors's mother recognized her daughter's ring, which had been held by the coroner, and was informed that her daughter was buried in Calvary Cemetery. This dropped the number of unidentified bodies to 42. Thirty-four people were known to have been lost in the fire without identifiable remains, leaving eight victims still unnamed.

The following year, a monument was put into place in Forest Home Cemetery through the generosity of individual donations. It listed the names of 64 of the 72 victims. There was talk by the Catholics of erecting a monument for the *Lady Elgin* victims as well as the Newhall House victims. But it was just talk. The 240 Milwaukeeans who were lost on the *Lady Elgin* would have no memorial then, just as they have none to date. A short time later, a monument, just for the Newhall House victims, was erected in Calvary Cemetery, also through donations, and it listed the names of 31 Catholic victims. Neither the Forest Home nor the Calvary monument included the names of two victims identified through recent research by this author—Bridget Bridgeman, age 62, and Mollie O'Connor, age 18. Thus, the number of unknown victims is now down to six.

Information about Bridget Bridgeman, and the fact that she was lost, was reported in the newspapers. Her probate records confirm that she perished in the blaze.[10] Mollie O'Connor's name not being included is a strange omission, considering that more was printed about her than any of the other female employees. Lizzie Anglim and another employee stated that O'Connor was Anglim's roommate on the fifth floor. Mollie O'Connor was the only servant named on the hotel floor plan published after the fire. Friends contacted her uncle, Stephen O'Connor, in Columbus, Ohio, with news of her death. When O'Connor came to town he told the story of Mollie's earlier life. She was born during the Civil War after her father joined the Union Army and never returned. When Mollie was an infant, her mother went insane and Mollie was taken in by a wealthy woman who died while Mollie was still a child. Her benefactor left money to a Pennsylvania convent for her care and education. Mollie was a good student and finished school when she was 16 years old, then came to Milwaukee. A friend who had contacted Mollie's uncle told him that she recognized Mollie's body at the morgue, which meant Mollie had jumped to her death. The assistant coroner told O'Connor that the body was claimed as Augusta Giese's by her brother and taken to the family home and then buried in Union Cemetery. Stephen O'Connor showed up at the Giese's door with his lawyer and an order to turn the body over to O'Connor. The Gieses apparently proved that the body was their daughter's because cemetery records show that Augusta Giese's body is still interred in Union Cemetery. That would indicate that Mollie remained in the burning building and was one of the remains discovered in the ruins, which fit with Lizzie Anglim's statement that she, Lizzie, ran through flames near the elevator with Mollie following her. As she ran downstairs, herself on fire, Lizzie glanced back and saw her roommate fall, her clothes on fire, on the steps above her.

Of the 66 known victims, 33 were either born in Ireland or raised by parents who were born there, and 29 of those were employees. Ten were German employees. The rest were guests: one African American, two Scotsmen, and twenty Yankees. Because most of the longterm boarders and employees lived on the upper floors, where the fatalities were higher, at least 59 of those who died were local people. The out-of-towners were lodged on the safer, lower floors and only seven of the known dead were non-Milwaukeeans. Four of the six unknown victims may have been

The Newhall House monument in Calvary Cemetery. (Photograph by the author)

employees. Ben Tice, the Newhall House's head clerk and bookkeeper, reported that 45 employees were lost, but only 41 employees are known victims.

Tice also said there were 67 employees in the hotel and 110 guests, for a total of 177 people in the building. Since 72 were known to have died, 105 should have survived, and there is evidence for the names of 104 survivors. This makes estimates that there may have been up to 90 victims of the fire groundless. Of the survivors, 13 were boarders, 63 were out-of-towners, and the rest employees. Many of the survivors went, or were taken, to nearby hotels, while others boarded trains and left town. Some who left, later read newspaper accounts that listed their names among the missing, and telegraphed authorities that they were safe, or if they were not on the list, notifying them that they had, in fact, been at the hotel.

On the morning of the fire, friends and family had crowded the morgue to identify victims. All were appalled at how the bodies in the morgue were treated—strewn about, naked, and in filthy conditions. The coroner was heavily criticized, and the criticism got stronger when the remains from the ruins were brought to the morgue and one box was set down roughly and a skull fell out. There were calls for the coroner to be removed for incompetency and inhumanity, but he managed to retain his job. Third Warder Hannah Kenneally, the aunt of victim Maggie

Sullivan, said the morgue was a disgrace and she was warmly praised for her work in cleaning and dressing not only her niece, but other victims as well.

A Fire Relief Fund was organized almost immediately. General Thumb and company gave two benefit performances two days later to standing room only crowds. The orchestra donated its services, and the sum of $735 was raised to help survivors who lost their possessions and for the families of victims. Other benefit performances were given in Milwaukee, Detroit, and Racine. The *Milwaukee Journal* started a fund for fireman hero Herman Stauss, but he requested that it be added to the general relief fund to help those who lost their jobs at the hotel. The Humane Society, which at that time dealt with humans as well as animals, cared for 14 injured employees, lodging them in private homes and hotels, and providing them with two sets of clothes. The society also contributed food to the Gillon family, which lost two sons who had provided the only support for the household.

Traveling salesmen donated $400 to the Commercial Travelers Fund, only to find that there were no salesmen in the Newhall House fire who needed financial help. The fund was then donated to employees who had survived and lost all their possessions. Twenty former employees received $20 in cash or were given the equivalent in the clothing, mittens, and overshoes needed for the cold winter.

The city's newspapers were unanimous in the opinion that the Newhall House was a firetrap. But the *Journal*, which had begun publishing only a few weeks earlier, wanted to place the responsibility for the deaths on the proprietor, John F. Antisdel, and the building's owners, led by Charles Nash, banker and treasurer of the Northwestern Mutual Life Insurance Company. The newspaper demanded their arrest. The *Journal* claimed that Antisdel was a liar and that he knew the hotel was a firetrap, which was why he refused to live in it himself. Articles alleged that Nash was greedy and that his grasping pursuit of money led to his dried-up, shriveled soul.[11] It was stated that Nash wanted a prorated refund on his property taxes, because they were paid through May and the building burned down in January. The newspaper's research showed that Nash had actually last paid taxes the previous May for 1882, and that he still owed taxes for the ten days in 1883 before the hotel burned. The Journal led off each article about the fire by printing an advertisement which had appeared in the *Milwaukee Sunday Telegraph* ten days before the fire:

Newhall House. Milwaukee, Wisconsin. John F Antisdel and Son, proprietors. Great reduction in rates. Room and Board $2, $2.50 and $3 per day. Bake and Dwight's patent fire escape provides means of exit from every floor in case of emergency. THE HOTEL EMPLOYEES ARE KEPT IN TRAINING AS A FIRE DEPARTMENT ON EVERY FLOOR, and every floor is supplied with water and hose.

The coroner's inquest jury would find that the advertisement was very misleading. There were the two fire escapes, but that was not enough; one on the alley side would have saved many lives. None of the fire escape exit doors were marked in any way and there was no signage pointing to

The Newhall House monument in Forest Home Cemetery. (FindaGrave.com, Newhall House Fire Monument)

them, so the doors to the fire escapes were mostly a secret. Witnesses testified that, a few weeks before the fire, at least one hose on the upper floors was rotten and that the other hoses were hanging on pegs, not on reels, making them difficult to unroll.

The city immediately began an intensive inspection of all buildings in town over two stories. Some hotels and other buildings were forced to install iron balconies beneath the level of the windows of all stories above the second floor, with an iron ladder between balconies. Hotels were also required to have an alarm bell or bells to warn guests. The Newhall House had a bell over the courtyard but the rope to ring it had rotted and fallen off.

The jury heard that Antisdel's claim that "THE HOTEL EMPLOYEES ARE KEPT IN TRAINING AS A FIRE DEPARTMENT ON EVERY FLOOR," was a fabrication. Under questioning, Antisdel admitted that he never trained any employee to fight fires and every employee questioned told the same story: they had not been trained. Despite the jury finding Antisdel guilty of negligence, he was not charged with any wrongdoing.

For any hotel to get the best fire insurance rates, it had to employ a watchman for each floor. The Newhall House had only one watchman, William McKenzie, and he had many duties to fulfill. He shined shoes, made transportation arrangements, filled in for the night clerk, and ran the elevator, leaving him little time to watch for fires. The jury found that the proprietors were guilty of culpable negligence in not employing more watchmen, but no charges were issued.

Antisdel and Nash did not want to accept any responsibility for the disaster. Both said everyone could have been saved if McKenzie, Delaney, and Linehan had awoken everyone in the building, ignoring the fact that they had been told to do otherwise, and neglecting to mention that John Antisdel Jr. was there too, and that he made no attempt to help anyone. Antisdel blamed his female employees for their deaths, claiming that the servants who jumped had no self-control, and the ones who burned were dallying because "that class had a weakness for waiting to collect their 'little all,'" as he referred to their possessions.[12] Nash said it was too bad the fire occurred while the servants were sleeping, causing them to lose control when they woke up. Neither man blamed any of their paying guests for dying.

The jury found that the Fire Department could have done a better job if it had more men on each truck, as well as the best quality extension ladders and firefighters well versed in their use. In Chicago, they said the Newhall House and their Tremont House were comparable, but in Chicago there would have been 21 steam engines to pump water, while Milwaukee had only 7 engines. Fire Chief Lippert resigned a month after the fire and was replaced by James Foley, who would become a highly-regarded fire chief. The disaster led to the city more than doubling the number of firemen and the amount of firefighting equipment. During the next nine years, up to the time of Third Ward Fire of 1892, the number of fire engines increased from seven to sixteen, ladder trucks from three to seven, chemical engines from one to seven, and a firefighting tug was added to the department's arsenal.

The jury also found that the telegraph wires had hindered the firefighting efforts. Over the next eight years, some downtown wires were buried. In 1892, the city passed an ordinance requiring that all of them be put underground. The fire was on the front page of every newspaper in the country, often for several days, and the danger of telegraph and telephone wires in downtown areas became a national issue.

The largest death toll in a United States hotel fire prior to the Newhall House fire appears to have been 14 people when the Southern Hotel in St. Louis burned in 1877.[13] The Newhall House's 72 deaths scared travelers and city officials all over the country. Hotel clerks in Chicago and New York complained that guests did not want rooms above the third floor. As in Milwaukee, the largest cities began requiring more inspections and more safety features in their buildings, such as enclosing elevator shafts in steel to prevent the rapid spread of fire. No one will ever know how many lives were saved due to changes made nationwide because of the Newhall House fire. Certainly, there were many. For example, three years later the Chicago Club House burned, and fifteen people were saved by a bridge put in place because of the Milwaukee disaster.

The jury also reached the conclusion, shared by just about everyone involved, that the fire was set intentionally. The one thing that employees and management agreed on was that the areas near the elevator shaft were kept free of anything that would easily burn because of the previous attempt at arson in the same place two years earlier.

Six days after the fire, George Scheller, keeper of the Newhall House barroom, was arrested and charged with arson. He was taken to an undisclosed location to avoid an attempted lynching by some Third Ward and Tory Hill residents. Scheller's attorney claimed that groups were forming on nearly every corner of the Third Ward and were talking hard about Scheller, but newspapers reported that there had been no lynching discussions. The Irish wrath was not directed at Scheller; it was focused on John Antisdel and Charles Nash. Third Ward resident Catherine Kelly, who lost her 20-year-old daughter, Lizzie, in the fire, spoke for many when she expressed her hope about where Antisdel and Nash would spend their very hot eternities.

George Scheller leased the bar and the billiard room from Antisdel, who in turn leased it, and most of the rest of the building, from the Newhall House owners. When questioned by the police, Scheller said he left the Newhall House bar at 2:30 the morning of the fire. His wife said, based on the time he got home, he must have left the bar closer to 3:30. Scheller had been gambling with friends between the time he left work and the time he got home, and the time discrepancy put him under scrutiny. He had been drinking a lot in recent months and asking acquaintances to lend him money. He was not doing well at the Newhall House and wanted to find a different location. The police reasoned that Scheller started the fire for insurance money. They also said it was suspicious that there were no billiard balls in the ruins, meaning he must have removed all seven sets of the expensive ivory balls before the fire. That theory was spoiled when some badly burned and split billiard balls were found in the ruins soon after. Scheller was tried and acquitted after two hours of jury deliberation.

The arsonist or arsonists were never discovered.

Many of the jobs at the Newhall House had been filled by Third Ward and Tory Hill residents from the time it opened. Bridget Bridgeman and Mary Conroy had worked there almost from the beginning, but most employees were much younger. Like the Owens girls from Tory Hill, Mary and Margaret, both in their early 20s, and Third Warders, Bessie Brown, 17, and Willie, 17, and Walter Gillon, 15, all of whom died. Jobs at the Newhall House were also a path away from the farm and drew young people from as far away as the Wisconsin Dells. There were more opportunities in the city, and farm life was not easy, so people had been leaving the farm and coming to Milwaukee since the Civil War ended. Now, in coffins, some were going back. Among them were: Julia Fogerty, 20, to Oconomowoc; Mary McDade, 25, to Mukwanago;

Mary McMahon, 25, to Seven Mile Creek; and Bridget O'Connell, 25, to the Dells. Two young German employees had only been in the United States for a few months: Ottilie Waltersdorf, 18, died from jumping, while Mathilda Tiegs, 19, made her escape down the servants' stairs and survived.

The *Journal*'s attacks on the proprietors and owners of the Newhall House were unique among the city's newspapers and appealed to a lot of people. The newspaper went from just barely existing a month earlier to being able to claim, three weeks after the fire, that it had the largest circulation of any newspaper in Milwaukee.

"Please help a poor woman who was in the Newhall Fire," read the sign over Mary McGuire's stand on the Wisconsin Avenue bridge.[14] She sold apples, candy, and peanuts, but because she had little money, the items she sold were of low quality, which resulted in low sales. She was described as an old woman, over 50, living in a room in Tory Hill but about to be evicted. McGuire, seriously burned, had crawled across a ladder over the alley the morning the Newhall House burned, and like her surviving coworkers, she had lost her job. The Relief Committee gave her $20 for her troubles.

There were those who tried to profit from the tragedy. Ida Daniels, an 18-year-old servant at the Newhall House, was first listed as missing, then later as a survivor. She was neither; she did not stay at the hotel the night it burned. She gave the Relief Committee a long list of expensive items she claimed to have lost, but they wisely rejected her story. Daniels begged on the streets, repeating her sad story often enough to collect $60. She was nabbed and turned over to the American Humane Society. They sent her out of town, so she would not be arrested. W. G. Dickey, a con man, collected money for Newhall House sufferers and then spent it in Chicago, where he told tales of having lost all in the fire to a group of merchants there. He was wined and dined as a sort of hero, but lost stature when he passed bad checks for their goods, after which they had him arrested.

The surviving employees were hopeful that the Newhall House would be replaced by another hotel where they could eventually get jobs, but there were no investors interested in the project. It would need a high occupancy rate to be successful, and the thinking was that the Plankinton House and a new hotel would just draw business away from each other.

A song, "The Milwaukee Fire or the Burning of the Newhall House," was written by J. W. Kelley shortly after the disaster. (Library of Congress)

Instead, a new office building for the Northwestern Mutual Life Insurance Company headquarters was built on the site. Today, after more than 125 years of housing offices, the building is again being used as a hotel, the Hilton Garden Inn.

Shortly after John Gilbert Donahue's astonishing recovery after jumping from the fifth floor, he sued John Antisdel and the Newhall House Company. He claimed that Antisdel falsely advertised that the hotel employees were trained to put out fires, and because they were not trained, and because they did not put out the fire, his wife was dead, and his career was ruined. Donahue won a settlement from the defendants, but his career, as it turned out, was not ruined. He continued touring, and each time he came to town he stayed at the Plankinton House, but never in a room above the second floor.

Tory Hill Gets Smaller

The core of Tory Hill today is literally concrete. Freeways, ramps, and streets cover the former neighborhood. The first bite was taken out of the neighborhood in 1885. The Milwaukee Road decided to build a railroad station on W. Clybourn Street between N. Third and N. Fourth streets, and the spur to the station would need to run through part of Tory Hill.

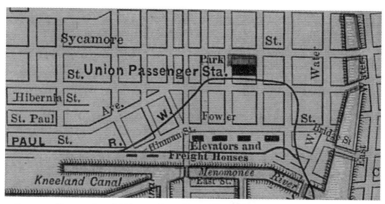

A spur from the Milwaukee Road's main line to the Union Passenger Station displaced 48 Tory Hill homes near Hinman Street. (American Geographical Society Library, University of Wisconsin-Milwaukee Libraries)

The city passed an ordinance condemning the property of 48 residents to allow railroad tracks to cross their land, but the amounts offered were considered too low. After an uproar by those residents, a satisfactory settlement was made between property owners and the railroad. The spur was built from N. Seventh Street and W. St. Paul Avenue to the new station at Union Square at N. Third and W. Clybourn streets. Most of the displaced residents did not want to leave Tory Hill and continued to live in the neighborhood.

The Sheridan Guard and the Bay View Massacre

The Wisconsin State Militia made the decision in 1884 to divide the state into four zones, with Milwaukee being the fourth zone, and the four companies in the city becoming known as the Fourth Battalion. The Sheridan Guard, as the oldest company, was designated Company A. The Polish company, the Kosciusko Guard, was called Company B, and the two German companies became C and D. A battalion staff was created with appointed officers in command. While companies were still allowed to elect their own officers, they were losing some identity and autonomy.

After nearly two decades in existence, the Sheridan Guard was known statewide for its drilling and shooting abilities. It had practiced and displayed its skills in parades and competitions. When it was finally called upon to provide actual militia services, the consequences were fatal.

In 1886, it was nearly impossible for unskilled workers to have satisfying lives. Most were paid between $1.25 and $1.50 per day. It was barely enough to live on and required ten to twelve hours of labor each day, six days a week. Many such workers joined the national Knights of Labor, which promoted an eight-hour workday at ten hours pay, leaving time for family, social, recreational, and cultural activities. One local influential employer, Edward P. Allis, seemed to agree, saying, "I believe 8 hours ought, and would under proper conditions, be sufficient for any man's daily support."[15] He would later accept his skilled workers having an eight-hour work day, but his unskilled employees either were not "under proper conditions" or not men, because he would not allow them the same benefit.

The loosely-knit Knights of Labor selected May 1 as the target date for the shorter work day. Workers around the country and in Milwaukee began striking at factories and workshops in February, and by late April it seemed they all would be on the eight-hour workday. Milwaukee strikes were relatively peaceful, but in a Texas incident, six people were killed or wounded in a battle between police and strikers, and in East St. Louis, nine strikers were killed and many more were wounded by deputies.

By Monday, May 3, there were still some large Milwaukee factories that had not agreed to worker demands and were still in operation. South Side strikers, mostly Polish, marched to those businesses and tried to convince workers, skilled and unskilled, to join them, and if that didn't work, many had clubs to try to physically force workers to leave their job sites. Mobs of strikers threw bricks and rocks at buildings of non-compliers and threatened to burn them down. Some workers fought back; those at Allis's plant used water hoses to disperse their attackers. Fearing more violence, most owners closed their factories.

That same day, Chicago police opened fire on strikers, killing at least two and wounding many others. Spooked by the Chicago turmoil, Milwaukee business leaders put pressure on local and state politicians to call out the Guard. The governor, Jeremiah Rusk, and his military advisors came to Milwaukee to take charge of the situation.

It did not help the South Side strikers' cause that they were Polish. As the most recent immigrant group, they were now the ones most looked down upon. That many did not speak English was held against them. They were not well liked by Germans and they were in a heavily German city. The *Sentinel* editorialized that the Polish were ignorant, illiterate, and had a harder time learning English than other immigrants. They were also hot-blooded and impulsive, "as is shown by the frequent rows that occur in their churches."[16] The newspaper did not have a problem with routinely using the derogatory term "Polack" in its news reporting, referring to a "Polack laborer," a "Polack woman," and even "Polack babies." The paper reported that the public was appalled at the destruction of property and violence against non-strikers by these "foreigners."

Early Tuesday morning, May 4, about 3,000 Polish strikers marched south from W. Mitchell Street to the rolling mills on E. Lincoln Avenue and S. Bay Street in Bay View, the last large factory to stay open, with the intention of forcing it to close. A committee of strikers discussed the situation with company officials, who told them they paid their workers by the ton of iron produced. Since time did not factor into this policy, they could not comply with the eight-hour plan. Additionally, the company's skilled workers refused to leave their jobs. But still, the strikers were determined to close the plant.

About 9 a.m., there were five double strikes on all fire bells in the city; the governor had called out the Fourth Battalion of the National Guard under Major George Traeumer. Two of the four companies, the Sheridan Guard and Lincoln Guard, the latter a German company, assembled at the armory on N. Broadway between E. Wisconsin Avenue and E. Mason Street. Sheridan Guard Captain John E. Coogan addressed the guardsmen after each had been given 20 rounds of ammunition, "... wait for the order to fire before you pull a trigger. And when you do fire, take an aim; pick out your man and kill him."[17] When the companies marched into the street from the armory, they were greeted by throngs of people lining the street, either loudly cheering or stridently jeering. As the guardsmen marched toward E. Wisconsin Avenue, "A number of vicious looking Polacks, armed with big clubs, shook them menacingly at the passing militia."[18]

The companies continued to the North Western Railway Station at the foot of E. Wisconsin Avenue, where they boarded a special train bound for the rolling mills. On the train they began singing "Marching through Georgia," "John Brown's Body," and other popular martial melodies. On the way to Bay View, the train made stops at stations along the way and picked up other militiamen.[19] At the Bay View station they were greeted by strikers screaming insults and threats. The militia was there to protect property, and their goal was to get through the company's gate and keep the strikers out. There wasn't enough room to get off the train and into formation, so each man had to push through the hostile crowd single file. A second train arrived, bringing the Polish Kosciusko Guard, and the guardsmen joined the queue that was pushing their way to the gates. They received the full wrath of the Polish strikers for opposing their countrymen. When the last few guardsmen in line were attacked by strikers, and others were showered with stones, some members of the company fired over the heads of the crowd, driving them back.

The strikers massed outside the gates throughout the afternoon, throwing stones over the fences, or trying to climb over them, and they beat two German guardsmen who were trying to report for duty. Eventually, the four militia companies all made it inside the factory complex, where the plant was closed and the workmen had been sent home. Guardsmen inside the compound had little to do as the day passed, except get hungry. At 6 p.m., a tugboat arrived at the mill's pier with the makings for sandwiches for the famished men. The four Milwaukee companies were joined later by two companies from Janesville, after the First Regiment was called to the city from communities across the southern part of the Wisconsin. The six companies spent an unpleasant night at the mills as the temperature dropped into the 40s along the shore of a cold Lake Michigan, and there were few overcoats or blankets to keep them warm. In Chicago, at Haymarket Square, a dynamite bomb thrown at police, and subsequent police gunfire, left eight dead and dozens wounded.

Wednesday morning, May 5, the governor sent word to Major Traeumer and the company captains to shoot at the crowd if it returned to the mills and did not disperse. A crowd gathered at St. Stanislaus Church, then moved down S. Kinnickinnic Avenue and E. Bay Street to the mills. What the 1,500 to 2,000 people were going to do is not known. They could not close the factory since it was closed already. They could not force the workers out because there were no workers. Battalion leader Traeumer said he was told that the strikers' goal was to "clear out the militia and set fire to the mills."[20] When the mob was about 600 feet from the gates, Traeumer ordered them to stop. At that distance, and with the noise the crowd was making, no striker could possibly have heard Traeumer's demand; they were also too far away to be any threat. But the soldiers had no problem hearing his order to fire. Four of the companies were on low ground and could not shoot because they were unable to see the crowd on the hill above. John Coogan's Sheridan Guard and

The Rolling Mills in Bay View was the site of the "Bay View Massacre." (Library of Congress Geography and Map Division)

Janesville's Bower City Rifles, who were on higher ground, each fired a volley. Nearly twenty of the seventy or eighty bullets fired found a target, killing five people, two of them innocent bystanders, and injuring others. All but one of those killed or wounded were Polish. As the strikers ran away, Traeumer ordered his men to march through the gates with fixed bayonets to assure that they did not come back.

On Thursday, May 6, the strike was over, and the streets were quiet. The Sheridan Guard and the rest of the Fourth Battalion were still at the rolling mills, exhausted, having had little sleep since Monday night. Most of the city's 170,000 people were relieved that the lawlessness of several thousand people had stopped. The strike had not been a success and the eight-hour workday was still decades away for most Americans.

On Friday, May 7, the 200 men of the battalion were finally dismissed. As the Sheridan Guard marched from the railroad station to their armory, there were spectators lining the streets, but they were mostly quiet. When the governor invited company officers to dine at the Plankinton House, they declined, saying they preferred to stay with their men. Rusk quickly changed his invitation to include all the men of the battalion and they spent the afternoon feasting at the hotel. Saturday, the wives of business leaders provided a banquet for the battalion at the armory in appreciation for their work in the "Battle of Bay View," more commonly remembered as the "Bay View Massacre."

Nationally and statewide, Rusk was considered a hero, and locally

Bay View's Rolling Mill marker discusses the "Bay View Massacre." (Photograph by the author)

Captain John Coogan's stock also went up. Coogan was a Tory Hill merchant, who was born in 1848 near Menomonee Falls to Irish immigrants from counties Kildare and Meath. He was offered a spot on the Republican ticket to run for County Treasurer, a position frequently filled by a Democratic Irishman, but he refused to run under any circumstances.

The Sheridan Guard presented Coogan with "an exceedingly handsome" sword and belt in appreciation for his leadership.[21] A few days after the riots, a group of 25 Irish women formed the Young Ladies' Legion, a sort of auxiliary of the Sheridan Guard. They requested that they drill under the direction of Captain Coogan and they named him president of the organization.

The riots also spurred the organization of at least three new militia companies in the city. One of those was formed by young Irishmen of Holy Name Catholic Church at N. 11th and W. State streets. Known initially as the Holy Name Cadets, the company name was changed to the Chapman Guard, honoring Chandler Chapman, the state's adjutant general. With some members as young as 16 years old, the company excelled. In its first year, the company ranked fifth of forty-two companies in the state in drilling and worked its way up to third place two years later. With the youngest officers of any company in the state, it was accepted into the National Guard as Company G of the Milwaukee Battalion 18 months after being formed.[22]

Home Rule for Ireland?

After the Land League movement fizzled out, Charles Stewart Parnell and the Home Rule Party of the English Parliament pushed for a bill to create an Irish parliament within the United Kingdom. With the support of English Prime Minister William Gladstone in 1886, Home Rule seemed a distinct possibility, and American Irish quickly showed their support by raising funds to support the Irish Parliamentary Party. Milwaukeeans, with significant financial support from German brewers Philip Best, Joseph Schlitz, and others, raised more money in proportion to the population than any other city in the United States, and enthusiasm and optimism were at a high point.[23]

William P. O'Connor, former captain of the Sheridan Guard, said of the bill that he felt "a great deal as the negroes felt when the emancipation proclamation was issued."[24] Comments from influential Irish in the city called it "a glorious thing for Ireland," "a grand effort," and "a great achievement." One man who was interviewed, John P. Murphy, was unimpressed, saying "it cannot be expected to go through."[25] He was right; the bill was defeated in the House of Commons.

The Home Rule fight continued, but it received another major setback in 1890 when it was revealed that Parnell was involved in a longterm, intimate relationship with a married woman, Kitty O'Shea. The Catholic Church in Ireland, along with many of Parnell's supporters, turned against him. Milwaukee's Irish leaders were divided on the issue. The city's newly elected mayor, Peter Somers, meatpacker Patrick Cudahy, and others called for Parnell's resignation. Others, like Jeremiah Quin, felt that it was a social issue, not a political one, and that Parnell should be supported. Most were disappointed that Parnell would imperil the cause and Judge Joseph Donnelly was so upset that he refused to even comment on the subject.

When Parnell died a year later, the city's Irish were hopeful that the Home Rule factions would be united, and that some autonomy for Ireland would become a reality. A Home Rule Bill passed the House of Commons in 1893 but was vetoed by the House of Lords. As would be seen later, it would take more than talk for the Irish to gain any measure of independence.

Chapter 7

1890–1899

The only data that exists from the 1890 census are the summaries; the actual censuses were destroyed by fire. The summaries show that there were 3,436 Irish-born people in Milwaukee's population of 204,000.[1] When considering the number of Irish Americans in the city whose parents or grandparents were born in Ireland, the percent of Milwaukeeans of Irish ancestry was probably close to eight percent.

Milwaukee's Third Irish Mayor

Peter J. Somers was born in Waukesha County in 1850 to County Roscommon natives Peter Somers Sr. and Honora Fitzgerald. In the early 1870s, he came to Milwaukee to study law and begin his practice. He served as president of the Hibernian Benevolent Society and was a member of the Sheridan Guard. In 1881 he went to Ireland to visit relatives in County Roscommon, and when he returned to Milwaukee he predicted that there would be armed rebellion in Ireland because of the poor treatment by the English. He estimated that 40,000 Irishmen could overtake every fort and barracks there. Back in Milwaukee, he was elected city attorney for two years, notwithstanding his opponent's claim that Somers, with his lengthy tresses, was "long on hair but short on law."[2]

1890 was a very busy year for Somers. In the spring elections he was elected alderman, defeating his German opponent by a large majority in the predominately German Ninth Ward. Despite his lack of experience, his peers immediately, and unanimously, elected him President of the

Before being elected an alderman and then mayor, Peter Somers ran for city attorney. His opponent claimed that Somers was "long on hair and short on law." (*Men of Progress, Wisconsin,* 1897)

Common Council. When the mayor, George Peck, resigned in November, Somers was elected mayor in the most Germanic city in the United States, also by a large majority, and was sworn in on December 6 of that year. He joined Hans Crocker and Edward O'Neill on the list of Milwaukee's Democratic Irish mayors.

Somers was re-elected in 1892 but did not complete his second term because he was elected to the United States Congress. At the end of his stint as a congressman, Somers retired from public life. He left Milwaukee in 1905 and died in Los Angeles, California, in 1924.

Even with Somers's success, the influence of the Irish in local politics was on the wane. As their percent of the population went down, so did their percent in the Democratic Party. They could no longer force deals with one faction against the other. Polish immigrants vastly outnumbered the Irish, so they became the group that could determine the balance. Additionally, the Irish were losing a center of power as the Third Ward became less Irish, with residents leaving for better neighborhoods. The next Irish-American mayor of Milwaukee would not be a Democrat, but a Socialist.

The Third Ward Fire

A massive low-pressure system over Lake Superior brought high winds and warm temperatures to Milwaukee on October 28, 1892. It also brought more destruction than the city had ever seen. In the Third Ward, 20 city blocks were completely or partially burned out by a windswept fire. Four hundred and sixty-five buildings, mostly small homes, were destroyed. More than 350 families, the majority of whom were Irish, were made homeless, and another 150 families had damage to their homes and furnishings. Five lives were lost, and the conflagration hastened the decline of the city's largest Irish neighborhood.

Early that Friday afternoon, the temperature was in the low 60s and the southwest wind was 38 miles per hour. Due to the unexpected warmth, a stranger asked a worker at the stable behind Kissinger's Wholesale Liquors on N. Water Street if he could leave his coat there while he worked nearby. By 3:30 the wind had switched to the northwest and increased to 50 miles per hour, which classified it as a strong gale. Dust and debris peppered store windows along N. Water Street and N. Broadway, and blowing newspapers collected in doorways. Signs detached from buildings, as did a few chimneys and roofs. Hats blown off by the gale had little chance of being recovered. Out on Lake Michigan, dozens of ships would be capsized or run aground.

The wind made fires especially dangerous. There were 18 fires in Milwaukee besides the Third Ward Fire that day. Five fire alarms were turned in during the hour before John Miller, a shipping clerk at the Union Oil and Paint Company on N. Water Street, left work with two fellow employees. The fact that Miller's wife was ill wound up saving their lives. Normal quitting time was 6 p.m., but Miller wanted to go home to her, and his coworkers had no problem leaving early, so they locked up at eighteen minutes to six and walked out into the night. The three had taken only a few steps down the sidewalk when there was an explosion from inside the building, showering glass onto N. Water Street. The investigation after the fire determined that the blast in the structure, located on the Milwaukee River midway between E. St. Paul Avenue and E. Buffalo Street, was probably due to spontaneous combustion caused

The fire boat *Cataract* was similar to the one pictured above. *(Wikivisually)*

by oily rags improperly stored. Miller's coworker, Jacob Mollerus, stated that if they had closed at the normal time, "we would certainly have been blown to atoms."[3] At Kissinger's stables, the stranger returned for his coat but stayed to help the stable hand in caring for the horses.

Thomas Patrick Dever, a broker whose business was located at E. St. Paul Avenue and N. Water Street, turned in the fire alarm at that corner at seventeen minutes to six, but because the fire companies were busy at other fires, no help came until six o'clock. Hundreds of shoppers, employees getting out of work, and people from the neighborhood watched fire pour from the building. The city's first fire boat, the three-year-old *Cataract*, under the command of Third Ward resident Captain Jeremiah O'Sullivan, was the first on the scene and began pouring water on the fire at the rate of 5,500 gallons per minute through a dozen 3.5-inch hoses.

Another Third Warder, Fire Chief James Foley, had left a fire at S. 16th Street and W. Greenfield Avenue and was headed for still another fire, at the Allis plant in Walker's Point, when he saw that the sky was lit up over the Third Ward. He detoured there to coordinate the firefighting efforts. The wind turned some of the streams from the hoses into a useless spray, but the efforts seemed be paying off. At 6:30 p.m., the excitement seemed over—the flames were gone and there was just black smoke streaming from the building—and most of the spectators went on their way. But at 6:45, flames shot up again and the howling gale, now from due west, sent sparks and pieces of burning material eastward. The buildings on the east side of N. Water Street did not seem to be in danger, but at 7 p.m. the burning debris started the seven-story Bub and Kipp upholstery building on N. Broadway and E. Buffalo Street, a block to the east, on fire. The burning material either landed on the roof or went into the building through an open window. The fire burned downward and in 20 minutes "the whole building came down in a heap," sending flames to surrounding buildings.[4]

Across N. Broadway, a wholesale grocery building began to burn, and then others caught fire. People began to gather again in the area to watch the spectacle. A three-story vacant building on N. Broadway burned so quickly that the crowd was just barely able to avoid being crushed as the façade crashed down onto the street. The burning sky above the Third Ward was drawing people from all over the city. An estimated 200,000 spectators would fill streets, bridges, docks, boats, and every other conceivable viewing space until dawn. It was said that if you were a Milwaukeean and were not there, you were either an invalid, an infant, or in jail.

With the wind shifting between the west and the north, the fire roared south down N. Broadway, and buildings that had been spared earlier on N. Water Street and N. Broadway began to burn. The stranger stayed to help remove the stable animals to safety. Bystanders yelled at him to save himself just as a wall collapsed, obscuring him from view.

Pleas for assistance were sent to fire departments within 100 miles of Milwaukee. A half dozen fire alarms sounded in other parts of the city. It was now certain that the fire would consume everything to the east until it reached Lake Michigan. Anyone living north of the Third Ward was thankful that the wind was coming from the west and northwest, and not from the south or southwest like the wind that fanned the Chicago Fire of 1871. A southerly wind could have destroyed the city from the Third Ward north to the city limits.

The fire department concentrated its efforts on the larger buildings more resistant to fire on N. Water Street and N. Broadway. A tug made repeated trips to supply the *Cataract* with the coal needed to keep it pumping river water on the fires. Fire engines, or "steamers," pumped more water on buildings on N. Water and E. Erie streets to try to prevent them from catching fire. But there was no point in trying to save the frame buildings to the east of N. Broadway, which were mostly two-story wooden cottages with wooden sheds and wooden outhouses in back.

Those not fighting the fire tried their best to remove as much from the fire's path as possible. Tug men were busy all night providing services to firemen as well as clearing vessels from Third Ward docks, the biggest and most expensive first. Employees at the freight yards east of the residential area worked to remove freight cars filled with merchandise from the path of the fire. Eight locomotives managed to push or pull about two hundred cars south across the river, but when the trainmen tried taking a burning car toward the river, the police, fearing the fire would be carried to Walker's Point, drew their revolvers and ordered that all train traffic be stopped.

In the residential area, the tiny 20-foot-wide lots meant that many of the little white wooden cottages were virtually touching. In many cases the only way to access the back yards, which were dotted with wooden outhouses, sheds, and barns, was to go through the houses or from the alleys. The barns housed everything from cows to pigs to horses to fowl. Many of the cottage windows were covered with green blinds. Gated fences enclosed many front yards and willow trees lined the blocks. Most yards had lilac bushes, which lent the Ward a pleasant fragrance in late spring, the only time of the year that neighborhood scents were agreeable.

For years people had looked at the Third Ward, with the small wooden buildings crowded together, and prayed that such a fire would never happen. Now it had, and a wall of flame was bearing down on them. Hundreds of residents had to make split-second decisions about what to take from their homes. For others, the fire moved so fast that there was no opportunity to save anything, not even a coat or jacket for protection in the now falling temperatures. People were racing back and forth, carrying items to relative safety in every kind of conveyance possible. In some instances, throwing or pushing furnishings out of windows was the quickest way to try to save them. A few people stored their belongings in a livery barn on E. Buffalo Street, assuming it to be safe from the fire. It wasn't, and the barn burned down with its contents. The entire police force was called out and many policemen helped residents gather their belongings. In the chaos, a young man, one of the "freaks of the city," rode his bicycle through the burning streets, shouting insults at people but encouraging the police and firemen.[5]

Teamster James McCarthy emptied sand from his wagon, hitched his team to it, and helped his neighbors load their furnishings onto it. But the furnishings and wagon began burning. McCarthy unhitched his horses and saved them, but the rest was lost. Michael McCormick, a

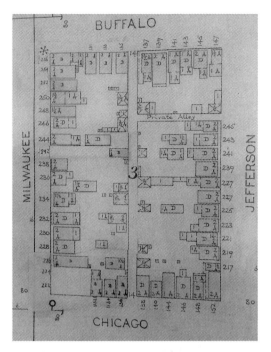

This fire insurance map shows how close the houses in the Third Ward were to one another. (*Rascher's Fire Insurance Atlas,* 1876 updated)

bridgetender, rushed to his home on E. Chicago Street to see his wife and their 11 children to safety, but neither he nor his brother, Tim, who lived next door, was able to save anything else. George Robinson, a 70-year-old man who had not walked in years, walked quite well as he quickly left his burning home on N. Milwaukee Street. Patrolman James Halsey was stationed on N. Water Street, but as the flames spread east his worry increased. His fear got the best of him and he ran to his home on E. Chicago Street near N. Jackson Street. He found his wife, Maria, so hysterical and out of control that he needed the help of fellow officer Cornelius Sullivan in removing her from their house, which, with everything in it, would soon be ashes.

One home that burned was that of William Aylward who, along with his brother, Philip, survived the sinking of the *Lady Elgin*. As fire approached his non-insured house, his neighbors, who had insurance, helped him remove his furnishings to safety rather than their own. It was reported that there were other instances of the insured sacrificing for the uninsured. Nearby, Maria Sullivan was attempting to leave the Third Ward and cross to Walker's Point on the railroad trestle with her baby in her arms. The fierce wind kept pushing her perilously close to the edge. She was nearly overwhelmed with relief when a man came along and helped the two across the bridge.

Some families were split up and parents feared the worst. James McManus, another *Lady Elgin* survivor who lost his first wife and sister-in-law in that disaster, now lost his house, and he and his wife could not find any of their six children. After hours of frantic searching, two children were found on the Broadway Bridge, another in Walker's Point, and three more at the Cathedral of St. John, where many went to escape the sinking temperatures, made colder by the strong wind.

Except for the Rose Callahan family, all Third Ward families were eventually reunited. Callahan, 35, was a widow of 10 years. She was raising two teenage daughters in their N. Milwaukee Street home, but her bad heart severely limited her capabilities. Neighbors took her to the Third Ward School, on the northeast corner of E. St. Paul Avenue and N. Jackson Street, where hundreds of residents were seeking shelter. She died there of heart failure.

Policeman Herman Marquardt went into a small cottage on E. Buffalo Street and carried out a frail Mary O'Brien, 63. Marquardt placed her in a grocery wagon and wheeled her to the emergency hospital, but she died on the way. Another Third Ward resident, Irish-born Margaret Reiter, 23, also was in poor health, and the exposure she suffered when she was removed from her home led to her death almost three weeks later.

"My canary, my canary, please save my canary," pleaded a young woman on E. Chicago Street to Deputy Sheriff John Abert. "I don't care if everything burns, please save my canary."[6] She pointed upstairs where Abert saw smoke and decided the bird was not worth the risk. He did save the reluctant young woman though.

There were reports that a great number of thieves were pillaging the houses of all that was valuable. On the fringes of the fire, some people sat in the cold with their possessions, afraid that they would be taken if left unprotected. In one reported incident, when John Kneeland carried his wife's trunk out of his burning house, a stranger offered to carry it to safety, but Kneeland later was unable to find it.

In another story, a man went to his burning house, took off his coat and set it on his fence, then went in to see what he could save. When he carried out a piece of furniture, his coat was gone. He went in for another item and when he came out, the first piece was missing.

Mary Smith, a widow on N. Jefferson Street, left her house just north of the burned area, but when it did not burn she returned and found the house ransacked and her money taken, although the thief's guilt got the better of him and he returned the money the next day.

Residents later said that reports of widespread looting were overstated, and many possessions thought to have been stolen were later recovered along the edges of what became known as the "burned district." The "looters" were mostly just helpful neighbors. There was not much of monetary value in this poor neighborhood to draw looters anyway.

One newspaper noted that the fire produced a study of Irish character, where everyone was trying to help one another and the "awful occasion could not stop outbursts of witticism."[7] Another reported a remark from one Irishman to another, "I knew such thumping, bumping Irishmen as you and me would burn together, but, begorra, I didn't know it would be so soon."[8]

After the fire raced through the residential area, it reached the freight yards. Two wooden freight buildings on N. Jackson Street between E. Buffalo and E. Menomonee streets, each a block long, started to burn. Between the buildings and the lake was nothing but freight cars, filled with a wide range of products. There was no water available to fight the fires, and neither buildings nor cars eluded the blaze. Even the planks and the top of the supports of the piers on the lakefront burned. Two of the freight cars held a total of twenty-five hundred geese and half a dozen men decided these birds were worth saving. Why should they roast for nothing? They broke through security lines and ran to the cars on the verge of burning and helped the geese escape. As the birds flapped and fluttered around the railroad tracks, the crowd chased them. Hundreds of geese found at least a temporary lease on life, but the rest perished.

On E. Michigan Street, a wagon filled with household goods, topped off with the family's two geese, worked its way through the crowded street when a fire engine approached from the other direction. The frightened geese flew off the wagon and onto the heads of onlookers, causing a small riot. Other animals fared better. Horses and cows from the Third Ward dispersed by the conflagration were later found wandering other parts of the city.

A dozen men took advantage of a burning saloon. A two-story shanty on N. Broadway provided whiskey free for the taking for those not afraid of the fires around them. While firemen aimed their hoses on the shanty, the men grabbed as many bottles as they could carry and ran off, delighted at their good luck. Also on N. Broadway, a vacant lot at E. Chicago Street, just north of the fire station, was hoped to be a buffer that would save the building. It did not, and the six-year-old fire station burned, the only fire station to be lost to fire in the city's history.

About 9 p.m., a huge explosion shook the ground. Most of the thousands of people who heard the blast assumed that the gasworks near E. Corcoran Avenue had blown up. But the explosion was caused by three kegs of dynamite that had been placed inside a building at the northwest corner of N. Broadway and E. Chicago Street by firefighters. The idea was that when the fire reached the building, the dynamite would explode, demolishing the building and preventing the fire from spreading to other buildings. It did not work. The wind was too strong, and the buildings were too densely packed for this firefighting technique.

Down at the gasworks, foreman Thomas Powers and a crew were fighting fires in the wooden structures around the works. His own home burned while Powers prevented what many had feared, the explosion of the gas holding tanks. Powers temporarily increased the pressure in the gas lines to clear them out. Gas lights throughout the city briefly blazed brighter, sputtered, and then went out. The move allowed Powers, who was proclaimed a hero, to lower the holding tanks below ground level and keep them safe from the fires. The parts of the city lit by gas suffered dark nights until the following Wednesday. Those who prepared their food on gas stoves were in for a few days of cold dinners.

The police could not handle everything that needed to be done. Crowd control was becoming an issue. The densely-packed crowd just north of the burning district was hampering firefighting operations as well as clogging up the streets, where fleeing residents were placing their possessions. The decision was made to call out the National Guard and buglers were sent through the crowds, calling to duty those belonging to the Guard. The first group of 50 guardsmen, under the command of Lieutenant John Manion of the Sheridan Guard, was deployed to clear the crowds from E. Clybourn Street. They were more effective than the police; a soldier with a bayonet was more intimidating than a policeman with a billy club.

Two guardsmen, the Winters brothers from the Third Ward, became heroes. They heard cries of distress from a burning cottage on E. Buffalo Street and rushed into the building. They emerged moments later with a mother and two babies in their arms, receiving prolonged cheers from those who watched. Another 150 militiamen joined in crowd control and worked to keep non-residents away from the burned district until the next afternoon.

Everyone on Jones Island, a fishing village south of the blaze, was on high alert for any sparks or embers coming their way. An unrelated fire broke out to the south in Walker's Point and several homes were destroyed. One spectator of the Third Ward Fire would later return to his Walker's Point house to find it ashes.

The Kenosha Fire Department was the first outside help to arrive when they reached Milwaukee at 9:57 p.m. after a 57-minute train trip. They brought along 1,300 feet of hose and set up near E. Erie Street and E. Corcoran Avenue. Mayor Peter Somers was there to help them set up their equipment, string out their hoses, and attach them to fire hydrants. Somers had been helping residents remove their possessions from burning homes and inspired onlookers to pitch in and help. One newspaper said the mayor was "a man to the very backbone and every inch a hero."[9]

Meanwhile, three large buildings on E. Buffalo Street caught fire simultaneously. The alcohol in the National Distilling Company assured that the entire block would burn. A tobacco warehouse burned, the tobacco giving the flames a blue tint. A building collapsed at E. Buffalo and N. Water streets and it showered bricks on a fire engine at the intersection. Ropes were attached to the engine and it was pulled to safety with the help of bystanders and was able to be used again. Three other engines started to burn but the fire department saved them, and they soon went back into use.

Shortly after the Kenosha Fire Department set up, the Racine firefighting contingent made it to the Third Ward. After being delayed by a broken-down locomotive, the Racine company still should have arrived before the Kenoshans, but they had to wait on a siding at the Milwaukee County line. The Kenosha train had priority and 16 Racine firemen fumed in frustration as they watched it pass them by. They would soon be stationed near the Kenosha firefighters on E. Erie Street. The Oshkosh Fire Department arrived with a fire engine, seven men, and a hose cart on a North Western train. Perhaps because they were unfamiliar with the city, the Oshkosh engine ended up on N. Prospect Avenue and did not help until the fire was under control.

The fires lit up and highlighted the newly built Pabst Building, a towering 14-story structure on N. Water Street and E. Wisconsin Avenue, against the night sky. The lighted sky over the city could be seen from Sheboygan to Waukegan. By far the brightest flames of the night were produced when a series of explosions in the Hilbert Chemical Company building on N. Water Street caused a "brilliant pyrotechnic display."[10] A store near the Broadway Bridge burned and its stock of fireworks exploded, providing another show. The fire at the Hanson malt elevator was a great spectacle, with green flames shooting high into the air from the tallest structure in the Ward. Some streets were carpeted with smoke as the wooden cedar pavers slowly burned. Stone pavers on other streets would warp and crack and need to be replaced.

By midnight the fire was contained. While there was still a "mountain of fire" on N. Water Street and many buildings were burning, there were no new fires. All the fire departments were still pouring water on fires, and the Chicago and Sheboygan firefighters would soon join them. Due to a series of mishaps, the Chicagoans, who left Chicago at 9 p.m., took over three and a half hours to reach Milwaukee. The Sheboyganites, who could not leave until they put out a fire in their own city, arrived at 3 a.m.

At 1 a.m., Chief Foley was with a crew working on the fires at the dynamited factory when the walls collapsed, killing two firefighters and injuring the chief. Charles Stahr, a truckman married only a year, left a wife and elderly mother. Henry Peddenbruch, 34, a pipeman, left a widow and three children.

The temperature dropped into the thirties, the wind was still strong, and more than 2,000 cold people, many of them broken-hearted and all of them miserable, did not have their warm homes to go to or their warm beds to sleep in. For the 300 women and children who slept on the bare floors of the rooms and corridors of the Third Ward School, it was at least warm, but their sleep was often broken by the sobs of those who had lost so much. The Cathedral of St. John was being redecorated and the walls were being painted, so scaffolding was taking up a lot of the

Many of the people left homeless spent the next few days living in the Third Ward School, on the northeast corner of E. St. Paul Avenue and N. Jackson Street. (Author's collection)

open floor space of the church. The vestibule and the last pews were filled with a jumble of cookery, bedding, trunks, sewing machines, clothing, furniture, and pictures brought to the church by the refugees. The other pews were filled with people trying to be as comfortable as possible. A man in one pew who had gone to his home only to find it burned down, said, "I cried and for the first time in years."[11] People were not any happier at St. Gall's Church on N. Third and W. Michigan streets, which was also filled with fire refugees and their possessions. Others spent the night in police stations or in the nearby North Western Railway Station at the foot of E. Wisconsin Avenue.

For several hundred other victims, things were better. There were 100 vacant rooms at the prestigious Plankinton House and more vacancies at the Pabst Hotel, and each offered their empty rooms free of charge to those who were burned out. So, over 200 newly homeless people were not only able to sleep in comfortable beds, but they also ate the hotels' excellent food. Some of the sufferers, as they were routinely referred to, were invited off the streets by fellow citizens who offered a warm place in their own homes to sleep. Many went to stay with relatives and friends in other parts of the city.

186

Regardless of where they slept, daybreak threw a light on what they had lost. Two girls were now orphans, three children had lost their father, and two women were widowed. About 2,500 people lost their homes and many lost some or all their worldly goods. Many lost their livelihood. The burning of factories, warehouses, and shops meant that 300 Ward men were without jobs. A half dozen people were injured but not seriously.

With the National Guard still standing duty, many residents went back to their homes in the morning to sift through the ashes, but with such small lots, it was not always easy to find which ashes to sift through. One resident said, "I have lived somewhere about here for the past fifty years, but I'm danged if I can tell where."[12] Most of them found nothing but ashes, but John Finan was lucky. In his haste the previous night, he had he left his house on N. Milwaukee Street without taking $125 in gold. He found it in the debris of his burned house.

At 9 a.m. on Saturday morning, the Chamber of Commerce met to discuss the needs of the homeless. Firemen continued to pour water on the fires that still burned and knocked down walls that posed a danger. Most of the buildings between E. St. Paul and E. Corcoran avenues east of N. Water Street were lost. The freight cars and railroad tracks at the freight yards were twisted into odd shapes. Workers cleaned up anything that was not burning or smoldering. Barley, oats, wheat, and many other products that had been stored in freight cars were in various states of ruin. Railroad officials reacted very quickly by sending wagons loaded with lumber for 200 carpenters to begin building new freight buildings, and one would be completed the next day. Burned railroad ties and twisted tracks were quickly replaced.

New poles were put up to hold new wires for electric streetcars, as well as telephone and telegraph lines. It was noted that the walls of the 40-year-old Union Oil and Paint Company building, the origin of the fire, were still standing, while the walls of newer buildings had fallen. The reason, it was observed, was that buildings in earlier times were built with more craftsmanship and better materials than the inferior construction of the buildings of the day.

The Chamber of Commerce organized the Third Ward Fire Relief Committee. The first order of business for the committee was to assure that the homeless were fed. Two thousand meal tickets for food at restaurants, hotels, and boardinghouses were disbursed. As a guideline for

The Third Ward fire started in the Union Oil and Paint Company building (center) on N. Water Street. (*After the Fire: 18 Photogravures*, 1892)

relief efforts, the committee used a publication detailing the experiences of the victims of the great Chicago Fire of 1871. The weather was becoming wintery, so providing clothing and shelter were the next items on the agenda. Donated food and clothing were already arriving at the Third Ward School.

Shelter was more challenging in the long run, but the school, churches, hotels, and other places were still willing to provide refuge from the elements temporarily. A plan was made to match available rental units with those who needed to rent, and a suggestion to build barracks for the victims was discussed. Mayor Somers wanted to employ those who had lost jobs in cleaning up the Third Ward. The committee felt it would be necessary to raise $100,000 to adequately take care of the homeless. Within six hours over $55,000 was donated, with former Milwaukeean Philip Armour, the Milwaukee Brewers Association, and a group of Democratic candidates topping the long list with contributions of $5,000 each.

That weekend, every train coming into Milwaukee was filled with farmers and other curiosity seekers from the surrounding areas. Every streetcar coming to the Third Ward was jammed. At 1 p.m. Saturday afternoon, the Guard was sent home and thousands of people entered the burned district. They wanted to see the destruction. Some, like the farmer who brought his lunch, wanted to take pictures. With his Kodak, he took a picture of a woman crying at the site of her former home. Others dug in the debris for souvenirs and gloated when they found a knife or a pot lid or a piece of melted glass. One woman in an expensive coat walked away with the handle of a pail and a set of bed castors. Having searched the ruins earlier in the day, residents resented the outsiders but there was not much they could do about it, so they stayed away and let the relic hunters have their way.

Over the weekend, circulars were passed throughout the Ward announcing that on Monday, those with insurance would be able to settle quickly so they could rebuild immediately. However, it was estimated that only about one in ten residents had any insurance, while most of the commercial buildings were covered. On Sunday, another 1,000 meal tickets were distributed, and fire crews continued their work.

There was talk that the burning of hundreds of homes was a blessing in disguise, that now better buildings could be built, resulting in better use of valuable property. The burned-out manufacturers could move to the newly developing industrial suburbs and their factories could be replaced by warehouses that could benefit from the water transportation and railroad facilities in the Ward. The Real Estate Board, a private organization that represented the interests of Milwaukee real estate dealers, said the fire was good for another reason, in that it drove out "a lot of people of ill-repute."[13] Third Ward alderman Cornelius Corcoran, who lost his home and grocery store in the fire, retorted that there were no people of that type in the Ward.

Monday it rained, and the rain ran through the ashes, creating little pools of lye. Over 100 men, mostly those who had lost their jobs, were hired by their former employers to clear up the debris created by the fire. Others were hired to dig in the rubble of business buildings, with the hope that they could locate safes that had been advertised as fireproof. Two voting booths for the presidential elections to be held the following week were built to replace those burned. Rose Callahan, Mary O'Brien, and fireman Charles Stahr were buried at Calvary Cemetery, the Catholic graveyard on W. Blue Mound Road. Men worked on repairing the gas lines at the gasworks, but that night businesses were closed and events cancelled throughout the city due to darkness. Guests at the Plankinton House were guided to their rooms by the light of candles stuck in Pabst bottles.

Victims lined up at the Third Ward School to receive donated clothing, and officers Halsey and O'Brien were there to ensure that it was done on a first come, first served basis. More donations of baby clothing were needed. Women around the city were sewing garments for the sufferers. One newspaper reported that later some donors of clothes felt a strange sensation when they saw other people wearing garments that used to be theirs. One man told a story of following a woman he thought was his wife because of her apparel, only to realize when he got closer that the woman was not his wife but his washerwoman. Another remarked on the incongruity of seeing a dirty-faced, ragged-haired Irish boy strutting down E. St. Paul Avenue in an expensive suit.

Another 1,500 meal tickets were distributed on that Monday. The Relief Fund reached nearly $100,000, but it was now estimated that another $50,000 would be required. There were more donations of money from individuals, businesses, and societies, and additional funds were raised by fairs, as well as by musical and theatrical benefit performances.

The committee decided that each destitute family, excluding any with insurance over $300, would receive $50, with an additional $5 for each dependent. The money was for a few weeks of food, clothing, rent, and other expenses, and totaled $21,565 paid to 356 families. Able-bodied single men would not receive any help.

In addition to the general Third Ward Fire Fund, specialized donations were made. The Gas Company donated a total of $5,000 to its employees who had lost their homes. The Hibernian Society gave money to its members who were victims. The *Milwaukee Sentinel* started a fund for the families of the dead firefighters, who were not Third Ward residents and not eligible to receive relief funds. Each burned-out member of St. Gall's and St. John's churches was given $25, as were members of the St. Patrick Foresters. The Master Plumbers association paid $50 to every journeyman plumber member who lost his home. The Letter Carriers Association helped affected members. The County Board Chairman, Timothy Driscoll, who lived with his father whose house burned down, proposed that the county give $5,000 in aid, but that proposal fell flat. Among the first to settle with the insurance adjusters was Bridget Gallagher of N. Milwaukee Street, who received $600.

The editors of newspapers around the country expressed their opinions on the fire. The *New York Mail* said there was too much prosperity and energy in this "model Western city" to be set back for long. Some said that Chicago, Boston, and Portland all had suffered major devastation and came out of it better than before, and they predicted the same for Milwaukee. The city was praised for taking care of its own and not requesting the help of others.

Tuesday the cleanup and repair work continued. Despite Monday's rain, the ruins were still hot and burning in some places. The Relief Fund now had over $110,000 in donations. Over 1,700 people had been supplied with clothing and another 1,500 meal tickets were dispersed. The committee decided that 30 large barracks would be built in Mitchell Park on S. Layton Boulevard, which was not close to Downtown, but was said to be the best option available.

Firefighter Peddenbruch was buried at Forest Home Cemetery. One woman, claiming to be the mother of five children, was turned away by relief workers because the previous day she was given clothing as the mother of twenty-one children. John Magee collected $65 for living expenses but returned it when he found that his wife had already received their allotment of $65.

On Wednesday, the body of the stranger was found under the collapsed walls at Kissinger's. His remains, what there were of them,

This residential block was totally destroyed.
(*After the Fire: 18 Photogravures*, 1892)

were buried on the grounds of the County Poor Farm. City newspapers printed lists of the people displaced by the fire and the addresses where they could currently be found. Although they were scattered around the city, they were told to vote in the Third Ward the following Tuesday. The number of meal tickets given out dropped dramatically to 500, and the relief committee was working to find jobs for the unemployed. All the supposed fireproof safes were recovered, but only one of them had protected its contents; the rest held only fragments and ashes.

Mitchell Park was taken out of the running as the site for the barracks. The park had recently been the first of the city's parks to be landscaped with new trees and shrubs, and some plantings would have had to be removed. There also was concern that the rest would be destroyed by barracks' tenants. Unimproved Lake Park was now considered the best site for the temporary housing, and it was agreed that any barracks would have to be removed during the following spring. The gasworks was repaired and that night lights once again burned brightly throughout the city.

Over the next few days, the *Milwaukee Journal,* the Democratic newspaper, announced that they would cancel any debts owed them by those burned out and that they would continue to provide subscribers with newspapers until they were able to pay. A local furniture store also cancelled any debts, saying that it was not fair to make people keep paying for furniture they no longer had. There was still a lot of residents' furniture along the streets north of the burned district, particularly on N. Prospect and N. Farwell avenues, but much had been ruined by the elements. The relief committee decided that Lake Park was too far away and thought that maybe the barracks should be built in the streets of the Third Ward. Regarding the fire, the *Wisconsin Afro-American* commented, "The colored people, (like everything else), were not in it. We are glad of that."[14]

Meanwhile, some of those who lost their homes were applying for building permits. Some wooden homes, a few saloons, and shops were springing up in the Ward. A few of the houses were cheap, flimsy, wooden shanties built to get their owners through the winter. Alderman Corcoran had a frame building moved from another part of the city and placed on his lot, where he reopened his grocery store.

The Real Estate Board reiterated its position that residences should not be rebuilt in the Third Ward, which was, according to them, suitable for warehouses only. Residents would not use the shipping facilities there, but businesses would. The Board wanted the city's fire limits, which up to this time only included commercial districts, extended so that residents would need to follow more fire-resistant building codes too. The codes would not allow any wooden structures without a brick veneer, but the brick requirement would double the cost, making it impossible for many residents to rebuild. In the Third Ward, buildings west of N. Milwaukee Street were within the fire limits, while those to the east did not have building codes.

By Thursday, the relief committee had helped 475 families and about 2,500 people. While the majority of those helped were Irish, there were also German families, some Italians, a few Polish, and three "olive skinned foreigners from the borders of the Red sea."[15] The Italians were causing some consternation within the committee because they all gave the same address of 246 N. Milwaukee Street. The building at that address was large, but not large enough to house nearly 100 Italians.

The Relief Committee was now leaning toward not building any barracks because there did not seem to be much need for them. They agreed to pay hospital and funeral expenses for those who suffered injuries or death.

A week after the fire, after the furniture that had been donated ran out, the committee determined that each family would receive $70 to $100 for furniture, depending on the family size. Over 360 families received this grant. New donations brought the fund total to $128,000. There were now fewer than 200 requests for meal tickets. Building Inspector Theodore Schuetz decided, without any authorization, that he would not issue any more building permits to those who wanted to build outside the fire limits, his rationale being that the city council should apply the building codes to the entire ward. He also said he would not issue any permits to build temporary housing, because an owner might stay permanently. This put residents in a position where they could not use their lots at all.

To add insult to injury, Matthew Parkhurst, a Yankee Hill minister at the Summerfield Methodist Church, caused a minor uproar when he gave a sermon claiming that 75 percent of all relief funds were being spent in saloons. Relief workers who had been dealing with the misery suffered by their clients denounced Parkhurst in the strongest terms and said he had done no investigating and had no evidence to support his false claims. They claimed that if Parkhurst had spent any time helping the unfortunates, he would not have said anything so absurd. Parkhurst said no more on the subject.

Two weeks after the conflagration, meal tickets were no longer being given out. The Third Ward School opened to a smaller student body. The building had been cleaned and was no longer serving as a relief distribution center, a task that was shifted to the Exposition Building on N. Sixth and W. State streets. But with residents scattered, there were fewer students when classes resumed. The school once claimed the highest attendance in the city; it even had a branch at one time. Now, the enrollment was lower than the minimum needed for it to be considered a district school, so there was talk of downgrading it to a primary school. Principal Patrick Donnelly wasn't thrilled with the idea; it would reduce his annual salary.

The Relief Committee said it would pay for replacing school books that were lost in the fire, and it found rental units for 40 homeless families. There were some complaints about the insurance adjusters' settlements. Mrs. Cornelius Smith carried a $500 policy on her E. Buffalo Street house, but the adjuster only would pay $350 because, he said, her home had depreciated. Ellen Lynch had her claim rejected because her home was leased, not owned, a distinction the insurance company was not concerned with when it accepted her premiums. The relief organization's Advisory Committee stepped in and helped the claimants in their dealings with the insurance companies. The adjusters were accused of being "guilty of trimming and of browbeating and bulldozing" insured residents.[16] Most businesses fared better with their insurance adjusters, but some cases ended in the courts and took several years to settle. The Third Ward Fire cost insurance companies $3,000,000, about 10 times their losses for an average year in Milwaukee. Overall, fire insurance rates went up in the city because, as one newspaper stated, the insurance companies had to make their profit in addition to paying high salaries to their officers.

By mid-November, the Relief Committee had found jobs for 33 men. They found that some men could not find work in their trade because their tools had burned, so they paid for tool replacement. The Relief Fund reached $135,000, and barracks for eight families were built in Lake Park.

One month after the fire, residents who had received building
before Schuetz's decision to stop issuing them had built dozens
wooden homes in the burned-out district. A temporary fire statio
set up in a barn on N. Jefferson and E. Clybourn streets until a new st
could be built. The city council considered extending the fire limits in
Third Ward, but the Ward's two aldermen, Cornelius Corcoran and I
Foley, objected because the Fourth, Fifth, and Seventh wards were n
included. This prompted the council to pass an ordinance that all fou
wards would have these stricter building codes. Third Warders converged
on the building inspector's office to obtain permits before Mayor Somers
signed the ordinance. The inspector issued a dozen permits and then
stopped, citing the city attorney's opinion that no permits for frame
houses could be issued. Those who were refused permits went home
extremely angry.

They were livid when they reached Schuetz's office the next day and
found a note on the door saying he had a cold and would not be in to
work. His deputy, George Krueger, refused to open the office because
he was afraid of the "wild Third Warders." The irritated permit seekers
quickly formed two committees. Patrick Murray, James Hogan, Thomas
Corcoran, Cornelius Sullivan, John Daly, and John Gallagher were

Fire Chief James Foley. (*Milwaukee
Sentinel*, March 20, 1898)

or. The women formed a second committee
chuetz showed up. He did not.

z did show up and the first thing he did was
not opening the office the previous day. Krueger
d said he would quit rather than open the office and
ird Ward women that Schuetz would not give permits
was resolved to the satisfaction of residents when Mayor
e would veto the ordinance because it was illegal; there had
pportunity for the people in the Third Ward to express their
on the topic.

nd the people of the Third Ward had plenty of opinions. In a petition
he Council they pointed out that the fire had started within the fire
mits, not outside the fire limits where they lived. They also said that
historically their neighborhood had fewer fires that any other similarly-
sized section of the city. They charged that the Real Estate Board was
talking up the fire danger so its members could buy the residential land
at low prices and then sell it at higher commercial rates. The petitioners
pleaded, "Do not deliver us over to the sharks who are sharpening their
teeth that they may fatten on the misfortunes of the poor." To the Real
Estate Board's assertion that the land was too valuable for the residents
to live on, they retorted, "If our property has become valuable who is
entitled to the reward, the patient toiler, or the greedy corporation and
grasping speculator?" The Third Warders said they had resided there in
peace for half a century and "here let us die."[17] The council did not have
enough votes to override Somers's veto, so residents were allowed permits
to rebuild. Aldermen finally did extend the fire limits in 1895.

In December, the source of the Third Ward Fire—the embers
blowing from the Union Oil and Paint Company building to Bub and
Kipp's furniture factory—came briefly into question. There had been a
rash of 13 major fires in November and December, killing and injuring
more firemen, and arson was suspected. Throughout the city, people
worried about where the next fire would be. Chief Foley thought all these
fires, including the one in the Third Ward, were started by firebugs.

Police investigators disagreed that arson played a role. One theory was
that the fires were started by members of the upholsterer's union because
Bub and Kipp's and two other burned buildings housed upholsterers, but
that did not explain the other fires. Another theory was that they were

set by disgruntled employees or that the owners were doing it themselves. Still another idea was that it was just bad luck and that big fires come in batches. The *Wisconsin Afro-American* took a different view when it said, "It looks as though Milwaukee is doomed to be burned up. Well, it has been said that 'the wicked will burn.'"[18]

At the end of December, Mayor Somers and Governor George Peck offered a $5,000 reward to anyone offering evidence that would convict the firebugs. The police force was increased by 100 men who would look for arsonists. But after two weeks with no major fires developing, the 100 extra police were let go. After more time with no significant fires, the general feeling was that the fire spree was just bad luck. And no one questioned that a spontaneous combustion at the Union Oil building was the source of the Third Ward Fire.

The Relief Fund ultimately reached a total of $138,000 in donations, which were used as follows: $1,260 for meal tickets; $37,440 in initial living expenses; $32,335 for furniture; $5,065 for clothing, shoes, etc.; $11,009 in special aid; $1,729 for tools; $208 for school books; $1,479 for doctor, hospital, and funeral expenses; $45,000 in permanent aid (estimated); and the balance in general expenses and incidentals.

The category for permanent aid was to support those who were "unable to earn their bread"—women, widows, and the aged. People who suffered from other disasters were added to the rolls of those receiving aid, including seven families who lost their homes the same night as the Third Ward Fire. The fund also gave aid to the families of some local men who drowned during a storm the following spring while working on the water intake in Lake Michigan that was to be used to flush the filth from the Milwaukee River into the lake. The Third Ward Fire Relief Fund was totally depleted in December 1895, when 22 widows were each given $10.07.

Rebuilding the Ward took much longer than expected. The members of the Real Estate Board had been raking in money for many years. It was a time of prosperity; the great economic expansion of the 1880s continued into the early 1890s. New neighborhoods were being developed and suburbs were rising from farmers' fields. The *Catholic Citizen* opined that Third Ward residents would find better housing in other parts of the city, and that they had benefitted from the quadrupling of land values in the Third Ward over the preceding ten years. But speculators were driving up the price of land beyond reason. And then the worst economic depression the country had seen arrived with the Panic of 1893.

Banks, railroads, and many businesses failed. The effect was worst in industrial cities, where nearly 20 percent of workers lost their jobs. Real estate values plummeted. Residents who had lost their homes to the fire and had no insurance could not afford to rebuild; nor could those without jobs. The 1895 ordinance requiring a brick veneer on all new construction in the Ward, effectively doubling the cost of building a new home, all but eliminated the possibility of rebuilding. Two years later it was noted that Ward construction was picking up, but it took the rest of the decade before it was completed. There were significantly fewer cottages and many fewer residents than before the fire, but more businesses and warehouses. There were calls to eliminate the Third Ward, which had a smaller population than the state's legal minimum required to form a city ward.

In one generation, between 1860 and 1892, three major disasters had befallen the Irish in the Third Ward: The *Lady Elgin* Disaster, the Newhall House Fire, and now the Third Ward Fire, all focusing their misery in this one neighborhood. It would be difficult to find Irish residents of the Ward who had not been affected by at least one of the disasters, and many had been affected by more than one.

As mentioned earlier, William Aylward and James McManus were both survivors of the *Lady Elgin* and both lost their homes to the fire, as did Martin Eviston and John Roper, other *Lady Elgin* survivors. The Irish-born Roper was a policeman at the time of the Newhall House fire and helped in fighting that blaze. Hannah Kenneally lost her niece, Maggie Sullivan, in the Newhall House fire and her home in the Third Ward Fire. Others, like Ann Malone and James Hoye, who lost their homes in this fire, also lost family members on the *Lady Elgin*. Malone lost her son, James, 19, and Hoye lost his wife, Hannah. Fire Chief James Foley and Alderman Paul Foley lost their father, Paul Sr., their brother, William, and cousin, Bridget Foley, in the sinking of the *Lady Elgin*. Thomas P. Dever, who turned in the Third Ward Fire alarm, was the son of *Lady Elgin* survivor William Dever, an Irish-born Milwaukee policeman who served with the ill-fated Union Guard.

Those who did not return to the Ward scattered throughout the city. The largest number moved to Tory Hill and further west, in a swath between the northern bluffs of the Menomonee River Valley and W.

Highland Avenue. Many others moved north to the East Side. Still others went to Walker's Point and west along the Menomonee River Valley. Some made their homes in the new manufacturing suburbs of Cudahy, South Milwaukee, and North Milwaukee, where they found employment.

Merrill Park, The New—and Last— Irish Neighborhood

The scattering of the Third Ward Irish meant that they took up residence in more ethnically diverse neighborhoods. Enough of them relocated to Merrill Park, centered around St. Rose of Lima parish at N. 30th and W. Michigan streets, though, that it was considered a new Irish neighborhood. It was not as densely Irish as either Tory Hill or the residential section of the Third Ward had been during their heydays, but the Irish were the largest ethnic group in Merrill Park. There were Germans, Yankees, and English there, and possibly the non-Irish outnumbered the Irish. But the Irish dominated the area's politics and held the better jobs at the Milwaukee Road railroad works located in the Menomonee River Valley below. The Merrill Park neighborhood was bordered by W. Wisconsin Avenue south to W. Park Hill Avenue between N. 27th and N. 35th streets, and from W. St. Paul Avenue south to W. Park Hill Avenue between N. 35th and N. 39th streets.

Most of the men in the neighborhood worked for the Milwaukee Road. The Irish had worked on the trains for decades as engineers, firemen, brakemen, and switchmen; positions that received higher wages. The non-Irish were paid less for jobs in the shops such as carpenters, machinists, and sweepers.[19] Like the Third Ward and Tory Hill, Merrill Park was near railroad yards and suffered from the soot and noise they generated. During the 1920s, some of the families that could afford it began to move from the neighborhood. And as in the two older Irish neighborhoods, new rail tracks replaced some of the homes in Merrill Park. These tracks were laid for rapid transit to the western suburbs. Rooming and boarding houses replaced some homes and the neighborhood lost some of its residential feel.

During the Great Depression of the 1930s, residents suffered without work, but World War II generated full employment. After the war, the exodus of Irish from the neighborhood continued, and they were replaced

Merrill Park was Milwaukee's last Irish neighborhood. (Photograph by the author)

by absentee landlords and people looking for low rents. By mid-century, Merrill Park was no longer an Irish neighborhood. The Irish were dispersed throughout the city and suburbs to such an extent that there were no longer any Irish neighborhoods in Milwaukee.

New Irish Catholic Churches

The Third Ward Fire sparked the growth of not only St. Rose parish, but also of the new parishes of Holy Rosary and St. Matthew. By 1884, the parish of the Cathedral of St. John had grown too big to administer, so it was divided into two parishes. Holy Rosary Church, on N. Oakland Avenue at E. LaFayette Place, was founded to serve the northern section of the old parish as a mission of St. John's Cathedral. Development of the new parish began slowly. William McGill was appointed the pastor of the new church, but he continued to live at Cathedral. Parishioners who had attended the Cathedral's services, school, and a wide range of other activities throughout their lives were reluctant make the change to Holy Rosary. The number who did was small, but the parish received a huge boost when the Third Ward Fire sent many new residents to the area and helped to make Holy Rosary a fully functioning parish.

To the south, St. Matthew's Church, at S. 25th and W. Scott streets, was dedicated in 1892 and held its first Mass two days after the Third Ward Fire. The church's first collection was for the fire victims, some of whom would join the congregation during the following months.

In 1894, the predominantly Irish Gesu Church was built at N. 12th Street and W. Wisconsin Avenue, replacing both Holy Name and Old St. Gall's churches. In 1895, a new, grander version of St. Patrick's Church, a structure of stone and brick, was built in Walker's Point. It served 1,500 parishioners, with an adjoining school of nearly 300 students.

Along with Immaculate Conception Church in Bay View and the Cathedral of St. John, these largely Irish parishes provided a place for their parishioners to focus their spiritual, educational, social, cultural, and recreational lives. Mass, Confession, and other church services catered to the spiritual side of parishioners, as did clerical counseling and visits

St. Patrick's church in Walker's Point. (Photograph by the author)

during times of need. Generally, students were taught by Catholic nuns at parish schools tuition-free, and for those who attended public schools, religion classes were available.

Social opportunities abounded. There was an organization for every member of the family. Sodalities, lay fellowship societies for religious and charitable purposes, existed for young boys, young girls, young women, and young men as well as married women and men. Parishioners could join choirs or ushers' groups. Joining benevolent societies provided an opportunity to visit the infirm and contribute to the needy of the parish.

The men of the congregation assisted in running their parish by serving on the church council, which decided how to raise funds to pay for church and school needs. Their role was mostly advisory because the clergy made the final decisions. As was the custom in the American Catholic Church at the time, the Archbishop held almost all the decision-making powers, and those that he didn't, the pastor did. Generally, the archbishop and other clergy were the parish's corporate officers, and the archbishop was the president of the parish boards, while the pastor was the vice-president. In keeping with the tradition of the day, women had no formal role in running the parish.

Finances were an important part of parish life. The renting of seats, known as "pew rental," became the primary means of paying the bills in parishes around the United States beginning in the early 1800s. Pewholders were entitled to sit in a reserved seat in a pew toward the front of the church for an annual fee, usually five or ten dollars, and in some cases, they were the only members of the parish given the right to vote in parish matters. Parishioners who were unwilling or unable to rent a pew were charged a door fee, or "seat money," for a seat toward the back of the church. Sunday Mass seat money charges ranged from five to ten cents.

When these revenue streams were inadequate, particularly when new buildings or equipment were needed, other sources were sought. Fundraisers like picnics, bazaars, festivals, concerts, raffles, card clubs, lectures, and dramatic performances by congregation members gave parishioners more opportunities for socializing. Parishioners had a good time while helping to fulfill parish needs. These parish activities also provided a social circle for young people and ultimately led to marriages of Irish Catholics to Irish Catholics, or at least other Catholics.

Over time, the Irish parishes were becoming less Irish as other English-speaking Catholics joined their churches, and as the Irish moved to newly created and more diverse neighborhoods. New English-speaking parishes were a mix of ethnicities. An example is St. Thomas Aquinas Church, which was organized in 1900 by Germans and Irish. The new church was constructed at N. 35th and W. Brown streets, a mile and a half north of Merrill Park. The Irish in the new parish had previously attended St. Rose's Church, but now they shared their church with English-speaking Germans. Unlike the Germans and Irish in the early days of St. John's Cathedral, the two ethnicities got along just fine, as evidenced by the many marriages between Irish and Germans documented in the parish records.

Cudahy: A Suburb Named for, and by, an Irishman

The 1880s and 1890s saw tremendous growth in manufacturing and population in the city. So much so that three new industrial suburbs were founded during the 1890s. In addition to South Milwaukee and North Milwaukee, Cudahy, a meatpacking town, was created south of the city.

The Cudahy Brothers' business had been operating in the Menomonee River Valley before it moved to the Cudahy location in 1893. In its infancy, a train running between the Third Ward and the packing plant provided workers. As housing was built in Cudahy, it drew new residents. The Irish and the Germans populated the northern section, and the Polish, the southern portion.

One potential resident that it did not draw was its founder, Patrick Cudahy. There was talk of him building a mansion on the east side of town, near Lake Michigan. But the poor relationship between owner and laborers quickly put an end to any thoughts of the Cudahys living in the same community. The family, famine era immigrants, had settled on a less common spelling of their surname, which is more typically rendered as Cuddihy. There can be little doubt that residents preferred the Cudahy family spelling to the Irish spelling of the name, Cuidighthigh.

Patrick Cudahy induced other industries to his village, and his company became one of the largest of its kind in the United States. In 1906, the community became a city, and by the mid-twentieth century it had a population of about 20,000. Today the packing plant is still in operation as a meat processing facility under the direction of a conglomerate. Patrick's brothers, John, Michael, and Edward, who also grew up in Milwaukee,

The founder of the city of Cudahy, Patrick Cudahy, was born on St. Patrick's Day in 1849. (Sculpture by Felix Weihs de Weldon)

later formed other packing plants around the country and all became very wealthy. The city of Cudahy, California, in Los Angeles County, was also named by the brothers.

The End of the Irish Militia

After the riots of 1886, neither the Sheridan nor the Chapman Guard was needed to quell any further violence in the city. Their biggest responsibility was crowd control, such as during the Third Ward Fire. Both companies were called to active duty during the Spanish-American War in 1898, marking the end of each of them as a city militia company. Being part of the Wisconsin National Guard destroyed their identity and reduced their opportunities to display themselves as crack units to the community, so they disbanded. There was talk after the war of creating a new Sheridan Guard unit, but it was just talk, and led nowhere. After 30

204

years of existence, the Sheridan Guard was no more.

The Third Ward Forever

The Third Ward began losing population in the 1880s, when the Chicago and North Western Railway bought out some residents and expanded its freight yards along Lake Michigan. Residents could keep their homes, they just needed to move them to other locations. By 1890, the number of Third Warders had dipped below 8,000, the minimum number needed for a city ward according to state law. Five years later, in the after-effects of the Third Ward Fire, the population was down to 4,500 and businesses were acquiring much of the Ward's real estate. Irish residents continued to move out faster than Italians could move in, but they still out-numbered Italians by more than two to one in 1900. The low population figures generated political pressure to eliminate the Ward by consolidating it with other wards, and to eliminate the upper grades of the Third Ward School and downgrade it to primary grades only.

Newspapers carried stories of how the Third Ward's political influence, which was always greater than its relatively small population would have indicated, was over. Obituaries of the Ward and the history of the many Irish leaders who had controlled the Ward and influenced city and county politics appeared. But the death notices were premature. The Third Ward was the birthplace of thousands of Irish Milwaukeeans and they were not happy about the possibility of losing the name of their old neighborhood. Their protests were successful—the Third Ward, and its borders, remained as they were when the city was founded.

The effort to downgrade the Third Ward School had been going on for more than a decade. As Third Ward School students completed the primary grades, many transferred to either St. Gall's or St. John's schools to complete their grade school education, leaving the Third Ward School with fewer pupils in the upper grades. The attempt to downgrade it in 1899, like others in the past, was unsuccessful, this time thanks to three "brilliant Irish orators."[20] The orators included school board directors Jeremiah Quin, James Sheridan, and Patrick Reilly, representing Tory Hill, Merrill Park, and the Third Ward respectively. They convinced the rest of the board that the per capita cost for the Third Ward School was less than that of schools in other wards, and that reducing the school to the primary grades only was not a wise economic decision.

This meant that Patrick Donnelly, who was born in Country Tyrone in 1836 and settled in Milwaukee in 1864 when he was hired as a teacher at St. Gall's School, would continue to serve as the principal of the school, a position he had held since 1873. Donnelly knew every man, woman, and child in the Ward and would continue in his position until he was in his 70s. His brother, Joseph Donnelly, was the Chief Judge of Milwaukee County's Civil Court.

Chapter 8

1900–Present

The number of Irish-born in Milwaukee in 1900 was 2,756, the lowest figure since before famine immigrants reached the city.[1] The city's population was just short of 300,000, and Irish and Irish Americans probably made up about 6 to 8 percent of that figure.

The number of city residents born in Ireland continued to decline, and by 1940 there were fewer than 600.[2] As the number of Irish-born went down, the number of residents of Irish descent continued to rise. By 2013, 160,000 people in the Milwaukee metro area, 8 percent of the population, claimed at least partial Irish ancestry.[3]

Irish Intermarriage

Due to a variety of factors, the Irish in Milwaukee did not marry outside of their ethnicity in great numbers during the nineteenth century. The most populous immigrant group in the city, the Germans, generally lived in German neighborhoods, and only about one third of them were Catholic. Many Germans could not speak English; they had no need to learn it. They were taught in German schools, they shopped in German stores, they went to German banks, and they worked in German shops. Many belonged to a higher economic class than the Irish, and there was a stigma attached to Germans who married the lowly Irish. The second largest immigrant group, the Polish, were Catholic, but many did not speak English and they were concentrated in Polish neighborhoods. Yankees were generally not Catholics and they were not anxious to marry

Irish Catholics.

In the twentieth century, the frequency of intermarriage began to increase as the Irish moved up the economic ladder. World War I cast a different light on being German in America, and Germans spoke their language less and English more. Newer neighborhoods in the city and the developing suburbs were ethnically mixed, as were the new Catholic parishes. St. Thomas Aquinas and St. Sebastian's in the city, as well as St. Frederick's in Cudahy and St. Bernard's in Wauwatosa, saw more ethnically mixed marriages. Many of Milwaukee's new children were not just Irish or German but were Irish and German, or German and Polish, or Irish and Yankee, or any of many permutations.

James Foley, Fire Chief Hero

James Foley was the third Irishman to lead the Milwaukee Fire Department. He was appointed when Henry Lippert resigned after the Newhall House fire in 1883. Foley joined the Fire Department in 1870 at age 25, and the next year he was in Milwaukee's firefighting contingent that was sent to help battle the Great Chicago Fire.

During his 20-year term as chief, Chief Foley gained a reputation for being innovative and was highly respected by his men. He added fire boats to the department's firefighting arsenal, which proved highly effective. Foley was a hands-on chief, and that led to his death. In 1903, a leak in a nitric acid container in a building on N. Water Street caused deadly fumes that overcame responding members of the fire department. They became ill, finding it difficult to breathe, and three men died that night. Foley also became sick and commented, "I'll bet $100 I'll be a dead man before morning."[4] He was right; he died a few hours later.

Foley was one of the best-known men in the city and was respected throughout the Midwest as well. City offices were closed, and the bodies of the men who died in the incident lay in state in City Hall and were viewed by 25,000 mourners. Fire chiefs and firemen from St. Paul, Minneapolis, Chicago, and many Wisconsin cities attended Foley's funeral at Gesu Church, and thousands of spectators lined the route to Calvary Cemetery as the Chief's buggy passed. It held only Foley's white coat, folded neatly on the seat.

Governor Francis McGovern

Francis E. McGovern was the first Milwaukee Irishman to be elected governor of Wisconsin. A lawyer, he began his political career by running for district attorney in 1904, promising to drive bribery out of city government. After his election, he did what he said he would, with the guilty being heavily fined or sent to prison. He was elected governor in 1910 as a progressive Republican and continued his anti-corruption campaign at the state level. He switched to the Democratic Party during the Great Depression. McGovern was born in 1866 in Sheboygan County to immigrant parents with roots in County Mayo, and died in 1946 in Milwaukee, where he is buried in Forest Home Cemetery.

Goodbye to the Old Irish Neighborhoods

The decline of Tory Hill as an Irish neighborhood is exemplified by the ethnic makeup of W. Hibernia Avenue over a 30-year period. The street, named with the Roman word for Ireland, was between W. Clybourn Street and W. St. Paul Avenue, running from N. 9th to N. 11th streets. An analysis of the 1880 census shows that Irish made up 92 percent of the street's residents. By 1900, the Irish population had dropped to 72 percent, and by 1910 it was no longer an Irish street, with only 12

Tory Hill today is largely concrete. (Photograph by the author)

percent of the residents of Irish ancestry. The new Tory Hill residents were mainly from Eastern Europe, with many from Slovenia and Croatia.

The changeover of the Third Ward from an Irish to an Italian neighborhood also occurred between 1900 and 1910. At the turn of the century, the Irish outnumbered the Italians two to one, while ten years later, Italians outnumbered the Irish eight to one. Many of the Irish from both neighborhoods had scattered to other parts of the city.

The Third Ward Expands

The Third Ward had the lowest population of any city ward in 1910 and the ward north of it, the Seventh, had the second lowest population. Neither met the state minimum of 8,000 people. Something had to be done but no one wanted to fight the Third Ward zealots, the Irish who no longer lived there, but still felt a spiritual connection to it. So, in 1912, the two wards were combined when the Third Ward's northern boundary was moved from E. Wisconsin Avenue to E. Knapp Street, and Juneautown became part of the Third Ward. This change allowed Alderman Cornelius Corcoran to move to Yankee Hill and still live in the Third Ward. In the 1970s, ward designations were eliminated when the city was divided into aldermanic districts. Then, part of the original Third Ward, the section south of Clybourn Street, took on the name "Historic Third Ward."

World War I and Irish Independence

After England declared war on Germany in 1914, Irish leaders decided to stage a rebellion before the war ended, while the British were occupied fighting the Germans. During 1915, formal planning proceeded. In America, Irish organizations, including the Ancient Order of Hibernians, the Clan na Gael, the United Irish League, and other groups, joined to form a national organization called the Friends of Irish Freedom. The Friends supported Irish independence by petitioning the United States government for support, and by raising money to help the effort and to aid the dependents of those who would participate in the rebellion. Patrick Cudahy was a member of the Milwaukee branch and vice-president of the national organization.[5]

The Easter Rising in Dublin in April 1916 was followed by five years of guerilla warfare against British military and police personnel in Ireland, finally leading to the Anglo-Irish Treaty of 1921. The treaty created the Irish Free State and gave semi-independent status to Ireland, like that of Canada, Australia, and New Zealand. The treaty left six counties in Ulster under complete British control and created the state of Northern Ireland. The Irish Republican Army (IRA) wanted total independence for all of Ireland, and a civil war broke out between the Republicans and those supporting the Free State. The Milwaukee Council of the American Association for the Recognition of the Irish Republic encouraged Milwaukee's Irish community not to take sides, noting that it was for Ireland to decide.

The war lasted a year and was won by the Free Staters in 1923. A Milwaukee-born man, Thomas Shaughnessy Jr., had been suggested by some political leaders to serve as the first Governor General of the Free State. Shaughnessy's grandparents, George Shaughnessy and Johanna Murphy of County Limerick, brought their family to the United States and settled on a farm in Granville in 1841. One of their sons, Thomas George Shaughnessy Sr., moved to the Third Ward and married Mary Kennedy of County Kerry. He was initially employed as a constable and later as a policeman.

Thomas Jr. was born in the Third Ward in 1853. He was educated at the Third Ward School and the school at St. Gall's before he started working for the Milwaukee Road at age 16. After studying law, Shaughnessy was elected an alderman from the Third Ward and for a brief time served as president of the Common Council. He was a member of the Curran Literary Society and lieutenant in the Sheridan Guard. In

Thomas Shaughnessy, born in the Third Ward, was knighted by the king of England. (Wikimedia Commons)

1880, Shaughnessy married Bridget Nagle of Tory Hill, who came from County Clare. In 1882, he was hired by the fledgling Canadian Pacific Railway and moved to Montreal, Canada. Nine years later he was named vice-president of the railroad and at age forty-six became its president. Because his leadership of the Canadian Pacific railroad was so important in the development of Canada, Shaughnessy was knighted by the King of England in 1901, and in 1916 he was made Baron of the City of Montreal and of Ashford in County Limerick, where his father was born.

Thomas Shaughnessy, now Lord Shaughnessy, was a supporter of the Irish Free State, and was considered by some to be the right man to run that country. Some thought his Irish ancestry would satisfy the Irish; that he was born in the United States would appeal to the Americans; and that he had become a Canadian citizen would please the Canadians. Shaughnessy was not interested, saying, "I have enough work to do just now without looking for a new job."[6] It is unlikely that anyone but an Irishman would have been accepted as Governor General anyway. Timothy Healy of County Cork was elevated to that position.

Ties Weaken

Now that Ireland had a measure of independence and the issues that had inspired the city's Irish for more than 80 years no longer existed, the ties between Milwaukee's Irish and Ireland were weakening. Repeal of the Acts of Union, the famines, the Young Irelanders, the Fenians, the Land League, and Home Rule were all in the past. There were only about 1,500 Irish-born in Milwaukee in 1920 and the many thousands with Irish ancestry were Americans now and they focused on their lives in the United States.

In 1937, the Irish Free State became the Republic of Ireland and, except for the six Ulster counties that formed Northern Ireland, which was part of the United Kingdom, the country was independent. One Milwaukee Irishman was in Ireland to watch the transformation. He was John Cudahy, the son of immigrant Patrick Cudahy and a United States diplomat to the Irish Free State and then to the Irish Republic.

In 1941, the Ancient Order of Hibernians held their last picnic in the city before they would be re-formed later in the century. In December, Pearl Harbor was attacked, and thoughts of Ireland were put on the back burner by the city's Irish, many of whom were dismayed by Ireland's position of neutrality during World War II.

Mayor Daniel Hoan

Daniel Webster Hoan, a Socialist, led Milwaukee as mayor for 24 years from 1916 to 1940. Hoan was born in 1881 in Waukesha County, the son of Daniel Webster Hoan Sr., whose parents were from Ireland and spelled their name Horan. Hoan, like many Irish, had sympathy for the underdog. At the time of his first election, Milwaukee was beset by many urban problems. Its leaders were corrupt. It was the second most densely populated city in the country after New York City. There were many poor immigrants who lived in substandard housing in unsanitary conditions, which contributed to health problems, crime, and juvenile delinquency. The Socialists worked to solve some of these problems.

Hoan is given credit for making city government honest, frugal, and efficient, and for many reforms from public health to harbor infrastructure. Hoan strongly believed that the lakefront should be enjoyed by all citizens and he oversaw the development of parks and beaches there. He is considered one of the best mayors in United States history. Hoan, who was not religious, died in 1961 and was buried in the Catholic Holy Cross Cemetery.

Hollywood Stars from Tory Hill and Merrill Park

Two of the city's Irish neighborhoods produced twentieth-century film stars. Tory Hill native Pat O'Brien (1899–1983) appeared in over 100 movies. His family lived on W. Clybourn Street near N. 12th Street the year William Joseph Patrick O'Brien was born.[7] His paternal grandparents were from County Cork and his mother's parents emigrated from County Galway. O'Brien often played Irish or Irish-American characters, frequently a priest or a policeman, in a career that lasted more than five decades. His last role was in 1982 in *Happy Days*, a television series set in Milwaukee. He died the next year.

Six months after O'Brien's birth, Spencer Tracy first saw the light of day in Merrill Park near N. 30th Street and W. St. Paul Avenue. Tracy's father, John, was born in Illinois to Irish immigrants. O'Brien and Tracy met when they attended Marquette High School while in their teens. During World War I they joined the U.S. Navy together and were stationed at the Great Lakes Naval Center until the war ended. They then

Pat O'Brien and Spencer Tracy, two local Irish boys who became twentieth century film stars. (Author's collection)

went to New York to begin their careers on the stage before turning to movie careers in Hollywood. Tracy, who appeared in 75 films, won two Oscars for best actor, one for his role as Father Edward Flanagan in *Boys Town*. Tracy died in 1967, a short time after his last film, *Guess Who's Coming to Dinner*, was completed.

Renewed Interest in Ireland

After World War II, prosperity returned to the United States. Most of the younger Irish Americans knew little of the trials and difficulties of their immigrant ancestors in America. While some were very aware of their Irish identity, others claimed they were Irish, but it was only in a vague sense. By the 1950s, it was possible for those enjoying the good times to travel. And with the arrival of cheaper air travel in the 1970s, Ireland became a destination for many Irish Americans, as well as for servicemen who had been stationed in Northern Ireland during the war.

Despite strong anti-Catholic resistance, Irish Catholic John F. Kennedy won the presidential election in 1960 by a slim margin. Locally, he won every ward in the city but lost the state. Kennedy was the nation's first Catholic president, something that had seemed impossible up to that time. A major barrier had been overcome and the status of Irish Catholics in America rose.

The same year Kennedy was elected, the Shamrock Club formed in Milwaukee. In 1963, Kennedy visited Ireland and the televised images of his trip renewed interest in the Emerald Isle. The Shamrock Club sponsored a trip to Ireland while Kennedy was there, and members heard the president speak while in Galway. They returned enthusiastic about learning more of Irish culture, history, and language. Traditional Irish music was brought to America by the Clancy Brothers and Tommy Makem when they appeared on national television in the early 1960s, kindling more interest.

During the late 1960s, when Catholics began protesting discrimination by the Protestant majority, the troubles in Northern Ireland became front page news. Violence followed the protests. The British government sent troops to Northern Ireland, which fueled the hostilities. Irish Milwaukeeans again sent money to Ireland, this time to support both Catholic political prisoners and their families as well as the Irish Republican Army. The conflict, including hunger strikes by political prisoners, would last into the 1990s and result in the loss of several thousand lives.

During this era, Irish music, dancing, language, sports, history, and drama flourished in Milwaukee. Irish Fest was founded in 1981 and is now billed as the largest celebration of Irish culture in the world. It draws over 100,000 people to Milwaukee's lakefront in the Historic Third Ward on the third weekend of August each year. Numerous local Irish dance and music groups were formed over the years, as well as organizations for playing Irish sports, learning the Irish language, and researching Irish roots. After a lapse of 45 years, a division of the Ancient Order of Hibernians was re-organized in 1986. One of the largest collections of Irish music in the United States, the Ward Irish Music Archives, was established in 1992 at the CelticMKE offices in Wauwatosa.

In 1996, the Irish Cultural and Heritage Center was opened at 2133 W. Wisconsin Avenue and has been the site of a myriad of Irish cultural events. Today, the University of Wisconsin – Milwaukee has a Center for Celtic Studies and the Marquette University History Department offers classes on Irish history.

Irish Cultural and Heritage Center. (Photograph by the author)

Fewer Catholics and Fewer Democrats

Besides an increased interest in Ireland and its culture, Milwaukee's Irish community saw another significant trend after World War II. Many left the Catholic Church and the Democratic Party. As they became better educated and society became more secularized, they questioned the many rules of the Church, particularly those regarding divorce, premarital sex, birth control, and abortion. Between 1970 and 2014, the Catholic population of the Milwaukee archdiocese declined by over 100,000 to 592,000, despite the large influx of Latino Catholics.[8] Although there are no specific numbers for Catholics of Irish descent who attend weekly services, they are likely similar to the overall Milwaukee Catholic population, of which fewer than 30 percent attended regular Sunday services in 2014.[9]

Nationally, Sunday Mass attendance among Catholics dipped from 70 percent in 1963 to 37 percent in 2005.[10] The Catholic clergy sex abuse scandal led to further loss of membership in Milwaukee as well as in Ireland, which also suffered child abuse by the clergy, and saw Sunday church attendance there decline from 91 percent in 1973 to 30 percent in 2011.[11]

During the nineteenth century, virtually all Irish Catholic immigrants supported the Democratic Party. The party helped the new arrivals get jobs, looked out for their welfare, and registered them to vote. Now, as they became successful, they began leaving the city for the suburbs, in many cases to avoid living in neighborhoods with African Americans and Latinos, and many began supporting the Republican Party.

When Lyndon Johnson, a Democrat, was elected in 1964, 22 percent of the Irish Catholics voted for the very conservative Barry Goldwater. In 1968, 36 percent supported the Republican, Richard Nixon, and a majority of Catholics voted for Ronald Reagan in 1980.[12] Today, Irish-American Catholics still lean Democratic, but significant numbers support the Republican Party.[13]

From Immigrants to Americans

Milwaukee's Irish immigrants, most of them poor and uneducated, suffered hardships, prejudice, and disaster after arriving in a city where being Irish was not easy. But they worked to improve life for themselves and their families, and in the process, helped make Milwaukee the city that it is today. For their descendants, life is much easier, and it is no longer a liability to be Irish. Most of them are of mixed ethnicity, and Milwaukeeans with names like Schmidt, Kowalski, and Hernandez proudly proclaim their Irish ancestry. They are an important part of the fabric of Milwaukee, and their descendants, and those of all immigrant groups, will continue to make contributions to every facet of the city for generations to come.

Afterword

Irish Names on Milwaukee's Map

Some of Milwaukee's Irish immigrants and their descendants are memorialized in local place names.

Archer Avenue in the Bay View neighborhood was named by Patrick Henry Archer, who was born in County Waterford in 1843. His parents settled in the Third Ward where he lived until moving to Bay View; there he subdivided land he owned and named this street in 1880. Archer died in Bay View in 1928.

Boden Street and Court, near W. College and S. Howell avenues, were named in 1981 for the Boden family who farmed nearby. Robert Boden was from Newry, County Down, where he was born about 1790. He and his family began farming in the area in 1842 and Boden died there during the 1850s.

Cannon Park on the West Side was named for Frank A. Cannon, a park commissioner who held that position at the time of his death in 1935. Cannon was born in Tory Hill in 1872 of Irish-born parents and was a promoter of good roads in Wisconsin. He was instrumental in introducing road signs in the state.

Callahan Place was named for St. Paul, Minnesota, native Robert N. Callahan who operated a tavern, the Callahan Club, in the Tory Hill neighborhood during the 1950s and 1960s. The bar drew students from Marquette University, some of whom later became influential. Among them was William Ryan Drew, who served as secretary of the City Redevelopment Authority, and was instrumental in naming this street in 1978. The Callahan Club, like the rest of Tory Hill, no longer exists.

Carpenter Avenue was named in 1892 during the development of the city of Cudahy, in which Michael Carpenter was an investor. Carpenter was born in the Tory Hill area in 1845 and later operated the Carpenter Baking Company, which could turn out 50,000 loaves of bread a day, in that neighborhood. He was an officer of the Ancient Order of Hibernians and the Hibernian Benevolent Society, a supporter of Irish causes like the Land League, and a donor for the relief of sufferers of the famine of 1879.

Carpenter died in Milwaukee in 1926.

Corcoran Avenue in the Third Ward was named in 1888. Cornelius J. Corcoran was born in County Limerick in 1809. He and his family settled in the Third Ward in 1849 and operated a grocery store and saloon on the corner of N. Jefferson and E. Chicago streets. His son, Cornelius L. Corcoran, was born there in 1864 and was elected a Third Ward alderman at the age of 27 in 1891. He was still a Third Ward alderman when he died at the age of 71 in 1936.

The **city of Cudahy, Cudahy Avenue**, and **Cudahy Park** were all named for Patrick Cudahy, who was born in County Kilkenny in 1849 and brought to Milwaukee as a six-month-old infant. The family settled in Tory Hill for a time before moving a few miles west to avoid the corrupting influence of that neighborhood. In 1892, Patrick Cudahy, the city's wealthiest Irishman, founded the community of Cudahy, with his slaughterhouse and meatpacking plant as the center of its economy, and where Cudahy Avenue was platted. He served on the Milwaukee County Park Commission, which led to Cudahy Park being named for him. He died in Milwaukee in 1919.

The Northwest Side's **Dineen Park** was named for Cornelius Dineen, a Milwaukee County Park commissioner from 1928 until his death in 1955. Dineen was born in 1866 in Mequon, where his grandparents settled after emigrating from counties Cork and Limerick. He graduated from Marquette Law School in 1912 and specialized in municipal law.

Doyne Park, overlooking the Menomonee River Valley, was named for the first Milwaukee County Executive, John Lyons Doyne. His family had roots in Merrill Park, but Doyne was born in Chicago in 1912. In 1937, he earned his law degree from Marquette University, paid for by his uncle, Willard P. "Mike" Lyons. Lyons served as a county supervisor and when he died, Doyne was appointed to fill his position. Doyne was later elected as a county supervisor on his own, then as County Board chairman, and when the new position of County Executive was created, he was elected to that position for three terms. Doyne died in Milwaukee in 1997.

On the North Side, **Finn Place** was the namesake of Richard Finn, a plumbing contractor and real estate developer. Finn was born in the Third Ward in 1853 to James Finn and Catherine McGrath, both of Ireland. Well on his way to financial success, Finn died at the age of 36 in 1890, leaving his wealth to his bride of two years, Rose Burke, and his one-year-old son, Richard Jr.

Graham Street was named for Wilson Graham, who was born in County Armagh in 1815. He was one of the city's first attorneys when he came to Milwaukee in 1838. Forty years later, he provided legal services for Joseph Williams, a Bay View farmer who subdivided his farm and named two of the new streets for Graham (see Wilson Street). He died in 1898 and is buried in Forest Home Cemetery.

Hackett Avenue was named for Edward Patrick Hackett, but not without controversy. Hackett was born in in 1857 in the Third Ward, where his County Meath-born father and grandfather settled in 1837. In 1893, Hackett, a successful real estate developer, helped in the creation of the exclusive Prospect Hill subdivision, bordered by N. Downer Avenue, N. Lake Drive, E. Park Place, and E. Kenwood Boulevard and which included N. Prospect Avenue. In 1895, the Common Council decided that N. Prospect Avenue should be three blocks to the west and changed the name of the Prospect Hill portion of Prospect to N. Hackett Avenue.

Homeowners on the street were enraged; they said the name Hackett Avenue lacked class and they suggested many alternatives. A friend of Hackett's, Joseph Donnelly, who was born in County Tyrone and grew up in the Third Ward, wrote a poem defending the choice of the name Hackett.

Peace, Prospect Hill! It seemeth ill
To raise this clamorous racket,
As if your street were too elite
To bear the name of Hackett.

'Tis true the name's unknown to fame;
No storied knight doth back it;
But we can cite full many a night
Made glorious by Hackett.

Not his renown to take a town
And ruthless raze and sack it.
He takes a farm and by his charm
Creates a town, does Hackett.

When Prospect Hill had prospects nil,
Who flashed the scheme to track it
With rich stone curb – this mere suburb –
And costly asphalt? Hackett!

Ah, Prospect Hill, it seemeth ill!
Let other tongues attack it.
Your tongue should wag and never flag
In grateful praise of Hackett.[1]

Donnelly's poem did the trick and we still have Hackett Avenue today. Edward Hackett died in 1910 and is buried in Calvary Cemetery.

The **Hoan Bridge** on Milwaukee's lakefront connects Downtown with Bay View and was named for Daniel Webster Hoan, Milwaukee's long-serving Socialist mayor.

On the far Northwest Side, **Kiley Avenue** and **Kiley Court** were named shortly after the death of Moses Kiley in 1953. Kiley had served as archbishop of the Milwaukee Archdiocese since 1940. He was born on Cape Breton Island in Nova Scotia, Canada, in 1876 of Irish parents. Kiley worked as a trolley motorman in Boston to finance his education

Daniel Hoan served as Milwaukee's
Socialist mayor for 24 years.
(FindaGrave.com)

221

and was ordained a priest in 1911.

While we do not know who **Killian Place** in the Riverwest neighborhood was named for in 1926, we can trace the name to St. Killian. The Irish missionary was active at the end of the seventh century and the beginning of the eighth century in Bavaria, Germany. Because he was held in high regard there, some Germans took on his name. Consequently, Killian, or Kilian as it is also spelled, can be either an Irish or a German surname, and Milwaukee has had citizens of both ethnicities with the name.

Lyons Park is the namesake of Willard Patrick (Mike) Lyons. A friend thought Willard was a "sissy" name so he called him Mike, a name that stuck. Lyons was a product of the Merrill Park neighborhood and graduated from St. Rose's School, West Division High School, and Marquette University. Lyons, a bachelor, served as a county supervisor for 30 years and was president of the County Board of Public Welfare for many years. He was born in 1886 and died in office in 1954.

West Allis's **McCarty Park** is named for a former Milwaukee County supervisor, William E. McCarty. McCarty was born in the Third Ward in 1870 to Irish immigrants. His father, Thomas, represented the Third Ward as an alderman and county supervisor, and in 1908 William McCarty followed in his father's footsteps when he was elected a county supervisor for the Third Ward. He was chairman of the county board when he died in 1932.

McGovern Park on the Northwest Side was named for William R. McGovern, who served as a park commissioner for 45 years, from 1919 to 1964. He began his career as a draftsman for the Wisconsin Telephone Company and retired as its president. McGovern was a strong advocate for moving the county airport from Curry Park to its present location, for building a stadium for major league baseball before the city had a team, and for creating parks along the lakefront. He was born in 1880 in Tory Hill and died in his N. Lake Drive home in 1964. His immigrant ancestors were from County Fermanagh. McGovern Park was the only Milwaukee County park named for a living person.

Running alongside I-94, **O'Connor Place** is named for Charles William (Chick) O'Connor, who was an alderman for 24 years between 1916 and 1944. He was born in 1885 in Milwaukee where his father, Michael, had been brought as an infant to escape the famine in Ireland.

O'Connor sponsored an ordinance to rename the streets and revise the addressing system to make it easier to navigate the city. That project was completed in 1930. He also wanted to consolidate the city and the county, an idea that was not accepted. O'Connor died in 1961.

O'Donnell Park, overlooking the lakefront, was named for William Francis (Bill) O'Donnell, the second Milwaukee County Executive. He was born in Tory Hill in 1922, the son of James O'Donnell, a plumber whose parents were Irish immigrants. O'Donnell was a big supporter of public transit and took the bus to work each day. He was elected a county supervisor in 1948, and for the next 40 years O'Donnell was always available to his constituents. His daughter, Bridget, recalled, "It was rare for us to ever finish a meal without someone calling or coming to the door."[2]

On the far South Side, **Parnell Avenue** was named for Charles Stewart Parnell, an Irish nationalist politician of the 1880s. He was born in County Wicklow to Protestant parents in 1846 and died in 1891. He headed the Land League and fought for Home Rule for Ireland. The street was named by real estate developer John Allen Goff, whose Goff immigrant ancestors were from counties Louth and Mayo.

Reynolds Place in the Walker's Point neighborhood was named for Thomas M. Reynolds, a labor leader, Socialist alderman, and saloonkeeper who was born in Tory Hill in 1866. Reynolds, who began his career as a pattern maker, was the son of Irish immigrants. He was elected to the Common Council representing Walker's Point in 1916 and served until his death in 1924. This street was named in 1940.

Russell Avenue in Bay View was named for Thomas Russell, who was born in County Cork in 1843. He was brought to the United States as an infant and lived in New York, Chicago, and Cincinnati before coming to Milwaukee. Russell, an employee of the rolling mills, was a village trustee when this street was named in 1880. Russell later left Bay View for Colorado.

Shea Avenue in the Silver City neighborhood was named for Thomas Shea, who was born in County Tipperary in 1830 and came to Milwaukee in his late teens. His early career as a teamster led to his wealth in the freight and real estate business, making him one of the richest Irishmen in the city. He was a sergeant in the Union Guard and a survivor of the sinking of the *Lady Elgin*. Shea was a member of the Police and Fire

Thomas Shea brought food to the Young Irelanders in hiding in 1848, survived the sinking of the *Lady Elgin*, and became one of the wealthiest Irishmen in Milwaukee. (*The Milwaukee Sentinel*)

Commission and an alderman. He died in 1894 in his mansion in Walker's Point, but was not buried from St. Patrick's Church there because it did not have adequate capacity for the crowd of mourners; his funeral services were held at St. John's Cathedral instead.

Sheridan Avenue on the North Side and **Sheridan Park** in Cudahy were both named for Civil War general Philip Sheridan. Sheridan, whose parents emigrated from County Cavan, was very popular with the city's Irish; they named the Sheridan Guard militia company for him when it was founded after the war. He was born in 1831 and died in 1888.

Somers Street was named for Peter Somers, the city's third Irish mayor. He was born on a farm near Menomonee Falls in 1850 to parents from County Roscommon. A lawyer by profession, he was an alderman, the mayor, and a congressman. The Hillside neighborhood's Somers Street, now only one block long, was named in his honor in 1926, two years after his death in Los Angeles. Somers's brother, John, was superintendent of Milwaukee Public Schools and an investor in the community of Cudahy, where **Somers Avenue** was named for him.

Wilson Street in Bay View was named for attorney Wilson Graham. It intersects Graham Street, which creates the only intersection in the city where both streets are named for one person (see Graham Street).

Appendix 1

Census Bureau Miscalculates Irish-Born Milwaukeeans

By Carl Baehr

A main concern of the U.S. Census Bureau each time it takes a census is that everyone in the country is enumerated. There is no way of knowing how well the job was done because there is no way to determine how many were not enumerated. But what of the statistics compiled from those who were enumerated? Did the Census Bureau do a good job there? No, not for the nativity of Milwaukeeans in 1850 and 1860, and possibly not for the rest of the country for those years either.

According to Census Bureau data there were 2,816 Irish-born Milwaukeeans in 1850[1] and 3,100 in 1860.[2] A search of the Ancestry.com census database for people born in Ireland and living in any of Milwaukee's wards in 1850 and 1860 yields totals of 3,019 and 4,272 respectively. If Ancestry.com's figures are correct, it means that the Census Bureau undercounted Milwaukee citizens born in Ireland by 7.2 percent in 1850 and 37.8 percent in 1860.

The only way to determine which figures are correct, if either, was to take an actual count from the census images. So, I did the counting. Because doing so is quite tedious, I did it in 15- to 30-minute sessions, sometimes several a day, over a period of about three weeks.

The results for 1850 show that 3,004 were born in Ireland and that the Ancestry.com figure was 15 too high and the Census Bureau figure was 188 too low. The Ancestry.com errors were primarily due to a page of Third Ward people being counted twice, once in the Third Ward (image 2) and then again in the Fifth Ward (image 62). The actual count shows that the Census Bureau undercounted the Irish-born by 6.7 percent in 1850.

The actual count of Irish-born in 1860, 4,381, shows that the Census Bureau total was 1,281 too low and the Ancestry.com total was 109 too low. The main reason for the low Ancestry.com number is that in the

Fourth Ward the enumerator sometimes listed a more specific birthplace than the country of birth. He listed people as born in Dublin, Limerick, etc. These people were not included in Ancestry's total for Ireland. The actual count shows that the Census Bureau undercounted the Irish-born by 41.3 percent in 1860.

If the Irish-born were undercounted by the Census Bureau, who was overcounted? Since Ancestry.com's data seems to be reasonably accurate, I continued to do searches in their database for other groups in Milwaukee in 1850. The results are listed below and show that all groups were undercounted by the Census Bureau except the Germans, who were overcounted by 23.6 percent.

1850 Census of Milwaukee City

Birthplace	Census Bureau	Ancestry .com	Difference
Ireland	2816	3004 (actual)	188
Britain	1457	1610	- 153
U.S.A.	7175	7890	- 715
Other	1342	1676	- 334
Germany	7271	5881	+1390

I did similar searches in Ancestry.com's 1860 census database in an effort to determine what group was overcounted by the Census Bureau to compensate for the undercounting of 1,281 Irish. I was unable to complete this task because Ancestry.com did not enter the birthplaces of about 6,000 people in the Sixth and Ninth wards. The enumerator of these wards left the place of birth blank when it was the same as that above it. To the experienced census researcher, it is obvious that the blank was meant as a ditto, but it was not handled that way by Ancestry.com.

The conclusion drawn by historians, and others who have used the Census Bureau data, was that between 1850 and 1860 Irish immigration to Milwaukee was relatively flat and insignificant. The new figures show a robust growth of Irish in the city during those years; additionally, they indicate that Milwaukee was not as German a city in 1850 as reported by the Census Bureau.

Population of Irish-Born in Milwaukee

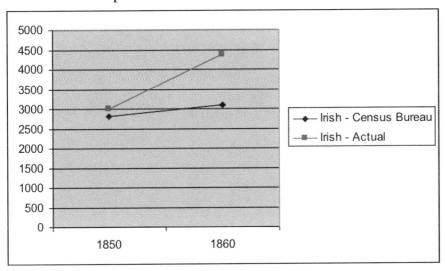

A comparison of the Census Bureau data on Irish-born Milwaukeeans in 1870 and 1880 with figures from Ancestry.com searches for those two censuses show variances of 4 (Census Bureau 3784[3], Ancestry.com 3788) and 35 (Census Bureau 3659[4], Ancestry.com 3624) respectively, which are statistically insignificant. Therefore, whatever technique the Census Bureau used to "count" in 1850 and 1860 seems to have been replaced by a better method starting in 1870.

Appendix 2

Lady Elgin Victims and Survivors

This list was compiled by Carl Baehr. It is based on research using inquest results printed in newspapers, church and cemetery burial records, tombstones, probate records, and other sources.

Lost on the *Lady Elgin*

Name		Age	Residence	Occupant Type	Ethnicity
Ahearn	Dennis	28	Milwaukee	Excursionist/Local Traveler	Irish
Ahearn	Margaret	28	Milwaukee	Excursionist/Local Traveler	Irish
Ahearn	Patrick	17	Milwaukee	Excursionist/Local Traveler	Irish
Alexander	Richard K.		Chicago, IL	Crew - 2nd Engineer	
Arnold	George	15	Milwaukee	Excursionist/Local Traveler	Yankee
Barron	Ann	30	Milwaukee	Excursionist/Local Traveler	Irish
Barry	Garrett	44	Milwaukee	Excursionist/Local Traveler	Irish
Barry	William	12	Milwaukee	Excursionist/Local Traveler	Irish
Bass	Henry	19	Milwaukee	Excursionist/Local Traveler	English
Bellew	James	46	Jackson, WI	Excursionist/Local Traveler	Irish
Birmingham	Cornelius	19	Milwaukee	Excursionist/Local Traveler	Irish
Bishop	Augustus	16	Milwaukee	Excursionist/Local Traveler	English
Bishop	Henry	18	Milwaukee	Excursionist/Local Traveler	English
Black	Hugh	29	Milwaukee	Excursionist/Local Traveler	Irish
Bloos	Philip	26	Milwaukee	Excursionist/Local Traveler	German
Bohan	Thomas	28	Milwaukee	Excursionist/Local Traveler	Irish
Bohan	Timothy	2	Milwaukee	Excursionist/Local Traveler	Irish
Bohan	Catherine	22	Milwaukee	Excursionist/Local Traveler	Irish
Bond	Eliza	28	Mineral Point, WI	Through Passenger	English
Bond	Eliza Jane	9	Mineral Point, WI	Through Passenger	English
Bond	Nathan B.	8	Mineral Point, WI	Through Passenger	English
Bossenburg	Fred	25	Milwaukee	Excursionist/Local Traveler	German
Boulger	Ann	18	Milwaukee	Excursionist/Local Traveler	Irish
Boulger	Margaret	19	Milwaukee	Excursionist/Local Traveler	Irish
Bulfin	Thomas	35	Milwaukee	Excursionist/Local Traveler	Irish
Bungard	Andreas	24	Milwaukee	Excursionist/Local Traveler	German
Burke	Mary	24	Milwaukee	Excursionist/Local Traveler	Irish
Burns	Fanny	26	Milwaukee	Excursionist/Local Traveler	Irish
Burns	James	16	Milwaukee	Excursionist/Local Traveler	Irish
Burns	Michael	30	Milwaukee	Excursionist/Local Traveler	Irish

Burns	William	27	Milwaukee	Excursionist/Local Traveler	Irish
Butler	Catherine	22	Milwaukee	Excursionist/Local Traveler	Irish
Campion	John L.	27	Milwaukee	Excursionist/Local Traveler	Irish
Canning	Patrick	28	Milwaukee	Excursionist/Local Traveler	Irish
Casey	Dennis	14	Milwaukee	Excursionist/Local Traveler	Irish
Casper	Francis	56	Milwaukee	Excursionist/Local Traveler	German
Chamberlain	Frank	59	Milwaukee	Excursionist/Local Traveler	Yankee
Churchill	Horace William	25	Milwaukee	Excursionist/Local Traveler	Yankee
Cline	Patrick	26	Milwaukee	Excursionist/Local Traveler	Irish
Codd	Bridget	23	Chicago, IL	Excursionist/Local Traveler	Irish
Codd	Margaret	20	Milwaukee	Excursionist/Local Traveler	Irish
Collins	James	21	Milwaukee	Excursionist/Local Traveler	Yankee
Commerford	Richard	18	Milwaukee	Excursionist/Local Traveler	Irish
Connaughty	Peter	17	Milwaukee	Excursionist/Local Traveler	Irish
Connolly	James	34	Milwaukee	Excursionist/Local Traveler	Irish
Connolly	Patrick	36	Milwaukee	Excursionist/Local Traveler	Irish
Connoly	Terrence	21	Milwaukee	Excursionist/Local Traveler	Irish
Conway	John	13	Milwaukee	Excursionist/Local Traveler	Irish
Cook	Eliza	24	Stockbridge, WI	Through Passenger	Canadian
Cook	Jane	46	Stockbridge, WI	Through Passenger	Canadian
Corbitt	Alexander	33	Milwaukee	Excursionist/Local Traveler	English
Corcoran			Milwaukee	Excursionist/Local Traveler	Irish
Cosgrave	James	16	Milwaukee	Excursionist/Local Traveler	Irish
Coughlin	John	24	Milwaukee	Excursionist/Local Traveler	Irish
Crean	Mary	19	Milwaukee	Excursionist/Local Traveler	Irish
Cuddihy	James	10	Milwaukee	Excursionist/Local Traveler	Irish
Cuddihy	Steven	32	Watertown, WI	Excursionist/Local Traveler	Irish
Cullen	Eliza	20	Milwaukee	Excursionist/Local Traveler	Irish
Curtin	Elizabeth	21	Milwaukee	Excursionist/Local Traveler	Irish
Curtin	Thomas	16	Milwaukee	Excursionist/Local Traveler	Irish
Delaney	Martin	33	Milwaukee	Excursionist/Local Traveler	Irish
Delaney	Mary	37	Milwaukee	Excursionist/Local Traveler	Irish
Delaney	Patrick	26	Milwaukee	Excursionist/Local Traveler	Irish
Delury	Ellen	24	Milwaukee	Excursionist/Local Traveler	Irish

Delury	John	24	Milwaukee	Excursionist/Local Traveler	Irish
Diehl	Elias	42	Milwaukee	Crew – Carpenter	Yankee
Dilersick	M.	19	Milwaukee	Excursionist/Local Traveler	German
Donavan	Mary	36	Milwaukee	Excursionist/Local Traveler	Irish
Dooley	Martin	18	Milwaukee	Excursionist/Local Traveler	Irish
Downer	Samuel A.	19	Milwaukee	Excursionist/Local Traveler	Yankee
Dressler	William	40	Milwaukee	Excursionist/Local Traveler	German
Duffy	James	19	Milwaukee	Excursionist/Local Traveler	Irish
Duffy	Margaret	23	Milwaukee	Excursionist/Local Traveler	Irish
Dunner	Hannah	40	Milwaukee	Excursionist/Local Traveler	Irish
Dwyer	Elizabeth	15	Milwaukee	Excursionist/Local Traveler	Irish
Dwyer	Ellen	44	Milwaukee	Excursionist/Local Traveler	Irish
Dwyer	Michael	21	Milwaukee	Excursionist/Local Traveler	Irish
Eichorn	Augustus	32	Milwaukee	Excursionist/Local Traveler	German
Ellis	Mary	45	Milwaukee	Excursionist/Local Traveler	Irish
Englehardt	John	27	Milwaukee	Excursionist/Local Traveler	German
Evarts	Charles	28	Milwaukee	Excursionist/Local Traveler	Yankee
Eviston	Bridget	31	Milwaukee	Excursionist/Local Traveler	Irish
Eviston	Thomas	10	Milwaukee	Excursionist/Local Traveler	Irish
Fahey	Mary Ann	30	Milwaukee	Excursionist/Local Traveler	Irish
Fahey	Mary	35	Milwaukee	Excursionist/Local Traveler	Irish
Fahey	Patrick	15	Milwaukee	Excursionist/Local Traveler	Irish
Fanning	Catherine	20	Milwaukee	Excursionist/Local Traveler	Irish
Fanning	Elizabeth	35	Milwaukee	Excursionist/Local Traveler	Irish
Faraby	George		Milwaukee	Excursionist/Local Traveler	English
Faraby	Mary	24	Milwaukee	Excursionist/Local Traveler	English
Farnsworth	William	64	Sheboygan	Through Passenger	Yankee
Fitzgerald	Ann	19	Milwaukee	Excursionist/Local Traveler	Irish
Fitzgerald	Ann	21	Milwaukee	Excursionist/Local Traveler	Irish
Fitzgerald	Maurice	17	Milwaukee	Excursionist/Local Traveler	Irish
Fitzgerald	Patrick Joseph	19	Milwaukee	Excursionist/Local Traveler	Irish
Fitzpatrick	Edward	23	Willow Springs, IL	Crew	Irish
Flanders	George	30	Dubuque, IA	Through Passenger	Yankee
Flynn	Ann	13	Milwaukee	Excursionist/Local Traveler	Irish

Foley	Bridget	22	Milwaukee	Excursionist/Local Traveler	Irish
Foley	Paul	45	Milwaukee	Excursionist/Local Traveler	Irish
Foley	William	20	Milwaukee	Excursionist/Local Traveler	Irish
Gannon	Margaret	18	Milwaukee	Excursionist/Local Traveler	Irish
Garth	Amanda	26	Paris, KY	Through Passenger	Yankee
Garth	Anna	23	Paris, KY	Through Passenger	Yankee
Garth	Mary	40	Paris, KY	Through Passenger	Yankee
Garth	William	45	Paris, KY	Through Passenger	Yankee
Gilligan	Ann	28	Milwaukee	Excursionist/Local Traveler	Irish
Goetz	Daniel William	42	Milwaukee	Excursionist/Local Traveler	German
Goff	Homer B.	16	Racine, WI	Through Passenger	Yankee
Grade	Ernest	8	Milwaukee	Excursionist/Local Traveler	German
Grade	Mary	26	Milwaukee	Excursionist/Local Traveler	German
Grady	Michael	44	Granville, WI	Excursionist/Local Traveler	Irish
Hackett	James	20	Milwaukee	Excursionist/Local Traveler	Irish
Hall	Benjamin F.	47	Aurora, IL	Through Passenger	Yankee
Hanley	Matthew	17	Milwaukee	Excursionist/Local Traveler	Irish
Hanley	Susan	20	Milwaukee	Excursionist/Local Traveler	Irish
Hanna	Theodore C.	22	Milwaukee	Excursionist/Local Traveler	Yankee
Hanson	Julia	14	Milwaukee	Excursionist/Local Traveler	Norwegian
Hanson	Louisa	21	Milwaukee	Excursionist/Local Traveler	Norwegian
Hayes	William	18	Milwaukee	Excursionist/Local Traveler	Irish
Hendrickson	John	23	Milwaukee	Excursionist/Local Traveler	Yankee
Hett	Fred	31	Milwaukee	Excursionist/Local Traveler	German
Hipelius	Godfrey	21	Milwaukee	Excursionist/Local Traveler	German
Hock	Christian		Milwaukee	Through Passenger	German
Hopkins	Lydia	32	Eagle River, WI	Through Passenger	Yankee
Hopkins	Willie	3	Eagle River, WI	Through Passenger	Yankee
Horan	John	30	Milwaukee	Excursionist/Local Traveler	Irish
Horner	William W.	20	Philadelphia, PA	Through Passenger	Yankee
Horrigan	Michael	19	Milwaukee	Excursionist/Local Traveler	Irish
Hoye	Hannah O'Brien	24	Milwaukee	Excursionist/Local Traveler	Irish
Hubby	William M.	56	Rochester, NY	Through Passenger	Yankee
Humbert	Sarah A.	25	Chicago, IL	Through Passenger	Yankee

Humbert	Theodora	8	Chicago, IL	Through Passenger	Yankee
Ingram	Herbert	49	England	Through Passenger	English
Ingram	Herbert Jr.	15	England	Through Passenger	English
Jarvis	Margaret	21	Milwaukee	Excursionist/Local Traveler	Irish
Johnson	Charles H.	17	Milwaukee	Excursionist/Local Traveler	Irish
Jothum	Charles	23	Chicago, IL	Excursionist/Local Traveler	Yankee
Kelly	John	31	Milwaukee	Excursionist/Local Traveler	Irish
Kennedy	Ann	20	Milwaukee	Excursionist/Local Traveler	Irish
Kennedy	Mary Johanna	0.5	Milwaukee	Excursionist/Local Traveler	Irish
Kennedy	Philip	18	Milwaukee	Excursionist/Local Traveler	Irish
Keough	Agnes	17	Milwaukee	Excursionist/Local Traveler	Irish
Kilroy	Bridget	27	Milwaukee	Excursionist/Local Traveler	Irish
Kilroy	James	28	Milwaukee	Excursionist/Local Traveler	Irish
Kilroy	May Cecelia	1	Milwaukee	Excursionist/Local Traveler	Irish
Kitto	Elizabeth	7	Mineral Point, WI	Through Passenger	English
Kitto	Elizabeth	31	Mineral Point, WI	Through Passenger	English
Kitto	Jane	12	Mineral Point, WI	Through Passenger	English
Kitto	Mary	3	Mineral Point, WI	Through Passenger	English
Kitto	Sophia	4	Mineral Point, WI	Through Passenger	English
Komarick	Anton	20	Milwaukee	Excursionist/Local Traveler	Bohemian
Komarick	Franz	23	Milwaukee	Excursionist/Local Traveler	Bohemian
Komarick	Joseph	17	Milwaukee	Excursionist/Local Traveler	Bohemian
Lacy	Charles		Chicago, IL	Crew - Barkeep	
Lanigan	Michael	29	Milwaukee	Excursionist/Local Traveler	Irish
Lasky			Milwaukee	Excursionist/Local Traveler	German
Ledden	Amelia	21	Milwaukee	Excursionist/Local Traveler	Irish
Leverenz	Otto	48	Milwaukee	Excursionist/Local Traveler	German
Locke	George R.	29	Chicago, IL	Through Passenger	Yankee
Loutz	John		Chicago, IL	Through Passenger	German
Loutz	Child		Chicago, IL	Through Passenger	German
Loutz	Child		Chicago, IL	Through Passenger	German
Loutz	Child		Chicago, IL	Through Passenger	German
Lumsden	Emma	4	New Orleans, LA	Through Passenger	Yankee
Lumsden	Francis Asbury	49	New Orleans, LA	Through Passenger	Yankee

Surname	First name	Age	Location	Category	Ethnicity
Lumsden	Frank	16	New Orleans, LA	Through Passenger	Yankee
Lumsden	Mrs Francis	32	New Orleans, LA	Through Passenger	Yankee
Lumsden	Female servant		New Orleans, LA	Through Passenger	
Lynch	Bloss	19	Milwaukee	Excursionist/Local Traveler	Irish
Malone	James	19	Milwaukee	Excursionist/Local Traveler	Irish
Maloney	Mary	19	Milwaukee	Excursionist/Local Traveler	Irish
Martin	Joseph	20	Milwaukee	Excursionist/Local Traveler	Irish
Mathews	Mary	27	Milwaukee	Excursionist/Local Traveler	Irish
McAuliffe	Daniel	30	Milwaukee	Excursionist/Local Traveler	Irish
McCormick	Francis	25	Milwaukee	Excursionist/Local Traveler	Irish
McCormick	Martha	19	Milwaukee	Excursionist/Local Traveler	Irish
McDonough	Patrick	40	Milwaukee	Excursionist/Local Traveler	Irish
McGarry	Hugh	35	Milwaukee	Excursionist/Local Traveler	Irish
McGee	Ann	18	Milwaukee	Excursionist/Local Traveler	Irish
McGill	Thomas	39	Milwaukee	Excursionist/Local Traveler	Irish
McGrath	Mary	22	Milwaukee	Excursionist/Local Traveler	Irish
McGrath	Nicholas	32	Milwaukee	Excursionist/Local Traveler	Irish
McGrath	Patrick	17	Milwaukee	Excursionist/Local Traveler	Irish
McKay	William	15	Milwaukee	Excursionist/Local Traveler	Irish
McLaughlin	Elizabeth	20	Watertown, WI	Excursionist/Local Traveler	Irish
McLaughlin	Hanora Ledden	24	Milwaukee	Excursionist/Local Traveler	Irish
McManus	Sara	26	Milwaukee	Excursionist/Local Traveler	Irish
Meyer	Wilhelm	38	Milwaukee	Excursionist/Local Traveler	German
Miller	Christian		Milwaukee	Excursionist/Local Traveler	German
Monaghan	Andrew	27	Milwaukee	Excursionist/Local Traveler	Irish
Monaghan	Catherine	22	Milwaukee	Excursionist/Local Traveler	Irish
Monaghan	Patrick	64	Milwaukee	Excursionist/Local Traveler	Irish
Morgan	Effort	21	Erie, PA	Crew	Yankee
Morrison	John		Racine, WI	Through Passenger	
Murphy	James	28	Milwaukee	Excursionist/Local Traveler	Irish
Murphy	Michael	35	Milwaukee	Excursionist/Local Traveler	Irish
Murphy	Sara	17	Milwaukee	Excursionist/Local Traveler	Irish
Murphy	Steven	28	Milwaukee	Excursionist/Local Traveler	Irish
Neville	Thomas	22	Milwaukee	Excursionist/Local Traveler	Irish

Last Name	First Name	Age	City	Type	Ethnicity
Newcomb	Sarah (Minnie)	32	Milwaukee	Excursionist/Local Traveler	Yankee
Newton	John M.	32	Superior, WI	Through Passenger	Yankee
Nichols	Christian	35	Milwaukee	Excursionist/Local Traveler	German
Nichols	Jacob	27	Milwaukee	Excursionist/Local Traveler	German
Oakley	George F.	37	Milwaukee	Excursionist/Local Traveler	Yankee
O'Brien	James	22	Milwaukee	Excursionist/Local Traveler	Irish
O'Brien	Mary	24	Milwaukee	Excursionist/Local Traveler	Irish
O'Brien	Michael	19	Milwaukee	Excursionist/Local Traveler	Irish
O'Brien	Richard	15	Milwaukee	Excursionist/Local Traveler	Irish
O'Grady	Anne	29	Milwaukee	Excursionist/Local Traveler	Irish
O'Grady	John	30	Milwaukee	Excursionist/Local Traveler	Irish
O'Leary	Daniel	40	Milwaukee	Excursionist/Local Traveler	Irish
O'Leary	Jeremiah	7	Milwaukee	Excursionist/Local Traveler	Irish
O'Mahoney	Cornelius	35	Milwaukee	Excursionist/Local Traveler	Irish
O'Neil	Thomas	22	Milwaukee	Excursionist/Local Traveler	Irish
Parsons	Oliver Morris	18	Milwaukee	Excursionist/Local Traveler	Yankee
Patterson	Albert	17	Milwaukee	Excursionist/Local Traveler	Yankee
Pengelly	Emma	10	Delta, MI	Excursionist/Local Traveler	Irish
Pentany	James	35	Milwaukee	Excursionist/Local Traveler	Irish
Persons	Henry	16	Milwaukee	Excursionist/Local Traveler	Yankee
Persons	John	17	Milwaukee	Excursionist/Local Traveler	Yankee
Philips	William Benjamin	18	Milwaukee	Excursionist/Local Traveler	English
Phillip	August F.	63	Milwaukee	Excursionist/Local Traveler	German
Pierce	Andrew M.	34	Milwaukee	Excursionist/Local Traveler	Yankee
Pine	Andrew O.	34	Milwaukee	Excursionist/Local Traveler	Yankee
Pine	Leveretia	20	Milwaukee	Excursionist/Local Traveler	Yankee
Plankinton	Eli	15	Milwaukee	Excursionist/Local Traveler	English
Pollard	Alice	22	Milwaukee	Excursionist/Local Traveler	Irish
Pollard	John C.	30	Milwaukee	Excursionist/Local Traveler	Irish
Pomeroy	William Cooper	15	Milwaukee	Excursionist/Local Traveler	Yankee
Potter	Edward	23	Milwaukee	Excursionist/Local Traveler	English
Purtell	Michael	26	Milwaukee	Excursionist/Local Traveler	Irish
Quail	John K.	28	Sparta, WI	Through Passenger	Irish
Quinlon	Patrick	24	Milwaukee	Excursionist/Local Traveler	Irish

Rapp	Jacob	33	Milwaukee	Excursionist/Local Traveler	German
Reynolds	George F.	20	Milwaukee	Excursionist/Local Traveler	Irish
Rice	Charles	7	Milwaukee	Excursionist/Local Traveler	Irish
Rice	James	37	Milwaukee	Excursionist/Local Traveler	Irish
Rice	Johannah	36	Milwaukee	Excursionist/Local Traveler	Irish
Rich	Michael		Chicago, IL	Excursionist/Local Traveler	
Ries	Anton	49	Milwaukee	Excursionist/Local Traveler	German
Riley	Peter	38	Milwaukee	Excursionist/Local Traveler	Irish
Ring	Robert	32	Milwaukee	Excursionist/Local Traveler	Irish
Ring	Sara Murphy	32	Milwaukee	Excursionist/Local Traveler	Irish
Rogers	Edward	18	Milwaukee	Excursionist/Local Traveler	Irish
Rooney	Christopher	25	Milwaukee	Excursionist/Local Traveler	Irish
Rooney	John	30	Milwaukee	Excursionist/Local Traveler	Irish
Rooney	Patrick	17	Milwaukee	Excursionist/Local Traveler	Irish
Rooney	Sarah	26	Milwaukee	Excursionist/Local Traveler	Irish
Ryan	Bridget	30	Milwaukee	Excursionist/Local Traveler	Irish
Ryan	James	30	Milwaukee	Excursionist/Local Traveler	Irish
Ryan	John	24	Milwaukee	Excursionist/Local Traveler	Irish
Ryan	Robert	26	Milwaukee	Excursionist/Local Traveler	Irish
Salzner	Margaret	20	Chicago, IL	Through Passenger	German
Schafer	Henry	35	Milwaukee	Excursionist/Local Traveler	German
Schneider	Henry		Milwaukee	Excursionist/Local Traveler	German
Scolian	James	25	Milwaukee	Excursionist/Local Traveler	Irish
Seibert	Frederick	19	Milwaukee	Excursionist/Local Traveler	German
Sentfleben	Henry	29	Milwaukee	Excursionist/Local Traveler	German
Sheehan	Thomas	30	Milwaukee	Excursionist/Local Traveler	Irish
Sheehy	James	33	Milwaukee	Excursionist/Local Traveler	Irish
Shehan	Bridget		Milwaukee	Excursionist/Local Traveler	Irish
Sherrod	John	22	Milwaukee	Excursionist/Local Traveler	Irish
Silk	Amelia	18	Milwaukee	Excursionist/Local Traveler	Irish
Simpson	Glover	25	Sterling, IL	Through Passenger	English
Slaughter	Thomas	32	Milwaukee	Crew	African American
Smith	Charles		Chicago, IL	Through Passenger	
Smith	James		Milwaukee	Excursionist/Local Traveler	Yankee

Smith	William G.	43	Milwaukee	Excursionist/Local Traveler	English
Smith	Franklin	19	Milwaukee	Excursionist/Local Traveler	Yankee
Sneider	Phillip	22	Milwaukee	Excursionist/Local Traveler	German
Spellane	Mary	15	Milwaukee	Excursionist/Local Traveler	Irish
Spellane	Michael	47	Milwaukee	Excursionist/Local Traveler	Irish
Struett	Herman		Chicago, IL	Excursionist/Local Traveler	German
Sullivan	Ellen	46	Milwaukee	Excursionist/Local Traveler	Irish
Sullivan	Jeremiah	20	Milwaukee	Excursionist/Local Traveler	Irish
Sullivan	Mary		Milwaukee	Excursionist/Local Traveler	Irish
Sullivan	Mary's brother				Irish
Tevlin	James	20	Milwaukee	Excursionist/Local Traveler	Irish
Tevlin	Jane	22	Milwaukee	Excursionist/Local Traveler	Irish
Tevlin	Mary	45	Milwaukee	Excursionist/Local Traveler	Irish
Thomas	Jeremiah		Chicago, IL	Crew	African American
Townsend	Milton	20	Milwaukee	Excursionist/Local Traveler	Yankee
Veale	James	32	Milwaukee	Excursionist/Local Traveler	Irish
Viig	Martha	25	Milwaukee	Excursionist/Local Traveler	Norwegian
Viig	Lena	24	Milwaukee	Excursionist/Local Traveler	Norwegian
Waegli	Samuel	30	Milwaukee	Excursionist/Local Traveler	German
Wagner	John		Philadelphia, PA	Through Passenger	
Waldo	Edwin	26	Ontonagon, MI	Through Passenger	Yankee
Walker	Emily	45	Chicago, IL	Through Passenger	Yankee
Wallace	W.H.	25		Crew - Drover	
Walradt	Cyrus	25	Milwaukee	Excursionist/Local Traveler	Yankee
Walsh	Patrick	20	Milwaukee	Excursionist/Local Traveler	Irish
Ward	Mary	22	Milwaukee	Excursionist/Local Traveler	Irish
Warner	Edward	26	Milwaukee	Excursionist/Local Traveler	Yankee
Weaver	Michael	23	Milwaukee	Excursionist/Local Traveler	Irish
Weiskoff	Henry	35	Milwaukee	Excursionist/Local Traveler	German
Williams	Allan	28	Milwaukee	Excursionist/Local Traveler	Irish
Williams	Theresa Ellen	30	Milwaukee	Excursionist/Local Traveler	Irish
Wilson	Jack	40	Niles, MI	Crew - Captain	Yankee
Wilson	William	37	Milwaukee	Excursionist/Local Traveler	English
Woods	Thomas	23	Milwaukee	Excursionist/Local Traveler	Irish

Survivors of the *Lady Elgin*

Name		Age	Residence	Occupant Type	Ethnicity
Ahearn	Ann	24	Milwaukee	Excursionist/Local Traveler	Irish
Aylward	Phillip	18	Milwaukee	Excursionist/Local Traveler	Irish
Aylward	William	20	Milwaukee	Excursionist/Local Traveler	Irish
Beeman	William		Milwaukee	Crew - 2nd Mate	
Bellman	James	33	Eagle Harbor, MI	Through Passenger	Yankee
Beverung	Charles	25	Milwaukee	Excursionist/Local Traveler	German
Boyd	Francis	19	Milwaukee	Excursionist/Local Traveler	Yankee
Bradford	W.		Brunswick, OH	Through Passenger	Yankee
Burke	Ed	33	Milwaukee	Excursionist/Local Traveler	Irish
Burke	Margaret	23	Milwaukee	Excursionist/Local Traveler	Irish
Caryl	H.S.		Buffalo, NY	Crew	Yankee
Christianson	Frank R.	40	Milwaukee	Excursionist/Local Traveler	Swedish
Collins	John H.	29	Chicago, IL	Crew - 2nd Pantry Man	African American
Connors	Michael	35	Milwaukee	Excursionist/Local Traveler	Irish
Cook	Jacob	19	Stockbridge, WI	Through Passenger	Yankee
Crilley	John J.	30	Milwaukee	Excursionist/Local Traveler	Irish
Crother	Terry		Chicago, IL	Crew	
Cummins	Thomas	35	Chicago, IL	Crew	Irish
Darnes	William A.		Chicago, IL	Crew	African American
Davis	George		Chicago, IL	Crew - First Mate	Yankee
Dempsey	Robert		Milwaukee	Excursionist/Local Traveler	Irish
Devarsky	Frederick		Milwaukee	Excursionist/Local Traveler	German
Dever	William	32	Milwaukee	Excursionist/Local Traveler	Irish
Doebert	Adelbart	28	Milwaukee	Excursionist/Local Traveler	Swiss
Doyle	John	21	Milwaukee	Excursionist/Local Traveler	Irish
Doyle	Michael	17			
Duffy	William	48	Milwaukee	Excursionist/Local Traveler	Irish
Eviston	Ellen	26	Milwaukee	Excursionist/Local Traveler	Irish
Eviston	John W.	31	Milwaukee	Excursionist/Local Traveler	Irish
Eviston	Martin	30	Milwaukee	Excursionist/Local Traveler	Irish

Furlong	George	19	Milwaukee	Excursionist/Local Traveler	Irish
Gardiner	Howard C.	30	Milwaukee	Excursionist/Local Traveler	Yankee
Gilmore	Henry Dennis	17	Milwaukee	Excursionist/Local Traveler	Irish
Grear	Robert		Buffalo, NY	Crew	
Gunnison	Henry W.	31	Milwaukee	Excursionist/Local Traveler	Yankee
Hartsuff	George Lucas	30	Ft Mackinac, MI	Through Passenger	Yankee
Hayes	Margaret	20	Milwaukee	Excursionist/Local Traveler	Irish
Herbert	John Cusack	28	Milwaukee	Excursionist/Local Traveler	Irish
Hetherman	John	23	Chicago, IL	Excursionist/Local Traveler	Irish
Hoepner	Frederick	35	Two Rivers, WI	Crew	German
Hogan	Eddy	14	Milwaukee	Through Passenger	Irish
Jacobsen	John		New York	Crew	Yankee
Jarvis	John	22	Milwaukee	Through Passenger	Yankee
Kennedy	Thomas	19	Milwaukee	Excursionist/Local Traveler	Irish
Keogh	Bridget	17	Milwaukee	Excursionist/Local Traveler	Irish
Keogh	Thomas B.	19	Milwaukee	Excursionist/Local Traveler	Irish
Kingsley	Isaac	50	Milwaukee	Excursionist/Local Traveler	Yankee
Kinsella	William	30	Milwaukee	Excursionist/Local Traveler	Irish
Kuetemeyer	Frederick	16	Milwaukee	Excursionist/Local Traveler	German
Leverrenz	Leopoldine	42	Milwaukee	Excursionist/Local Traveler	German
Loutz Mrs.	John		Chicago, IL	Through Passenger	German
Maher	Patrick	32	Milwaukee	Excursionist/Local Traveler	Irish
May	Charles	26	Milwaukee	Excursionist/Local Traveler	German
McCredan	Terry		Milwaukee	Crew	
McDonough	Terrence E.	13	Detroit, MI	Excursionist/Local Traveler	Irish
McGlone	Andrew Jackson	18	Milwaukee	Excursionist/Local Traveler	Irish
McGrath	Michael	35	Milwaukee	Excursionist/Local Traveler	Irish
McIntyre	Michael	25	Kenosha	Crew	
McLaughlin	Charles B.	34	Milwaukee	Excursionist/Local Traveler	Irish
McLinden, Jr.	John	19	Milwaukee	Excursionist/Local Traveler	Irish
McManus	James	22	Milwaukee	Excursionist/Local Traveler	Irish
Mellon	Edward	41	Milwaukee	Excursionist/Local Traveler	Irish
Miller	John H.	22	Milwaukee	Excursionist/Local Traveler	Irish
Mills	Wildman	25	Sandusky, OH	Through Passenger	

Appendix 2

Surname	Given Name	Age	Residence	Category	Ethnicity
Moots	William	30	Lansing, MI	Through Passenger	Yankee
Murphy	Thomas	21	Milwaukee	Crew	Irish
Murray	John H.	14	Milwaukee	Excursionist/Local Traveler	Irish
Myers	Patrick	30	Chicago, IL	Excursionist/Local Traveler	Irish
Nelson	Edward			Through Passenger	
O'Brien	John	46	Milwaukee	Excursionist/Local Traveler	Irish
O'Brien	Tim	26	Milwaukee	Excursionist/Local Traveler	Irish
O'Leary	Catherine		Milwaukee	Excursionist/Local Traveler	Irish
O'Neil	John		Milwaukee	Excursionist/Local Traveler	Irish
Owens	Patrick		Milwaukee	Excursionist/Local Traveler	Irish
Parks	George	36	Delta, MI	Through Passenger	Yankee
Pengelly	Mary Ledden		Milwaukee	Excursionist/Local Traveler	Irish
Powers	E.J.	17	Milwaukee	Excursionist/Local Traveler	
Pritchard	Thomas	34	Milwaukee	Excursionist/Local Traveler	Welsh
Regan	John		Chicago, IL	Excursionist/Local Traveler	Irish
Rice	Fred		Milwaukee	Crew - Steward	Yankee
Rivers	Frank		Milwaukee	Excursionist/Local Traveler	
Rodee	Jerome B.	29	Milwaukee	Excursionist/Local Traveler	Yankee
Rogers	James	16	Milwaukee	Excursionist/Local Traveler	Irish
Rollins	Frank			Through Passenger	
Rooney	John H.	23	Milwaukee	Excursionist/Local Traveler	Irish
Roper	John	26	Milwaukee	Excursionist/Local Traveler	Irish
Rossiter	Martin	22	Milwaukee	Excursionist/Local Traveler	Irish
Roughan	Thomas	28	Chicago, IL	Excursionist/Local Traveler	Irish
Shea	William G.	22	Milwaukee	Excursionist/Local Traveler	
Simon	William			Through Passenger	Irish
Singer	Michael E.	18	Ontonagon	Excursionist/Local Traveler	German
Smith	Fred	32		Crew	Irish
Snyder	Louis		Milwaukee	Excursionist/Local Traveler	Yankee
Steinke	Hugh	35	Milwaukee	Excursionist/Local Traveler	
Sullivan	Lyman	29	Milwaukee	Excursionist/Local Traveler	Irish
Updike	Peter		Waupun, WI	Through Passenger	Yankee
Walsh	Edward	39	Milwaukee	Excursionist/Local Traveler	Irish
Westlake		22	Milwaukee	Crew - Porter	English

Appendix 2

| White | Edward | 29 | Milwaukee | Excursionist/Local Traveler | Yankee |
| Winslow | Edward | 23 | Chicago, IL | Crew | African American |

Appendix 3

Newhall House Hotel Fire Victims

This list was compiled by Carl Baehr. It is based on research using inquest results printed in newspapers, church and cemetery burial records, tombstones, probate records, and other sources.

Name		Age	Residence	Occupant Type	Ethnicity
Anderson	Mary	23	Newhall House	Hotel Staff	Irish
Anglim	Lizzie	22	Newhall House	Hotel Staff	Irish
Barker	Fred	18	Newhall House	Hotel Staff	Yankee
Bridgeman	Bridget	62	Newhall House	Hotel Staff	Irish
Brown	Ann B.	55	Newhall House	Resident/Boarder	Yankee
Brown	Bessie	17	Newhall House	Hotel Staff	Irish
Brown	Quintus C.	33	Philadelphia, PA	Traveler/Guest	Yankee
Burke	Mary		Newhall House	Hotel Staff	Irish
Burns	Rosa	26	Newhall House	Hotel Staff	Irish
Casey	Annie	31	Newhall House	Hotel Staff	Irish
Chellis	Libbie	42	Newhall House	Resident/Boarder	Yankee
Connors	Kate (Kittie)	23	Newhall House	Hotel Staff	Irish
Conroy	Mary	45	Newhall House	Hotel Staff	Irish
Donahue	Gertie	22	Chicago, IL	Traveler/Guest	Yankee
Dunn	Jane	41	Newhall House	Hotel Staff	Irish
Eliott	Theodore B.	47	Newhall House	Resident/Boarder	Yankee
Finnegan	Maggie	22	Newhall House	Hotel Staff	Irish
Flanagan	Nora	20	Newhall House	Hotel Staff	Irish
Fogerty	Julia	20	Newhall House	Hotel Staff	Irish
Foley	John H.	30	Newhall House	Resident/Boarder	Irish
Fredericks	Gussie		Newhall House	Hotel Staff	German
Fulmer	Wyman E.	20	Newhall House	Hotel Staff	Yankee
Giesler	Emil		Newhall House	Hotel Staff	German
Giese	Augusta	16	Newhall House	Hotel Staff	German
Gillon	Walter	12	Newhall House	Hotel Staff	Irish
Gillon	William "Willie"	15	Newhall House	Hotel Staff	Irish
Goggin	Richard	61	Newhall House	Resident/Boarder	Irish
Groesbeck	Julia F.	56	Brooklyn, NY	Traveler/Guest	Yankee
Haak	Justine	34	Newhall House	Hotel Staff	German
Hager	Anna	22	Newhall House	Hotel Staff	German
Hall	William H.	33	LaPorte, IN	Traveler/Guest	Yankee
Hough	Judson J.	36	Maroa, IL	Traveler/Guest	Yankee

Last Name	First Name	Age	Location	Category	Ethnicity
Howie	Robert T.	24	Newhall House	Resident/Boarder	Scottish
Johnson	Allan	58	Newhall House	Resident/Boarder	Yankee
Johnson	Martha	53	Newhall House	Resident/Boarder	Yankee
Kellogg	Joseph Bradford	24	Ashton, SD	Traveler/Guest	Yankee
Kelly	Lizzie	21	Newhall House	Hotel Staff	Irish
Kelsey	Charles	22	Brdigeport, CT	Traveler/Guest	African American
Krause	Amelia		Newhall House	Hotel Staff	German
Linehan	Kate (Kittie)	26	Newhall House	Hotel Staff	Irish
Lowry	George	59	Newhall House	Hotel Staff	Irish
Martelle	David H.	29	Newhall House	Resident/Boarder	Yankee
Mason	Benjamin	56	Newhall House	Resident/Boarder	Yankee
McDade	Mary	25	Newhall House	Hotel Staff	Irish
McMahon	Annie	29	Newhall House	Hotel Staff	Irish
McMahon	Mary	25	Newhall House	Hotel Staff	Irish
Miller	Mary	52	Newhall House	Hotel Staff	Irish
Monaghan	Kate	42	Newhall House	Hotel Staff	Irish
Moynahan	Daniel	17	Newhall House	Hotel Staff	Irish
O'Connell	Bridget	25	Newhall House	Hotel Staff	Irish
O'Connor	Mollie	18	Newhall House	Hotel Staff	Irish
Owens	Margaret	25	Newhall House	Hotel Staff	Irish
Owens	Mary	23	Newhall House	Hotel Staff	Irish
Power	David Gratton	67	Newhall House	Resident/Boarder	Irish
Reed George	H.	73	Newhall House	Resident/Boarder	Yankee
Schloessner	Martha		Newhall House	Hotel Staff	German
Schoenbucher	Ernst	14	Newhall House	Hotel Staff	German
Scott	Walter H.	25	Newhall House	Resident/Boarder	Scottish
Smith	George G.	52	Newhall House	Resident/Boarder	Yankee
Smith	Louis K.	23	Newhall House	Resident/Boarder	Irish
Sullivan	Maggie	17	Newhall House	Hotel Staff	Irish
Trapp	Augusta	18	Newhall House	Hotel Staff	German
Van Loon	Thomas E.	54	Newhall House	Resident/Boarder	Yankee

Vose	James P.	40	Newhall House	Resident/Boarder	Yankee
Waltersdorf	Ottilie	18	Newhall House	Hotel Staff	German
Wiley	William E.	32	Newhall House	Resident/Boarder	Yankee
Unknown #1					
Unknown #2					
Unknown #3					
Unknown #4					
Unknown #5					
Unknown #6					

Endnotes

Chapter 1: 1835-1839

[1] Kirby Miller, *Emigrants and Exiles: Ireland and the Irish Exodus to North America* (Oxford: Oxford University Press, 1985), 21.

[2] Ibid, 193.

[3] The Jeremiah Curtin House at S. 84th and W. Grange streets was built in 1846 by David Curtin and is listed on the National Register of Historic Places. It is owned by the Milwaukee County Historical Society.

[4] The Matthew Keenan house at 777 N. Jefferson Street has been designated a Milwaukee landmark.

[5] Steven M. Avella, *In the Richness of the Earth* (Milwaukee: Marquette University Press, 2002), 30.

Chapter 2: 1840-1849

[1] Humphrey J. Desmond, "Early Irish Settlers in Milwaukee," *The Wisconsin Magazine of History* 13, no. 4 (June 1930): 366–367.

[2] Kathleen Neils Conzen, *Immigrant Milwaukee 1836–1860* (Cambridge, MA: Harvard University Press, 1976), 88.

[3] "St. Patrick's Adopted Soil—the Old Third Ward Before the Fire," *Milwaukee Sentinel*, 19 March 1933.

[4] James S. Buck, *Pioneer History of Milwaukee* (Milwaukee: Swain and Tate, 1890), 1:135.

[5] Mario A. Carini, *Milwaukee's Italians: The Early Years* (Milwaukee: Italian Community Center of Milwaukee, 1999), 43.

[6] "Tory Hill," *Catholic Citizen*, 2 September 1916, 3.

[7] "Letter From New York," *Semi-Weekly Wisconsin*, 30 January 1863, 1.

[8] "Declaring War—Tory Hill Property," *Milwaukee Sentinel*, 31 July 1885, 3.

[9] "City Matters," *Milwaukee Sentinel*, 29 December 1864; "Fourth Ward Politics," Milwaukee Sentinel, 22 March 1866.

[10] "Local Miscellany," *Milwaukee Sentinel*, 10 August 1877, 8.

[11] "James Kneeland Dead," *Evening Wisconsin*, 7 September 1899, 5.

[12] "City Matters," *Milwaukee Sentinel*, 14 June 1875, 8.

[13] "Tory Hill," *Catholic Citizen*, 2 September 1916, 3.

[14] "William Kelly Death Notice," *Milwaukee Journal*, 27 February 1950, 18.

[15] "Jail and Stations Jottings," *Milwaukee Daily Sentinel*, 25 July 1881.

[16] "Saint Patrick's Day," *Milwaukee Sentinel*, 30 March 1844.

[17] "Saint Patrick's Day," *Milwaukee Sentinel*, 23 March 1844.

[18] Kirby Miller, *Emigrants and Exiles: Ireland and the Irish Exodus to North America* (Oxford: Oxford University Press, 1985), 284.

19 Ibid., 291.
20 James S. Buck, *Pioneer History of Milwaukee* (Milwaukee: Swain and Tate, 1884), 3:381.
21 "City Matters," *Milwaukee Daily Sentinel*, 2 April 1858, 1.
22 Charles King, "The Wisconsin National Guard," *Wisconsin Blue Book 1923* (Madison: The State Printing Board, 1923), 346.
23 "The City Guard's Ball," *Milwaukee Sentinel and Gazette*, 21 December 1848, 2.
24 Grace McDonald, *The History of the Irish in Wisconsin in the Nineteenth Century* (North Stratford, NH: Ayer Publishing Company, 1954), 138.
25 Ibid., 139.
26 John J. Finan, "The Boys School," *Fifty Years at Saint John's Cathedral* (Milwaukee: St. John's Cathedral, 1897?), 170.
27 Kathleen Neils Conzen, *Immigrant Milwaukee 1836–1860* (Cambridge, MA: Harvard University Press, 1976), 92.
28 Frank Flower, *History of Milwaukee, Wisconsin: from pre-historic times* (Chicago: Western Historical Co., 1881), 519.

Chapter 3: 1850-1859

1 Carl Baehr, see "Appendix 1: Census Bureau Miscalculates Irish-Born Milwaukeeans" in this publication.
2 Frank Flower, *History of Milwaukee, Wisconsin: from pre-historic times* (Chicago: Western Historical Co., 1881), 519.
3 Kathleen Neils Conzen, *Immigrant Milwaukee, 1836–1860* (Cambridge: Harvard University Press, 1876), 91.
4 *Garland v. Robert and Peter Lynch*, Milwaukee County Circuit Court, Volume D: 408 (1849).
5 *Catherine Lynch v. Robert B. Lynch*, Milwaukee County Circuit Court, Volume L: 95 (1851).
6 Ibid.
7 Ibid.
8 Robert G. Carroon, "John Gregory and Irish Immigration to Milwaukee," *Historical Messenger* (Milwaukee: Milwaukee County Historical Society, 1971), 27:57.
9 Ibid., 59.
10 Grace, McDonald, *The History of the Irish in Wisconsin in the Nineteenth Century* (North Stratford, NH: Ayer Publishing Company, 1954), 20–22.
11 Ibid., 189.
12 Kathleen Neils Conzen, *Immigrant Milwaukee, 1836–1860* (Cambridge: Harvard University Press, 1876), 73.
13 James S. Buck, *Pioneer History of Milwaukee* (Milwaukee: Swain and Tate, 1886), 4:86.

14 Ibid., 4:326.

15 James S. Buck, *Pioneer History of Milwaukee* (Milwaukee: Swain and Tate, 1881), 2:163

16 James S. Buck, *Pioneer History of Milwaukee* (Milwaukee: Swain and Tate, 1886), 4:39

17 Ibid., 4:85

18 James S. Buck, *Pioneer History of Milwaukee* (Milwaukee: Swain and Tate, 1881), 2:300.

19 "Death of Tim O'Brien," Wisconsin Local History & Biography Articles, http://www.wisconsinhistory.org/wlhba/article.

20 "The Excliements [sic] of the Week," *Bangor (Maine) Daily Whig & Courier*, 12 October 1850.

21 Frederick J. Zwierlein, "Know Nothingism in Rochester, New York," *Historical Records and Studies*, United States Catholic Historical Society: 14:20.

22 "A Feast of Flat Things," (Milwaukee) *Daily Free Democrat*, 10 April 1851, 2.

23 James S. Buck, *Pioneer History of Milwaukee* (Milwaukee: Swain and Tate, 1884), 3:335.

24 "Circuit Court," *Milwaukee Daily Sentinel and Gazette*, 5 June 1851.

25 Herbert C. Damon, *History of the Milwaukee Light Guard* (Milwaukee: Sentinel Company, 1875), 12.

26 Zwierlein, 14:25.

27 "Presentation of a Flag to the City Guards," *Milwaukee Daily Sentinel*, 18 March 1852, 2.

28 "Disgraceful Riot and Bloodshed!" *Milwaukee Daily Sentinel*, 8 March 1854, 1.

29 "Disturbance at the Polls," *Daily Evening Wisconsin*, 8 March 1854, 3.

30 "United States Commissioner's Court," (Milwaukee) *Daily Free Democrat*, 1 April 1854, 3.

31 "City Matters," *Milwaukee Daily Sentinel*, 28 June 1854, 2.

32 "Slander Suit," (Milwaukee) *Daily Free Democrat*, 10 May 1855, 2.

33 "The Ball of the Union Guards," *Milwaukee Sentinel*, 27 November 1858.

Chapter 4: 1860-1869

1 Carl Baehr, see "Appendix 1: Census Bureau Miscalculates Irish-Born Milwaukeeans" in this publication.

2 Kathleen Neils Conzen, *Immigrant Milwaukee, 1836–1860* (Cambridge, MA: Harvard University Press, 1976), 25–26.

3 James S. Buck, Pioneer *History of Milwaukee* (Milwaukee: Swain and Tate, 1886), 4:157.

4 Valerie Van Heest, *Lost on the Lady Elgin* (In-Depth Editions, 2010), 39.

Endnotes

5 "The Union Guards," *The (Madison) Wisconsin Daily Patriot*, 9 March 1860, 3.

6 "The Scene in the Third Ward," *Milwaukee Sentinel*, 10 September 1860, 1.

7 Van Heest, 95.

8 *Journal of Board of Supervising Inspectors*, National Archives Record Group 41, Volume 1, 42–43.

9 "Fred Snyder's Statement," *Daily* (Milwaukee) *Wisconsin*, 10 September 1860, 1.

10 "Requiescat in Pace," *Milwaukee Daily Sentinel*, 13 September 1860, 1.

11 *The Metropolitan Catholic almanac and laity's directory for the year of our Lord 1860* (Baltimore: F. Lucas), 199; *The Metropolitan Catholic almanac and laity's directory for the year of our Lord 1861*, (Baltimore: F. Lucas), 174.

12 (Milwaukee) *Daily Enquirer*, 9 October 1860.

13 "The City," *Milwaukee Daily Sentinel*, 7 November 1860, 1.

14 "Lady Elgin," (Milwaukee) *Daily Wisconsin*, 24 September 1860.

15 "The Loss of the Lady Elgin," *Milwaukee Sentinel*, 4 September 1892, 10.

16 Charles M. Scanlan, *The Lady Elgin Disaster*, September 8, 1860 (Cannon Printing Co.: 1928), 42.

17 Susannah Ural Bruce, *The Harp and the Eagle: Irish-American Volunteers and the Union Army*, 1861–1865 (New York: University Press, 2006), 70–71.

18 "With the Grand Army," *Milwaukee Sentinel*, 3 June 1895, 5.

19 Lance J. Herdegen and William J. K. Beaudot, *In the Bloody Railroad Cut at Gettysburg* (Dayton, Ohio: Morningside, 1990), 120.

20 "When Johnny Comes Marching Home," Captain John O'Rourke Blogger, accessed 23 November 2014, http://inorourkesfootsteps.blogspot.com/.

21 Michael J. Pfeifer, "The Northern United States and the Genesis of Racial Lynching: The Lynching of African Americans in the Civil War Era," *The Journal of American History* 97, Issue 3, 1 December 2010, 621–635, https://doi.org/10.1093/jahist/97.3.621.

22 "Mob on Saturday Night," *Daily Milwaukee*, 10 September 1861, 3

23 Ibid: 2.

24 "Terrible Stabbing Affray," *Daily Milwaukee*, 8 September 1861, 3.

25 "Tragic Sequel to the Stabbing Affray," *Daily Wisconsin*, 9 September 1861, 3.

26 "Mob on Saturday Night," *Daily Milwaukee*, 10 September 1861, 3.

27 "Diabolical Outrage," (Milwaukee) *Daily Life*, 14 September 1861.

28 "Trial of the Lynchers of Geo. M. Clark," *Milwaukee Sentinel*, 16 November 1861, 1.

29 *Civil War Database*, Wisconsin Veterans Museum, accessed 23 November 2014, http://museum.dva.state.wi.us/CivilWar.

30 *Annual Reports of the Adjutant General of the State of Wisconsin for the years*

of 1860, 1861, 1862, 1863, 1864 (Madison: Democrat Printing Co.: 1912), 130.

[31] "'Faugh A Ballagh!': The 17th Wisconsin at Corinth," *Irish in the American Civil War*, accessed 23 November 2014, http://irishamericancivilwar. com/2012/01/07/faugh-a-ballagh-the-17th-wisconsin-at-corinth/.

[32] "War Items—Suggestion to Volunteers," *Milwaukee Daily Sentinel*, 14 August 1862, 1.

[33] "Civil War Medal of Honor Recipients, Thomas Toohey entry," U.S. Army Center of Military History, accessed 23 November 2014, http://www. history.army.mil/moh/civilwar_sz.html#TOOHEY.

[34] "Civil War Medal of Honor Recipients, Michael McCormick entry," U.S. Army Center of Military History, accessed 23 November 2014, http://www. history.army.mil/moh/civilwar_sz.html#MCCORMICK.

[35] "The Fenian Movement," *Daily Wisconsin*, 2 June 1866, 5.

[36] J.A. Cole, *Prince of Spies, Henri le Caron* (Boston: Faber and Faber, 1984), 30.

[37] Peter Leo Johnson, *Crosier on the Frontier: A Life of John Martin Henni* (Madison: State Historical Society of Wisconsin, 1959), 135.

[38] Grace McDonald, *The History of the Irish in Wisconsin in the Nineteenth Century* (North Stratford, NH: Ayer Publishing Company, 1954),143.

[39] "The Fenian Picnic," *Milwaukee Sentinel*, 21 September 1865.

[40] Wilfried Neidhardt, *Fenianism in North America* (University Park: Pennsylvania State University Press, [1975]), 91.

[41] Ibid, 11.

[42] "The Fenians," *Milwaukee Sentinel*, 10 April 1866, 1.

[43] "The Fenian Movement," *Daily Wisconsin*, 2 June 1866, 5.

[44] McDonald, 143.

[45] *Appletons' annual cyclopaedia and register of important events of the year 1866: Embracing political, military, and ecclesiastical affairs; public documents; biography, statistics, commerce, finance, literature, science, agriculture, and mechanical industry,* Volume 6 (New York: D. Appleton and Company, 1867), 286.

[46] "The Invasion of Canada," *Milwaukee Sentinel*, 2 June 1866.

[47] "Fenian Activities," *Milwaukee Daily News*, 8 June 1866.

[48] *Portrait and Biographical Album of Des Moines County, Iowa* (Chicago: Acme Publishing, 1888), 340.

[49] *Garland v. Robert and Peter Lynch*, Milwaukee County Circuit Court, Volume D: 408 (1849).

[50] *Lynch v. Lynch*, Milwaukee County Circuit Court, Volume L: 95 (1857).

[51] Ibid, Letter from Robert Lynch to Peter Lynch, 24 Apr 1852.

[52] "Editorial," *Milwaukee Sentinel*, 15 April 1859.

[53] "Compiled Military Service file: Robert B. Lynch," National Archives (NATF 86).

[54] "Lynch, Robert," United States Serial Set, J04 S. Exdoc 42 (40–2) 1317.

[55] "Letter from Lynch," *Daily Wisconsin*, 2 November 1866.

[56] Neidhardt, 106.

Chapter 5: 1870-1879

[1] Brachman, Arlene, "Business Owners Missed on The 1870 US Federal Census For Milwaukee Wisconsin," Milwaukee County Genealogical Society, https://milwaukeegenealogy.org/cpage.php?pt=88, 4etrieved 15 September 2017.

[2] "Tribute of Respect," *Milwaukee Sentinel*, 3 July 1871.

[3] "Local Miscellany," *Milwaukee Daily Sentinel*, 29 September 1877.

[4] *Directory of the City of Milwaukee, being a complete General and Business Directory for 1860/61* (Milwaukee: Starr & Son, 1860).

[5] *Milwaukee City Directory for 1870–71* (Milwaukee: John Thickens, 1870), 360.

[6] "He is Unfit for the Place," *Milwaukee Daily Sentinel*, 17 February 1880, 2.

[7] Kathleen Neils Conzen, *Immigrant Milwaukee, 1836–1860* (Cambridge: Harvard University press, 1876), 86.

[8] "Multiple News Items," *Milwaukee Daily Sentinel*, 7 February 1880, 4.

[9] "For Irish Relief," *Milwaukee Daily Sentinel*, 25 February 1880.

[10] "Multiple Classified Advertisements," *Milwaukee Sentinel*, 19 August 1894, 15.

[11] "Multiple Classified Advertisements," *Milwaukee Sentinel*, 22 August 1895, 7.

[12] "Germans in the Third Ward," *Milwaukee Sentinel*, 2 August 1895, 4.

[13] "Summary," *Milwaukie [sic] Sentinel*, 2 July 1842.

[14] "Gleanings," *Milwaukee Daily Sentinel*, 30 March 1866, 2.

[15] Gorge W. Peck. *Grocery Man and Peck's Bad Boy* (Chicago: Belford, Clark and Co., 1883), Chapter 5.

[16] Peck, Chapter 6.

[17] "St. Patrick's Adopted Soil—the Old Third Ward Before the Fire," *Milwaukee Sentinel*, 19 March 1933.

[18] "Hand Ball Redevivus [sic]—The Irish National Game to Be Revived in Milwaukee," *Milwaukee Daily Journal*, 11 August 1883.

[19] Ibid.

[20] T. J. McElligott, *The Story of Handball: The Game, the Players, the History* (Dublin: Wolfhound Press, c.1984.), 121–147.

[21] Dennis Pajot, *The Rise of Milwaukee Baseball* (Jefferson, N.C.; McFarland and Co., 2009), 8–9.

[22] "The Base Ball Tournament," *Milwaukee Daily Sentinel*, 29 June 1866, 1.

[23] Dennis Pajot, *The Rise of Milwaukee Baseball* (Jefferson, N.C.; McFarland and Co., 2009), 114.

[24] Bob Buege, Borchert Field: *Stories from Milwaukee's Legendary Ballpark* (Madison: Wisconsin Historical Society Press, 2017), 70–74.

[25] "Police Stopped Bouts," *Milwaukee Sentinel*, 16 February 1898, 6.

[26] Grace McDonald, *The History of the Irish in Wisconsin in the Nineteenth Century* (North Stratford, NH: Ayer Publishing Company, 1954), 209.

[27] McDonald, 212.

[28] Steven M. Avella, *In the Richness of the Earth* (Milwaukee: Marquette University Press, 2002), 181.

[29] Thomas Gildea Cannon, "Solonus Casey," *The Irish Genealogical Quarterly* 10, issue 4 (Milwaukee: Irish Genealogical Society of Wisconsin, 2001): 4.

[30] Martin Hintz, *Irish Milwaukee* (Charleston, SC: Arcadia Publishing, 2003), 90

[31] *1850–1940 United States Federal Censuses* [database on-line]. Provo, UT: Ancestry.com Operations, Inc., 2009.

Chapter 6: 1880-1889

[1] *1880 United States Federal Census* [database on-line]. Lehi, UT: Ancestry. com Operations Inc., 2010.

[2] Grace McDonald, *The History of the Irish in Wisconsin in the Nineteenth Century* (North Stratford, NH: Ayer Publishing Company, 1954), 238.

[3] "Sure and 'Tis All Irish When Hibernians Meet," *Milwaukee Journal*, 9 July 1941, 14

[4] "For the Cause of Old Erin," *Milwaukee Daily Journal*, 26 July 1885.

[5] "Great Financial Success," *Milwaukee Daily Journal*, 27 July 1885.

[6] "Irishmen Ready for A Row," *New York Times*, 5 August 1886, 5.

[7] "Chief Lippert Sworn," *The* (Milwaukee) *Daily Journal*, 30 January 1883, 1.

[8] "A Body Found," *The* (Milwaukee) *Daily Journal*, 12 January 1883, 1.

[9] Julius Bleyer, *Burning of the Newhall House* (Milwaukee: Bleyer Brothers: 1883), 40–41. Bleyer's victim count was 71 people, 43 unidentified and 28 identified. He does not count Catherine Monaghan as identified, although she was in several newspapers accounts. Bringing the number of identified to 29 and the victim count to 72. "Day of Horror Five Bodies Brought to Light—Work of the Undertakers," *Milwaukee Sentinel*, 13 January 1883, 1.

[10] Bridget Bridgeman, Probate case number 5384. Wisconsin. Milwaukee County. Court of Probate. Probate records. Microfilm no. 1234567, Item 1. Family History Library, Salt Lake City, UT.

[11] "The Journal Would Like to Offer Mr. C. D. Nash a Little Advice," *The* (Milwaukee) *Daily Journal*, 31 January 1883, 2.

[12] "Ben Tice's Tale," *Milwaukee Sentinel*, 27 January 1883, 5.

[13] "Fourteen Lives Lost," *St. Louis Post-Dispatch*, 18 April 1877, 2.

[14] "Old and Lonely," *Milwaukee Sentinel*, 24 July 1885: 4.

[15] "As Seen by Them," *Milwaukee Sentinel*, 2 May 1886, 6.

[16] "A Mistake of Eastern Journals," *Milwaukee Sentinel*, 29 May 1886, 4.

[17] "Mob and Militia," *Milwaukee Sentinel*, 5 May 1886.

[18] Ibid.

[19] Ibid.

[20] Jerry M. Cooper, "The Wisconsin National Guard in the Milwaukee Riots of 1886," *Wisconsin Magazine of History* (Autumn 1971): 31–48.

[21] "Interesting Lacrosse Game," *Milwaukee Sentinel*, 11 July 1886, 2.

[22] "It's a Crack Company," *Milwaukee Sentinel*, 26 March 1893, 11.

[23] "Ireland's Cause," *Milwaukee Sentinel*, 18 October 1885, 6.

[24] "As They View It," *Milwaukee Sentinel*, 10 April 1886, 7.

[25] Ibid.

Chapter 7: 1890-1899

[1] *Eleventh census of the United States, 1890* (Washington: U.S. Govt. Print. Off., 1890–1896), Part 1.

[2] "Topic of the Times," *Milwaukee Daily Journal*, 10 October 1883.

[3] "Origin of the Big Fire," *Milwaukee Sentinel*, 2 November 1892, 4.

[4] "The Big Losses," *Milwaukee Sentinel*, 29 October 1892.

[5] "Bonfire of Household Goods," *Milwaukee Journal*, 29 October 1892, 1.

[6] "Cinders from the Fire," *Milwaukee Sentinel*, 31 October 1892, 10.

[7] "Work of the Department," *Milwaukee Journal,* 29 October 1892, 1.

[8] "The Shifting Colors in Milwaukee's Old Third Ward," *Milwaukee Journal*, 25 September 1921.

[9] "Incidents of the Fire," *Milwaukee Journal*, 29 October 1892, 1.

[10] "The Big Losses," *Milwaukee Sentinel*, 29 October 1892.

[11] "Twenty-Five Hundred People Left Homeless," *Milwaukee Journal*, 29 October 1892, 1.

[12] "Notes About the Fire," *Evening Wisconsin*, 31 October 1892, 3.

[13] "Defends His Ward," *Milwaukee Journal*, 7 November 1892: 1.

[14] "Cream City Items," (Milwaukee) *Wisconsin Afro-American*, 5 November 1892, 4.

[15] "After the Big Fire," *Milwaukee Sentinel*, 6 November 1892, 21.

[16] "Funds for Fire Sufferers," *Milwaukee Sentinel*, 15 November 1892, 2.

[17] "Petition of Third Warders," *Milwaukee Sentinel*, 8 December 1892, 3.

[18] Cream City Items," (Milwaukee) *Wisconsin Afro-American*, 19 November 1892, 4.

[19] John Gurda, *The West End* (Madison: University of Wisconsin Board of Regents, 1980), 28.

[20] "Third Ward Wins," *Milwaukee Journal*, 17 June 1899.

Chapter 8: 1900-Present

[1] *1900 United States Federal Census* [database on-line]. Provo, UT: Ancestry. com Operations Inc., 2004.

[2] *1940 United States Federal Census* [database on-line]. Provo, UT: Ancestry. com Operations, Inc., 2012.

[3] Timothy McMahon, "Irish," *Encyclopedia of Milwaukee*, downloaded 11 January 2018.

[4] R.L. Nailen and James S. Haight, *Beertown Blazes: A Century of Milwaukee Firefighting* (Milwaukee: NAPCO Graphic Arts, Inc., 1971), 100.

[5] William George Bruce, *History of Milwaukee, City and County* (Chicago: S. J. Clarke Publishing Co., 1922), 3:875.

[6] "Sees Canada Out of Europe," *Milwaukee Journal*, 14 May 1922, 2.

[7] *Wright's Directory of Milwaukee for 1899* (Milwaukee: Alfred G Wright, 1899), 726.

[8] *"Demographic Portrait—Archdiocese of Milwaukee,"* Center for Applied Research in the Apostolate, Georgetown University: Washington, DC, November 2014: 7. http://www.archmil.org/ArchMil/ ArchbishopListeckiLetters/Synod 2014/District Gatherings/CARA Report/MilwaukeeDemographicReportFINAL.pdf, downloaded 10 January 2018.

[9] Brian T. Olszewski, "It's All About Sunday Mass," (Milwaukee) *Catholic Herald* 11 (February 2016), https://catholicherald.org/news/local/it-s-all-about-sunday-mass/.

[10] Jay P. Dolan, *The Irish Americans* (New York: Bloomsbury Press, 2008), 285.

[11] "Religion in the Republic of Ireland," Wikipedia, wikipedia.org/wiki/ Religion in the Republic of Ireland, accessed 5 January 2018.

[12] Dolan, 295.

[13] How Irish America Thinks, Votes and Acts," *The Irish Times*, 3 June 2017, https://www.irishtimes.com/life-and-style/abroad/how-irish-america-thinks-votes-and-acts-1.3104336, downloaded 10 January 2018.

Afterword

[1] Carl Baehr, *Milwaukee Streets: The Stories Behind their Names* (Milwaukee: Cream City Press, 1994): 110

[2] "William F. O'Donnell, 1922–2004," *Milwaukee Journal Sentinel*, 7 September 2004, 1.

Appendix 1: Census Bureau Miscalculates Irish-Born Milwaukeeans

[1] *Mortality Statistics of the Seventh Census of the United States, 1850* (Washington: A.O.P. Nicholson, 1855), 41.

[2] *Population of the United States in 1860; compiled from the original returns of the eighth census, under the direction of the secretary of the interior* (Washington:

Government Printing Office, 1864), xxxii.

3 *Ninth Census of the United States. Statistics of Population: Tables I to VIII Inclusive*, (Washington: United States Government Printing Office, 1872), 389.

4 *Compendium of the Tenth Census (June 1, 1880)*, Part One (Washington, Government Printing Office, 1883), 549.

Index

Page numbers followed by *f* indicate figures.

Index

Menomonee River, 5, 6, 18
Menomonee Street, 17
merchant class. *See* middle class
Merchant Guard, 100
Merrill Park, 199–200, 205, 213–214
"Merrill Park" historical marker, 200*f*
Messmer, Sebastian, 139
Methodist Church, 51, 52*f*
Mexican-American War (1846-1848), 30
Michigan Street
  about, 4, 5, 6, 14–15
  Newhall House fire rescue at, 149–154
  Newhall House location, 144–146, 146*f*
  Tory Hill border and, 18
middle class
  Civil War draft and, 101
  Irish immigrants of, 2, 3
  occupations, 44–45, 60–61, 64
migration
  about, 2–4
  from Canada, 2, 7, 116–117
  to and from Chicago, 116–117
  cholera epidemic and, 34–36
  to company towns, 118–119
  from Ireland, 1–4, 7–10, 20–21, 27–28, 41–43
  of Irish Americans, 115–117
  recruitment and aid for, 41–43
  voting rights after, 20–21
  of Yankees, 4
militias. *See* Wisconsin's militias and guards; *specific militias and guards*
Miller, John, 176–177
Milwaukee. *See also* migration; occupations; *specific ethnic groups; specific neighborhoods, places, and wards*
  about, 1, 4–6, 5*f*
  development controversies, 14–15

historical markers, 58*f*, 83–85, 84*f*, 134, 134*f*, 171 171*f*, 200*f*
Irish mayors of. *See* Hoan, Daniel Webster, Jr.; O'Neill, Edward; Somers, Peter J.
Irish place names in, 13, 59, 118, 209, 218–224
local time discrepancies, 34
maps of, xii*f*, xiii*f*, xiv*f*, 17*f*
marshes of, 5–6, 15, 33, 137
population demographics. *See* United States Census Bureau
street names, original and current, xi
Milwaukee and Prairie du Chien Railroad, 100–101
Milwaukee and Rock River Canal Company, 12
Milwaukee Badgers (militia), 97
Milwaukee Battalion, 32, 48
Milwaukee Brewers (baseball team), 135
Milwaukee Brewers Association, 188
Milwaukee Council of the American Association for the Recognition of the Irish Republic, 211
Milwaukee Diocese, 137
"The Milwaukee Fire or the Burning of the Newhall House" (song), 165*f*
Milwaukee Independent Union Guard, 65–66
Milwaukee Journal (newspaper)
  on Newhall House fire, 159–160, 164
  prejudice jokes and cartoons in, 131, 131*f*
  relief fundraising by, 159, 192
Milwaukee Light Guard, 53, 67, 76
Milwaukee Police Department, 123–124
Milwaukee Protestant Orphan Asylum, 78

Wisconsin's militias and guards
  First Regiment, 169
  Fourth Battalion, 166, 168, 170
  Irish Brigade. *See* Irish Brigade
  Light Artillery, 89
  Second regiment, 86–87, 88–89
  Seventh regiment, 88–89
  Sixth Regiment, 87–89, 90
  State Militia, 120, 122–123, 166
  Third regiment, 86–87
  Twenty Fourth Regiment. *See*
    Milwaukee Regiment
Wisconsin Rangers, 94
Wisconsin State Emigrant Agency,
  43
Wisconsin Supreme Court, Fugitive
  Slave Law ruling by, 65
Wolfe Tone Circle, 105
women
  occupations for, 64
  prejudice and bigotry towards, 161
  in workforce, 116
Wood National Cemetery, 103*f*
Work, Henry C., 82*f*
workers' strikes, 167–168
workforce. *See* occupations
World War I, 208, 210–212
World War II, 212–213

Yankee Hill, 14–15, 40, 60, 210
Yankees
  Civil War recruitment of, 101
  fundraising by, 26
  on immigrant voting, 20–21
  in Irish Brigade, 96
  on Irish independence, 22–24
  on Irish militia, 86, 88–89
  Know Nothing movement and,
    32–33
  migration of, 4
  militia companies, 59, 121
  mob actions against, 49, 55, 87–88,

95
  Newhall House fire victims, 157
  political influence of, 16
  population, 11, 14, 22
  on temperance, 15–16
  Third Ward ownership by, 17–18
  Tory Hill land ownership by, 19
Young Irelander Rebellion (1848),
  28–29, 59, 223*f*
Young Ladies' Legion, 171
Young Men's Christian Association,
  132

Zouaves company, 88

About the Author

Carl Baehr, a native Milwaukeean, is the author of *Milwaukee Streets: The Stories Behind Their Names*, which was awarded the 1994 Gambrinus Prize. He has also written many local history articles, including the City Streets column for *Urban Milwaukee*. He is a graduate of Cardinal Stritch University and the University of Wisconsin–Milwaukee School of Information Studies. Baehr is a former IT director, reference librarian, library director, and professional genealogist.

Baehr has ten Irish immigrant ancestors and despite his Teutonic-sounding name, neither documentation nor DNA indicate any German ancestry. His great-grandfather adopted the Baehr name from his stepfather.